AF663436

ENCYCLOPAEDIC DICTIONARY OF COMPUTER SCIENCE

Volume 3

Edited by

Dr. Akshaya Kumar Nayak
Dr. Avinash Chiranjeev
Er. Haojam Rocky S.

JNANADA PRAKASHAN (P&D)
in association with
THE GLOBAL OPEN UNIVERSITY
NAGALAND (INDIA)

Published by :
JNANADA PRAKASHAN (P&D)
4837/2, 24, Ansari Road, Daryaganj
New Delhi-110 002, India
Phone : +91-11-23272047
Mobile : +91-9212137080

Assisted by :
Text Book Promotion Society of India
4837/2, 24, Ansari Road, Daryaganj
New Delhi-110 002, India
Phone : +91-11-23272047
Mobile : +91-9212137080

Edition : 2016

Encyclopaedic Dictionary of Computer Science

ISBN: 978-81-7139-362-6 (Set)

Typesetting by :
Vardhman Computers
New Delhi-110 017, India

Published by Mrs. S. Chowdhary for M/s. Jnanada Prakashan (P&D) Daryaganj, Ansari Road, New Delhi-110002, India and printed at Balaji Offset, Navin Shahdara, Delhi-110032, India.

PREFACE

As we enter the 21st century, technology involving computer science proliferates in most areas of our lives. How we work, how we study, how we run errands, how we spend our leisure time, and how we communicate all entail the use of computers. The past decade has seen an explosion of new growth on the internet and the introduction of personal computers into millions of homes. Along with this growth has come the proliferation of specialised terminology—related not just to the internet, but to software, multimedia systems, information processing, and more. The Dictionary of Computer Science includes the newest terminology and makes it accessible to anyone who works with a computer at home, school, or work. This dictionary contains over 6,000 entries in the first edition—as well as a comprehensive cross-referencing system, providing clear and concise definitions for the newest terms in computing.

The wide range of topics covered include computer applications in industry, the office, science, education, and the home; the means of achieving these applications—the hardware, software, computer organisation, telecommunications, and user interaction; security, safety, and legal issues; underlying concepts and theories in computing and associated fields; and major computer manufacturers and organisations. Special emphasis is placed on terms widely used in relation to the latest advances in personal computing, computer graphics, networking, artificial intelligence, and computer security. Full coverage is also given to the Internet, World Wide Web, and multimedia programmes.

From browser and sniffer programme to millennium bug and spam, the Dictionary of Computer Science, First Edition will prove invaluable to students and teachers of computing, and everyone who uses computers in the home, lab, or business.

— Editors

R

R&D *n.* Acronym for research and development.

Race condition *n.* 1. A condition in which a feedback circuit interacts with internal circuit processes in a way that produces chaotic output behaviour. 2. A condition in which data propagates rapidly through a logic circuit far ahead of the clock signal intended to control its passage.

Rack-mounted *adj.* Built for installation in a metal frame or cabinet of standard width (typically 19 inches or 23 inches) and mounting arrangements.

RAD *n.* Acronym for rapid application development. A method of building computer systems in which the system is programmed and implemented in segments, rather than waiting until the entire project is completed for implementation. Developed by programmer James Martin, RAD uses such tools as CASE and visual programming. See also CASE, visual programming.

Radian *n.* The angle between two radii of a circle such that the length of the arc between them is equal to the radius. The circumference of a circle is equal to 2p times the radius, so one radian contains 360/(2p) = 180/p = approximately 57.2958 degrees. Conversely, multiplying the number of degrees by p/180 gives the number of radians; 360 degrees equals 2p radians. See the illustration.

Radio *n.* 1. Electromagnetic waves longer than about 0.3 mm (frequencies lower than about 1 THz). Radio is used to transmit a wide variety of signals, using various frequency ranges and types of modulation, such as AM and FM broadcasts, microwave relays, and television broadcasts. See also hertz, radio frequency. 2. Audio signals transmitted over the Interne of quality comparable to those broadcast by commercial radic stations. See also Internet Talk Radio, MBONE, RealAudio.

Radio button *n.* In graphical user interfaces, a means of selecting one of several options, usually within a dialog box. A radic button appears as a small circle that, when selected, has a smaller, filled circle inside it. Radio buttons act like the statior selector buttons on a car radio. Selecting one button in a se deselects the previously selected button, so one and only one of the options in the set can be selected at any given time. In contrast, check boxes are used when more than one option in the set can be selected at the same time.

Radio clock *n.* A device that receives a broadcast containing a standard time signal. Radio clocks are used in networl communications to synchronise the host's hardware clock to the Universal Time Coordinate format in accordance with th Network Time Protocol (NTP). See also NTP, Universal Tim Coordinate.

Radio frequency *n.* The portion of the electromagnetic spectrun with frequencies between 3 kilohertz and 300 gigahertz. Thi corresponds to wavelengths between 30 kilometers and 0. millimeter. Acronym: RF. See also radio (definition 1).

Radio frequency interference *n.* See RFI.

Radiosity *n.* A method used in computer graphics to rende photographic-quality, realistic images. Radiosity is based o dividing an image into smaller polygons, or patches, fo purposes of calculating the global illumination emitted b sources of light and reflected from surfaces. Unlike ray tracing which follows rays of light between a light source and th objects it illuminates, radiosity takes into account both th light emitted from a light source and the light reflected by a objects in the image environment. Radiosity thus account not only for a source of illumination (such as a lightbulb) bu also for the effects of that illumination as it is absorbed by and reflected from, every object in the "picture." See als form factor.

RADIUS *n.* Acronym for Remote Authentication Dial-In User Service protocol. A proposed Internet protocol in which an authentication server provides authorisation and authentication information to a network server to which a user is attempting to link. See also authentication, communications protocol, server (definition 2).

Radix *n.* The base of a number system—for example, 2 in the binary system, 10 in the decimal system, 8 in the octal system, and 16 in the hexadecimal system. See also base (definition 2).

Radix-minus-1 complement *n.* In a system for representing numbers using a fixed number of possible digits (radix) and a fixed number of positions for them, the number obtained from another number by subtracting each of the digits of the other number from the largest possible digit (equal to the radix minus 1). For example, in a system of five-digit decimal numbers, the radix-minus-1 complement of 1,234 is 98,765. Adding any number to its radix-minus-1 complement produces the largest possible number in the system (in the example, 99,999). Adding another 1 to this number produces, in our example, 100,000—but since only the lower five digits are used, the result is zero. Thus, the negative of any number in the system is its radix-minus-1 complement plus 1, because –a + a = 0. In the binary system, the radix-minus-1 complement is the one's complement, which is easily formed electronically by inverting all bits.

Radix point *n.* The period or other character that separates the integer portion of a number from the fractional portion. In the decimal system, the radix point is the decimal point, as in the number 1.33.

Radix sort *n.* See digital sort.

Radix sorting algorithm *n.* A sorting algorithm that sorts by grouping elements according to successive parts of their keys. A simple example is sorting a list of numbers in the range 0–999. First the list is sorted by the hundreds digit into a set of (up to) 10 lists; then each list, one at a time, is sorted into a set of (up to) 10 lists based on the tens digit; and finally each of those lists is sorted by the ones digit. This algorithm is usually most efficient when the sorting is done using binary values, which simplifies comparisons (is a given bit on or off?) and reduces the number of lists (each pass produces at most two lists).

RADSL *n.* Acronym for rate-adaptive asymmetric digital subscriber line. A flexible, high-speed version of ADSL (asymmetric digital subscriber line) that is capable of adjusting transmission speed (bandwidth) based on signal quality and length of the transmission line. As the signal quality improves or deteriorates while a transmission line is being used, the transmission speed is adjusted accordingly. See also ADSL, xDSL.

Rag *n.* Irregularity along the left or right edge of a set of lines of text on a printed page. Rag complements justification, in which one or both edges of the text form a straight vertical line. See the illustration. See also justify, ragged left, ragged right.

Ragged left *adj.* Of, relating to, or being lines of text whose left ends are not vertically aligned but form an irregular edge. Text may be right-justified and have a ragged left margin. Ragged-left text is used infrequently—typically, for visual effect in advertisements. See also rag, right-justify.

Ragged right *adj.* Of, relating to, or being lines of text whose right ends are not vertically aligned but form an irregular edge. Letters and other word-processed documents are commonly left-justified, with ragged-right margins. See also left-justify, rag.

RAID *n.* Acronym for redundant array of independent (or inexpensive) disks. A data storage method in which data is distributed across a group of computer disk drives that function as a single storage unit. All the information stored on each of the disks is duplicated on other disks in the array. This redundancy ensures that no information will be lost if one of the disks fails. RAID is generally used on network servers where data accessibility is critical and fault tolerance is required. There are various defined levels of RAID, each offering differing trade-offs among access speed, reliability, and cost. See also disk controller, error-correction coding, Hamming code, hard disk, parity bit, server (definition 1).

RAID array *n.* See RAID.

RAM *n.* Acronym for random access memory. Semiconductor-based memory that can be read and written by the central processing unit (CPU) or other hardware devices. The storage locations can be accessed in any order. Note that the various types of ROM memory are capable of random access but cannot be written to. The term RAM, however, is generally understood to refer to volatile memory that can be written to as well as read.

RAMAC *n.* 1. Acronym for Random Access Method of Accounting Control. Developed by an IBM team led by Reynold B. Johnson, RAMAC was the first computer disk drive. It was introduced in 1956. The original RAMAC consisted of a stack of 50 24-inch platters, with a storage capacity of 5 megabytes and an average access time of 1 second. 2. A high-speed, high-capacity disk storage system introduced by IBM in 1994. Based on the original RAMAC storage device, it was designed to fulfill enterprise requirements for efficient and fault-tolerant storage.

RAM cache *n.* Short for random access memory cache. Cache memory that is used by the system to store and retrieve data from the RAM. Frequently accessed segments of data may be stored in the cache for quicker access compared with secondary storage devices such as disks. See also cache, RAM.

RAM card *n.* Short for random access memory card. An add-in circuit board containing RAM memory and the interface logic necessary to decode memory addresses.

RAM cartridge *n.* See memory cartridge.

RAM chip *n.* Short for random access memory chip. A semiconductor storage device. RAM chips can be either dynamic or static memory. See also dynamic RAM, RAM, static RAM.

RAM compression *n.* Short for random access memory compression. This technology was an attempt by a number of software vendors to solve the problem of running out of global memory under Windows 3.x. Compression of the usual contents of RAM may lessen the system's need to read or write to virtual (hard disk-based) memory and thus speed up the system, as virtual memory is much slower than physical RAM. Because of the falling prices of RAM and the introduction of operating systems that handle RAM more efficiently, such as Windows 9x, Windows NT, and OS/2, RAM compression is generally used only on older PCs. See also compression, RAM, Windows.

RAMDAC *n.* Acronym for random access memory digital-to-analog converter. A chip built into some VGA and SVGA video adapters that translates the digital representation of a pixel into the analog information needed by the monitor to display it. The presence of a RAMDAC chip generally enhances overall video performance. See also SVGA, VGA.

RAM disk *n.* Short for random access memory disk. A simulated disk drive whose data is actually stored in RAM memory. A special programme allows the operating system to read from and write to the simulated device as if it were a disk drive. RAM disks are extremely fast, but they require that system memory be given up for their use. Also, RAM disks usually use volatile memory, so the data stored on them disappears when power is turned off. Many portables offer RAM disks that use battery-backed CMOS RAM to avoid this problem. See also CMOS RAM.

RAM refresh *n.* See refresh (definition 2).

RAM resident *adj.* See memory-resident.

RAM-resident programme *n.* See terminate-and-stay- resident programme.

Random *adj.* Specifically, a reference to an arbitrary or unpredictable situation or event. The term is also given an extended, pejorative or semi-pejorative meaning, however, in which it is used in the sense of nonspecific, incoherent, poorly organised, loser, and so on.

Random access *n.* The ability of a computer to find and go directly to a particular storage location without having to search sequentially from the beginning location. The human equivalent of random access would be the ability to find a desired address in an address book without having to proceed sequentially through all the addresses. A computer's semiconductor memory (both RAM and ROM) provides random access. Certain types of files stored on disk under some operating systems also allow random access. Such files are best used for data in which each record has no intrinsic relationship to what comes physically before or after it, as in a client list or an inventory. Also called: direct access. See also RAM, ROM (definition 2).

Random access memory *n.* See RAM.

Random noise *n.* A signal in which there is no relationship between amplitude and time and in which many frequencies occur randomly, without pattern or predictability.

Random number generation *n.* Production of an unpredictable sequence of numbers in which no number is any more likely to occur at a given time or place in the sequence than any other. Truly random number generation is generally viewed as impossible. The process used in computers would be more properly called "pseudorandom number generation."

Range *n.* 1. A block of cells selected for similar treatment in a spreadsheet. A range of cells can extend across a row, down a column, or over a combination of the two, but all cells in the range must be contiguous, sharing at least one common border. Ranges allow the user to affect many cells with a single command—for example, to format them similarly, enter the same data into all of them, give them a name in common and treat them as a unit, or select and incorporate them into a formula. 2. In more general usage, the spread between specified low and high values. Range checking is an important method of validating data entered into an application.

Range check *n.* In programming, a limit check of both the upper and lower limits of a value, thus determining whether the value lies within an acceptable range. See also limit check.

RAPI *n.* See Remote Application Programming Interface.

RARP *n.* Acronym for Reverse Address Resolution Protocol. A TCP/IP protocol for determining the IP address (or logical address) of a node on a local area network connected to the Internet, when only the hardware address (or physical address) is known. While RARP refers only to finding the IP address and ARP technically refers to the opposite procedure, ARP is commonly used for both senses. See also ARP.

RAS *n.* 1. See remote access server, Remote Access Service. 2. Acronym for reliability, availability, serviceability. See high availability.

Raster *n.* A rectangular pattern of lines; on a video display, the horizontal scan lines from which the term raster scan is derived.

Raster display *n.* A video monitor (typically a CRT) that displays an image on the screen as a series of horizontal scan lines from top to bottom. Each scan line consists of pixels that can be illuminated and coloured individually. Television screens and most computer monitors are raster displays. See also CRT, pixel.

Raster fonts *n.* Fonts that are stored as bitmaps. Raster fonts are designed with a specific size and resolution for a specific printer and cannot be scaled or rotated. If a printer does not support raster fonts, it will not print them. The five raster fonts are Courier, MS Sans Serif, MS Serif, Small, and Symbol. Also called: bitmapped fonts. See also font, printer.

Raster graphics *n.* A method of generating graphics that treats an image as a collection of small, independently controlled dots (pixels) arranged in rows and columns.

Raster image *n.* A display image formed by patterns of light and dark or differently coloured pixels in a rectangular array. See also raster graphics.

Raster image processor *n.* A device, consisting of hardware and software, that converts vector graphics or text into a raster (bitmapped) image. Raster image processors are used in page printers, phototypesetters, and electrostatic plotters. They compute the brightness and colour value of each pixel on the page so that the resulting pattern of pixels re-creates the vector graphics and text originally described. Acronym: RIP.

Rasterisation *n.* The conversion of vector graphics (images described in terms of mathematical elements, such as points and lines) to equivalent images composed of pixel patterns that can be stored and manipulated as sets of bits. See also pixel.

Raw data *n.* 1. Unprocessed, typically unformatted, data, such as a stream of bits that has not been filtered for commands or special characters. See also raw mode. 2. Information that has been collected but not evaluated.

Raw infrared *n.* A method of receiving data through an infrared (IR) transceiver. Raw infrared treats the IR transceiver like a serial cable and does not process data in any way. The application is responsible for handling collision detection and other potential problems.

Raw mode *n.* A way in which the UNIX and MS-DOS operating systems "see" a character-based device. If the identifier for the device indicates raw mode, the operating system does not filter input characters or give special treatment to carriage returns, end-of-file markers, and linefeed and tab characters.

Ray tracing *n.* A sophisticated and complex method of producing high-quality computer graphics. Ray tracing calculates the colour and intensity of each pixel in an image by tracing single rays of light backward and determining how they were affected on their way from a defined source of light illuminating the objects in the image. Ray tracing is demanding in terms of processing capability because the computer must account for reflection, refraction, and absorption of individual rays, as well as for the brightness, transparency level, and reflectivity of each object and the positions of the viewer and the light source.

RCA connector *n.* A connector used for attaching audio and video devices, such as stereo equipment or a composite video monitor, to a computer's video adapter. See the illustration. See also composite video display.

RDBMS *n.* Acronym for relational data base management system. See relational database.

RDRAM *n.* Acronym for Rambus dynamic random access memory. A type of DRAM designed by Rambus, Inc. In its fastest form, known as Direct RDRAM, this technology provides a 16-bit data path and a peak bandwidth of 1.6 GB per second (approximately eight to ten times faster than synchronous DRAM, or SDRAM). RDRAM has been used in graphics and video chips; Direct RDRAM is expected to replace DRAM and SDRAM in personal computers. Also called: Rambus DRAM. See also dynamic RAM, SDRAM.

Read 1 *n.* The action of transferring data from an input source into a computer's memory or from memory into the CPU (central processing unit).

Read 2 *vb.* To transfer data from an external source, such as from a disk or the keyboard, into memory or from memory into the central processing unit (CPU).

Read-after-write *n.* A feature of certain data storage devices, such as tape drives, in which the device reads data immediately after it is written as a means of verifying data integrity.

Read error *n.* An error encountered while a computer is in the process of obtaining information from storage or from another source of input.

README *n.* A file containing information that the user either needs or will find informative and that might not have been included in the documentation. README files are placed on disk in plain-text form (without extraneous or programme-specific characters) so that they can be read easily by a variety of word processing programmes.

Read notification *n.* An e-mail feature providing feedback to the sender that a message has been read by the recipient.

Read-only *adj.* Capable of being retrieved (read) but not changed (written). A read-only file or document can be displayed or printed but not altered in any way. Read-only memory (ROM) holds programmes that cannot be changed; a read-only storage medium, such as CD-ROM, can be played back but cannot be used for recording information.

Read-only attribute *n.* A file attribute, stored with a file's directory entry, indicating whether or not a file may be changed or erased. When the read-only attribute is off, the file can be modified or deleted; when it is on, the file can only be displayed.

Read-only memory *n.* See ROM.

Read-only terminal *n.* See RO terminal.

Read/write *adj.* Able to be both read from and written to. Abbreviation: R/W.

Read/write channel *n.* See input/output channel.

Read/write head *n.* See head.

Read/write memory *n.* Memory that can be both read from and written to (modified). Semiconductor RAM and core memory are typical read/write memory systems.

Real address *n.* An absolute (machine) address specifying a physical location in memory. See also physical address.

RealAudio *n.* Streaming audio technology developed by RealNetworks, Inc., for distributing radio and FM-quality sound files over the Internet in real time. RealAudio is based on two components: client software for decompressing the sound on the fly and server software for delivering it. The client software is free, distributed either as a downloadable programme or as part of browser software. See also RealPlayer, RealVideo, stream, streaming.

Reallocate *n.* A function in C that allows the programmer to request a larger portion of heap memory than was previously assigned to a particular pointer. See also dynamic memory allocation, heap (definition 1).

Reallysafe palette *n.* A colour look-up table (CLUT) consisting of 22 colours from the 216-colour websafe palette that are completely consistent when viewed with all Web browsers on all major computer platforms. The reallysafe palette arose from an experiment that indicated that most of the colours of the websafe palette shift to some degree in different viewing environments. See also browser CLUT, websafe palette.

Real mode *n.* An operating mode in the Intel 80x86 family of microprocessors. In real mode, the processor can execute only one programme at a time. It can access no more than about 1 MB of memory, but it can freely access system memory and input/output devices. Real mode is the only mode possible in the 8086 processor and is the only operating mode supported by MS-DOS. In contrast, the protected mode offered in the 80286 and higher microprocessors provides the memory management and memory protection needed for multitasking environments such as Windows. See also 8086, privileged mode.

Real-mode mapper *n.* An enhancement for Windows 3.x systems that allows 32-bit file system access. The real-mode mapper provides a 32-bit disk access interface to the DOS device driver chain. Acronym: RMM.

Real number *n.* 1. A number that can be represented in a number system with a given base, such as the decimal system, by a finite or infinite sequence of digits and a radix point. For example, 1.1 is a real number, as is 0.33333.... See also irrational number. 2. A data type, in a programming language such as Pascal, that is used for storing, to some limit of precision, values that include both integer and fractional parts. See also double-precision, single-precision.

RealPlayer *n.* An Internet media player and browser plug-in developed by RealNetworks, Inc., that supports playback of RealAudio and RealVideo, as well as certain other formats, after installation of appropriate plug-ins. The current version allows RealPlayer users to surf for media content directly from the player or through a Web browser. See also RealAudio, RealVideo. Real Soon Now adv. Soon, but not really expected to be as soon as claimed. One might say, for example, that a commercial programme will have some desired feature Real Soon Now if several versions ago the vendor knew of the need for the feature and has done nothing. Acronym: RSN.

Real storage *n.* The amount of RAM memory in a -system, as distinguished from virtual memory. Also called: physical memory, physical storage. See also virtual memory.

RealSystem G2 *n.* An open, standards-based platform for delivery of streaming audio and video over the Internet and other TCP/IP networks developed by RealNetworks, Inc. RealSystem G2 was introduced by RealNetworks in its audio and video players, servers, and development tools in 1998. Among other features, RealSystem G2 scales to different bandwidths, includes streaming that adjusts delivery to available bandwidth, and supports SMIL (Synchronised Multimedia Integration Language) for multimedia presentations. See also RealPlayer, RealVideo, SMIL, streaming.

RealSystem Producer *n.* A software application developed by RealNetworks that converts most types of video and sound files into RealMedia formats for use as streaming media over the Internet or within a corporate intranet.

RealSystem Server *n.* Software developed by RealNetworks to enable a server to broadcast streaming media. Several versions of RealSystem Server are available, designed to meet needs ranging from small intranet servers to large proxy servers.

Real-time *adj.* Of, or relating to, a time frame imposed by external constraints. Real-time operations are those in which the machine's activities match the human perception of time or those in which computer operations proceed at the same rate as a physical or external process. Real-time operations are characteristic of aircraft guidance systems, transaction-processing systems, scientific applications, and other areas in which a computer must respond to situations as they occur (for example, animating a graphic in a flight simulator or making corrections based on measurements).

Real-time animation *n.* Computer animation in which images are computed and updated on the screen at the same rate at which the objects simulated might move in the real world. Real-time animation allows dynamic involvement by the user because the computer can accept and incorporate keystrokes or controller movements as it is drawing the next image in the animation sequence. Arcade-style animation (such as in a flight simulator programme) makes use of real-time animation in translating game plays into onscreen actions. In contrast, in animation done in virtual time, image frames are first calculated and stored and later replayed at a higher rate to achieve smoother movement. See also animation, bit block.

Real-time clock *n.* In PCs, a circuit or other hardware element that provides the system with real-world time. Upon startup of the system, the real-time clock puts the date and time in memory, where it can then be systematically incremented by the BIOS. A real-time clock generally has a battery that is separate from the rest of the system, so it's not dependent upon the system's power source. This is not the same thing as a system clock, which synchronises the processor. Acronym: RTC. See also clock (definition 2).

Real-time conferencing *n.* See teleconferencing.

Real-Time Control Protocol *n.* A scalable transport control protocol that works with the Real-Time Protocol (RTP) to monitor real-time transmissions to multiple participants over a network—for example, during videoconferencing. The Real-Time Control Protocol, or RTCP, transmits packets of control information at regular intervals and is used to determine how well information is being delivered to recipients. Acronym: RTCP. See also Real-Time Protocol, Real-Time Streaming Protocol, Resource Reservation Setup Protocol.

Real-time operating system *n.* An operating system designed for the needs of a process-controlled environment. A real-time operating system recognises that responses must be made and tasks handled instantly, with no lag time. Real-time operating systems are typically used as embedded systems in devices and applications requiring time-critical reaction, such as telecommunications, air traffic control, and robotic functions. Acronym: RTOS. See also real-time system.

Real-Time Protocol *n.* An Internet-standard network transport protocol used in delivering real-time data, including audio and video. The Real-Time Protocol, or RTP, works with both unicast (single sender, single recipient) and multicast (single sender, multiple recipients) services. RTP is often used in conjunction with the Real-Time Control Protocol (RTCP), which monitors delivery. Acronym: RTP. See also Real-Time Control Protocol, Real-Time Streaming Protocol, stream.

Real-time streaming *n.* The process of delivering a streaming media file via a specialised streaming media server using real-time streaming protocol (RTSP). With real-time streaming, the file itself actually plays on the streaming media server, even though it is viewed on the computer that opened the file. Real-time streaming transmits at a higher bandwidth than HTTP streaming. It is often used to broadcast live events, such as concerts or keynote conference addresses. See also HTTP streaming.

Real-Time Streaming Protocol *n.* A control protocol for the delivery of streamed multimedia data over Internet Protocol (IP) networks. The Real-Time Streaming Protocol, or RTSP, was developed by Columbia University, Progressive Networks, and Netscape and has been submitted as a proposed standard to the IETF (Internet Engineering Task Force). RTSP is designed to deliver real-time, live, or stored audio and video efficiently over a network. It can be used either for groups of recipients or for on-demand delivery to a single recipient. Acronym: RTSP. See also Advanced Streaming Format, Real-Time Protocol, Resource Reservation Setup Protocol, stream.

Real-time system *n.* A computer and/or a software system that reacts to events before the events become obsolete. For example, airline collision avoidance systems must process radar input, detect a possible collision, and warn air traffic controllers or pilots while they still have time to react.

RealVideo *n.* The streaming technology developed by RealNetworks, Inc., for distributing video over intranets and the Internet. RealVideo transmits video from a server in encoded (compressed) form. The video and accompanying sound are viewed on the client end with the help of a software player. RealVideo works with both IP and IP multicasting and, as with RealAudio, does not require transmission of complete files before playback can begin. See also RealAudio, RealPlayer, streaming.

Reboot *vb.* To restart a computer by reloading the operating system. See also boot2, cold boot, warm boot.

Receipt notification *n.* An e-mail feature providing feedback to the sender that a message has been received by the recipient.

Receive *vb.* To accept data from an external communications system, such as a local area network (LAN) or a telephone line, and store the data as a file.

Receive Data *n.* See RXD.

Rec. newsgroups *n.* Usenet newsgroups that are part of the rec. hierarchy and whose names have the prefix rec. These newsgroups cover topics devoted to discussions of recreational activities, hobbies, and the arts. See also newsgroup, traditional newsgroup hierarchy, Usenet. newsgroups, sci. newsgroups, soc. newsgroups, talk. newsgroups.

Recompile *vb.* To compile a programme again, usually because of changes that needed to be made in the source code in response to error messages generated by the compiler. See also compile.

Record1 *n.* A data structure that is a collection of fields (elements), each with its own name and type. Unlike an array, whose elements all represent the same type of information and are accessed using an index, the elements of a record represent different types of information and are accessed by name. A record can be accessed as a collective unit of elements, or the elements can be accessed individually. See also array, data structure, type1 (definition 1).

Record2 *vb.* To retain information, usually in a file.

Record format *n.* See record structure.

Record head *n.* The device in a tape machine that places data on the tape. In some tape machines, the record head is combined with the read head.

Record layout *n.* The organisation of data fields within a record. See also record1.

Record length *n.* The amount of storage space required to contain a record, typically given in bytes. See also record1.

Record locking *n.* A strategy employed in distributed processing and other multiuser situations to prevent more than one user at a time from writing data to a record. See also record1.

Record number *n.* A unique number assigned to a record in a database in order to identify it. A record number can identify an existing record by its position (for example, the tenth record from the beginning of a database), or it can be assigned to the record to serve as a key (for example, the number 00742 assigned to the tenth record from the beginning of the database). See also record1.

Record structure *n.* An ordered list of the fields that compose a record, together with a definition of the domain (acceptable values) of each field. See also record1.

Recover *vb.* 1. To return to a stable condition after some error has occurred. A programme recovers from an error by stabilising itself and resuming execution of instructions without user intervention. 2. To put back into a stable condition. A computer user may be able to recover lost or damaged data by using a programme to search for and salvage whatever information remains in storage. A database may be recovered by restoring its integrity after some problem has damaged it, such as abnormal termination of the database management programme.

Recoverable error *n.* An error that can be successfully managed by software. For example, when the user enters a number when a letter is required, the programme can simply display an error message and prompt the user again.

Recovery *n.* The restoration of lost data or the reconciliation of conflicting or erroneous data after a system failure. Recovery is often achieved using a disk or tape backup and system logs. See also backup.

Recreational Software Advisory Council *n.* An independent, nonprofit organisation established in the fall of 1994 by a group of six trade organisations, led by the Software Publishers

Association. The Council's goal was to create a new, objective content-labeling rating system for recreational software and other media such as the Internet. Acronym: RSAC.

Rectangle ad *n.* An Internet ad format that is larger than a traditional banner ad and is generally inserted directly into page content for greater visibility.

Rectifier *n.* A circuit component that passes current flowing in one direction but stops current flowing in the other direction. Rectifiers are used to convert alternating current to direct current.

Recto *n.* The right-hand page of two facing pages. A recto is characteristically an odd-numbered page.

Recursion *n.* The ability of a routine to call itself. Recursion enables certain algorithms to be implemented with small, simple routines, but it does not guarantee speed or efficiency. Erroneous use of recursion can cause a programme to run out of stack space during execution, causing the programme, and sometimes the entire system, to crash. See also call1 (definition 2), routine.

Recycle Bin *n.* A folder in Windows 9x, Windows CE, Windows NT, Windows 2000, and Windows XP represented by an icon on the screen resembling a basket decorated with the recycling logo. To remove a file, the user drags its icon to the Recycle Bin. However, a file in the Recycle Bin is not actually deleted from the disk until the user opens the Recycle Bin, selects the file, and presses the Delete key; until then, the user can retrieve it.

Red Book *n.* 1. The standards documents of the U.S. National Security Agency entitled "Trusted Network Interpretation of the Trusted Computer System Evaluation Criteria (NCSC-TG-005)" and "Trusted Network Interpretation (NCS-TG-011)." These documents define a system of ratings from A1 (most secure) to D (nonsecure), indicating the ability of a computer network to protect sensitive information. 2. A specifications book written by the Sony Corporation and Philips Corporation and endorsed by ISO, covering audio compact discs. 3. Telecommunications standards published by the CCITT.

Red-green-blue *n.* See RGB.

Redirection *n.* The process of writing to or reading from a file or device different from the one that would normally be the target or the source. For example, the MS-DOS or OS/2 command dir >prn redirects a directory listing from the screen to the printer.

Redirector *n.* Software on a client computer that intercepts requests for information and, when appropriate, directs them to the network. Redirectors can either be built into the client operating system or be part of an added networking package.

Redlining *n.* A feature of a word processing application that marks changes, additions, or deletions made to a document by a coauthor or editor. The purpose of redlining is to produce a record of the changes made to a document during the course of its development.

Redraw *n.* See refresh (definition 1).

Reduce *vb.* In a graphical user interface, to decrease the size of a window. A user can reduce a window either by clicking the appropriate button in the title bar or by clicking the mouse on the border of the window and dragging the border toward the middle of the window. See also maximise, minimise.

Reduced Instruction Set Computing *n.* See RISC.

Redundancy *n.* Using one or more servers on a Web site to perform identical tasks. If one of the servers crashes, another server assumes its tasks. Redundancy ensures that the Web site will continue to function if one of the servers stops working.

Redundancy check *n.* See CRC, LRC.

Redundant code *n.* Code that duplicates a function performed elsewhere—for example, code to sort a list that has already been sorted.

Reengineer *vb.* To rethink and redefine processes and procedures. In the context of computer systems, to reengineer means to change the way work is done in order to maximise the benefits of new technology.

Reengineering *vb.* 1. With regard to software, changing existing software to strengthen desirable characteristics and remove weaknesses. 2. With regard to corporate management, using information technology principles to address the challenges posed by a global economy and to consolidate management of a rapidly expanding work force.

Reentrant code *n.* Code written so that it can be shared by several programmes at the same time. When a programme is executing reentrant code, another programme can interrupt the execution and can then start or continue execution of that same code. Many operating-system routines are written to be reentrant so that only one copy needs to reside in memory to serve all executing applications. See also relocatable code.

Refactoring *n.* An optimisation process in object-oriented programming intended to improve the design or structure of a programme without changing its functionality. The goal of refactoring is to make the programme clearer and easier to work with—in part by removing duplication, abstracting common behaviours, and refining class hierarchies—and to improve the extensibility and reusability of existing code.

Reference1 *n.* A data type in the C++ programming language. A reference must be initialised with a variable name. The reference then becomes an alias for that variable but actually stores the address of the variable.

Reference2 *vb.* To access a variable, such as an element in an array or a field in a record.

Reference parameter *n.* A parameter in which the address of a variable, rather than the explicit value, is passed to the called routine. See also parameter.

Reference type *n.* A data type that is represented by a reference (similar to a pointer) to the type's actual value. If a reference type is assigned to a variable, that variable references (or "points to") the original value. No copy is made. Reference types comprise classes, interfaces, delegates, and boxed value types. See also data type, value type.

Reflecting software *n.* See reflector.

Reflective liquid-crystal display *n.* A liquid crystal display that is not equipped with edge light or backlight to enhance readability but rather depends on reflecting ambient light, making it difficult to read in brightly lit environments such as the outdoors. Also called: reflective LCD.

Reflective routing *n.* In wide area networks, the process of using a reflector to distribute data, thereby reducing the load of the network server. See also reflector.

Reflector *n.* A programme that sends messages to a number of users upon receipt of a signal from a single user. A common type of reflector is an e-mail reflector, which forwards any e-mail sent to it to the multiple recipients currently on its list. See also multiple recipients.

Reformat *vb.* 1. In applications, to change the look of a document by altering stylistic details, such as font, layout, indention, and alignment. 2. In data storage, to prepare for reuse a disk that already contains programmes or data, effectively destroying the existing contents.

Refresh *vb.* 1. To retrace a video screen at frequent intervals, even if the image does not change, so as to keep the phosphors irradiated. 2. To recharge dynamic random access memory chips (DRAMs) so that they continue to retain the information stored in them. Circuitry on the memory board automatically performs this function. See also refresh cycle.

Refreshable *adj.* In programming, referring to a programme module capable of being replaced in memory without affecting processing of the programme or the information being used by the programme.

Refresh cycle *n.* The process in which controller circuitry provides repeated electric pulses to dynamic random access memory chips in order to renew the stored electric charges in those locations that contain binary 1. Each pulse is one refresh cycle. Without constant refreshing, dynamic semiconductor RAM loses any information stored in it—as it does when the computer is turned off or when the power fails. See also dynamic RAM, static RAM.

Refresh rate *n.* In reference to video hardware, the frequency with which the entire screen is redrawn to maintain a constant, flicker-free image. On TV screens and raster-scan monitors, the electron beam that lights the phosphor coating on the inner surface of the screen typically refreshes the entire image area at a rate of about 60 hertz, or 60 times per second. Interlaced monitors, which redraw alternate lines during each sweep of the electron beam, actually refresh any particular line only 30 times per second. Because odd and even lines are refreshed on successive sweeps, however, the effective refresh rate is 60 times per second. See also refresh (definition 1).

Region *n.* 1. An area dedicated to or reserved for a particular purpose. 2. In video programming, a contiguous group of pixels that are treated as a unit. On the Apple Macintosh, for example, a region is an area in a grafPort that can be defined and manipulated as an entity. The visible working area within a window is an example of a region. See also grafPort.

Region code *n.* Codes on DVD movie titles and DVD-ROM drives that prevent playback of certain DVDs in certain geographical regions. Region codes are part of the DVD specification. See also CSS, DeCSS.

Region fill *n.* In computer graphics, the technique of filling a defined region on the screen with a selected colour, pattern, or other attribute. See also region (definition 2).

Register *n.* A set of bits of high-speed memory within a microprocessor or other electronic device, used to hold data for a particular purpose. Each register in a central processing unit is referred to in assembly language programmes by a name such as AX (the register that contains the results of arithmetic operations in an Intel 80x86 processor) or SP (the register that contains the memory address of the top of the stack in various processors).

Registered file type *n.* File types that are tracked by the system registry and are recognised by the programmes you have installed on your computer. See also file type.

Registration *n.* The process of precisely aligning elements or superimposing layers in a document or a graphic so that everything will print in the correct relative position. See also registration marks.

Registration marks *n.* Marks placed on a page so that in printing, the elements or layers in a document can be arranged correctly with respect to each other. Each element to be assembled contains its own registration marks; when the marks are precisely superimposed, the elements are in the correct position. See the illustration.

Registry *n.* A central hierarchical database in Windows 9x, Windows CE, Windows NT, and Windows 2000 used to store information necessary to configure the system for one or more users, applications, and hardware devices. The Registry contains information that Windows continually references during operation, such as profiles for each user, the applications installed on the computer and the types of documents each can create, property sheet settings for folders and application icons, what hardware exists on the system, and which ports are being used. The Registry replaces most of the text-based .ini files used in Windows 3. x and MS-DOS configuration files, such as AUTOEXEC.BAT and CONFIG.SYS. Although the Registry is common to the several Windows platforms, there are some differences among them. Also called: system registry. See also hierarchical database, .ini, input/output port, property sheet, Registry Editor.

Registry Editor *n.* An application under Windows that allows the user to edit the entries in the registry. Acronym: REGEDIT. See also registry.

Regression analysis *n.* In statistics, an analysis of the degree to which variations in an independent variable affect a dependent variable (a variable whose value depends on the value of another variable). See also multiple regression.

Regression testing *n.* Complete retesting of a modified programme, rather than a test of only the modified routines, to ensure that no errors have been introduced with the modifications.

Relation *n.* A structure composed of attributes (individual characteristics, such as name or address, corresponding to the columns in a table) and tuples (sets of attribute values describing particular entities, such as customers, corresponding to the rows in a table). Within a relation, tuples cannot be repeated; each must be unique. Further, tuples are unordered within a relation; interchanging two tuples does not change the relation. Finally, if relational theory is to be applicable, the domain of each attribute must be atomic—that is, a simple value, rather than a structure such as an array or a record. A relation in which the domains of all attributes are atomic is said to be normalised or in first normal form. See also normal form (definition 1).

Relational algebra *n.* A collection of rules and operators that permits relations (tables) to be manipulated. Relational algebra is usually described as having the following operators: SELECT, PROJECT, PRODUCT, UNION, INTERSECT, DIFFERENCE, JOIN (or INNER JOIN), and DIVIDE. In a relational database, relational algebra is used to develop procedures to build new relations based on the existing relations.

Relational calculus *n.* In database management, a nonprocedural method for manipulating relations (tables). There are two families of relational calculus: domain calculus and tuple calculus. The two families of relational calculus are mathematically equivalent to each other and to relational algebra. Using either family, one can formulate a description of a desired relation, based on the existing relations in the database.

Relational database *n.* A database or database management system that stores information in tables—rows and columns of data—and conducts searches by using data in specified columns of one table to find additional data in another table. In a relational database, the rows of a table represent records (collections of information about separate items) and the columns represent fields (particular attributes of a record). In conducting searches, a relational database matches information from a field in one table with information in a corresponding field of another table to produce a third table that combines requested data from both tables. For example, if one table contains the fields EMPLOYEE-ID, LAST-NAME, FIRST-NAME, and HIRE-DATE, and another contains the fields DEPT, EMPLOYEE-ID, and SALARY, a relational database can match the EMPLOYEE-ID fields in the two tables to find such information as the names of all employees earning a certain salary or the departments of all employees hired after a certain date.

Relational database management system *n.* See relational database.

Relational expression *n.* An expression that uses a relational operator such as "less than" or "greater than" to compare two or more expressions. A relational expression resolves to a Boolean (true/false) value. See also Boolean, relational operator.

Relational model *n.* A data model in which the data is organised in relations (tables). This is the model implemented in most modern database management systems.

Relational operator *n.* An operator that allows the programmer to compare two (or more) values or expressions. Typical relational operators are greater than (>), equal to (=), less than (<), not equal to (<>), greater than or equal to (>=), and less than or equal to (<=). See also relational expression.

Relational structure *n.* The record organisation used in the implementation of a relational model.

Relative address *n.* A location, as in a computer's memory, that is specified in terms of its distance (displacement or offset) from a starting point (base address). A relative address is typically computed by adding an offset to the base. In everyday terms, this is similar to creating the address 2001 Main Street, in which the base is the 2000 block of Main Street and the offset is 1, which specifies the first house from the beginning of the block. Also called: indirect address.

Relative coordinates *n.* Coordinates that are defined in terms of their distance from a given starting point, rather than from the origin (intersection of two axes). For example, from a starting point on the screen, a square defined by relative coordinates can be drawn as a series of lines, each representing a displacement in distance and direction from the end of the preceding point. The entire square can be redrawn at another location simply by changing the coordinates of the starting point rather than by recalculating the coordinates of each corner with reference to the origin.

Relative movement *n.* 1. Motion whose distance and direction are relative to a starting point. For example, when a mouse pointer is moved on the screen, the coordinates of its new position are relative to the previous location of the pointer. See also relative coordinates, relative pointing device. 2. In computer graphics and cinematography, the movement of one object in relation to another, such as the movement of horse A from the perspective of horse B on a racetrack.

Relative path *n.* A path that is implied by the current working directory. When a user enters a command that refers to a file, if the full pathname is not entered the current working directory becomes the relative path of the file referred to.

Relative pointing device *n.* A cursor-control device, such as a mouse or a trackball, in which the movement of an onscreen cursor is linked to the movement of the device but not to the position of the device. For example, if a user picks up a mouse and puts it down in a different location on a desk, the position of the onscreen cursor does not change because no movement (rolling) is detected. When the user rolls the mouse again, the cursor moves to reflect the mouse movement against the surface of the desk. Relative pointing devices differ from absolute pointing devices, such as graphics tablets, in which the device's location within a defined area is always associated with a predefined onscreen position. See also relative coordinates, relative movement (definition 1).

Relative URL *n.* Short for relative uniform resource locator. A form of URL in which the domain and some or all directory names are omitted, leaving only the document name and extension (and perhaps a partial list of directory names). The indicated file is found in a location relative to the pathname of the current document. Acronym: RELURL. See also file extension, URL.

RELAX NG *n.* An XML schema language based on Tree Regular Expressions for XML (TREX) and Regular Language Description for XML (RELAX). RELAX NG supports XML namespaces, uses XML syntax, maintains the information set of the XML document, and provides unrestricted support for mixed or unordered content.

Relay *n.* A switch activated by an electrical signal. A relay allows another signal to be controlled without the need for human action to route the other signal to the control point, and it also allows a relatively low-power signal to control a high-power signal.

Release 1 *n.* 1. A particular version of a piece of software, most commonly associated with the most recent version (as in "the latest release"). Some companies use the term release as an integral part of the product name (as in Lotus 1-2-3 Release 2.2). 2. A version of a product that is available in general distribution.

Release 2 *vb.* 1. To relinquish control of a block of memory, a device, or another system resource to the operating system. 2. To formally make a product available to the marketplace.

Reliability *n.* The likelihood of a computer system or device continuing to function over a given period of time and under specified conditions. Reliability is measured by different performance indexes. For example, the reliability of a hard disk is often given as mean time between failures (MTBF): the average length of time the disk can be expected to function without failing. See also MTBF, MTTR.

Reliability, availability, serviceability *n.* Acronym: RAS. See high availability.

Reload *vb.* 1. To load a programme into memory from a storage device again in order to run it, because the system has crashed or the program's operation was otherwise interrupted. 2. To retrieve a new copy of the Web page currently visible in a Web browser.

Relocatable address *n.* In programming, an address that is to be adjusted to reflect the actual place in memory into which a programme is loaded for execution. In "Get the byte located 12 bytes from this instruction," the address is relocatable; in "Get the byte located at address 255," the address is not relocatable. This convention is comparable to describing the "address" of a parked car as "level 2, row G" on one day and "level 5, row B" on another.

Relocatable code *n.* A programme written in such a way that it can be loaded into any part of available memory rather than having to be placed in one specific location. In relocatable code, address references that depend on the program's physical location in memory are calculated at run time so that programme instructions can be carried out correctly. See also reentrant code.

Relocate *n.* To move programmes and blocks of memory about within available space so as to use memory resources flexibly and efficiently. A relocatable programme can be loaded by the operating system into any part of available memory rather than into only one specific area. A relocatable block of memory is a portion of memory that can be moved around by the operating system as required; for example, the system might collect several available, relocatable blocks of memory to form one larger block of the size requested for use by a programme.

RELURL *n.* See relative URL.

Remailer *n.* A service that will forward e-mail while concealing the e-mail address of the originator of the message. Remailers may be used by individuals who wish to retain their privacy or avoid unsolicited commercial e-mail (UCE). Remailers may also be used to hide the identities of individuals and businesses sending spam or malicious or fraudulent e-mail.

Remark *n.* See comment, REM statement.

Remote *adj.* Not in the immediate vicinity, as a computer or other device located in another place (room, building, or city) and accessible through some type of cable or communications link.

Remote access *n.* The use of a remote computer.

Remote access server *n.* A host on a LAN (local area network) that is equipped with modems to enable users to connect to the network over telephone lines. Acronym: RAS.

Remote Access Service *n.* Windows software that allows a user to gain remote access to the network server via a modem. Acronym: RAS. See also remote access.

Remote administration *n.* The performance of system administration–related tasks via access from another machine in a network.

Remote Application Programming Interface *n.* A Remote Procedure Call (RPC) mechanism that enables an application running on a desktop computer to make function calls on a Windows CE–based device. The desktop computer is known as the Remote Application Programming Interface (RAPI) client, and the Windows CE device is known as the RAPI server. RAPI runs over Winsock and TCP/IP. Acronym: RAPI. See also remote procedure call.

Remote communications *n.* Interaction with a remote computer through a telephone connection or another communications line.

Remote computer system *n.* See remote system.

Remote Data Objects *n.* An object-oriented data access tool featured in Visual Basic 4 and later. Remote Data Objects have no native file format of their own; they can be used only with databases complying with the most recent ODBC standards. This feature is popular for its speed and minimal coding requirements. Acronym: RDO. See also ODBC, Visual Basic.

Remote Installation Services *n.* Software services that allow an administrator to set up new client computers remotely, without having to visit each client. The target clients must support remote booting. Acronym: RIS.

Remote login *n.* The action of logging in to a computer at a distant location by means of a data communications connection with the computer that one is presently using. After remote login, the user's own computer behaves like a terminal connected to the remote system. On the Internet, remote login is done primarily by rlogin and telnet. See also rlogin1 (definition 1), telnet1.

Remote monitoring *n.* See RMON.

Remote network monitoring *n.* See RMON.

Remote PC *n.* See remote system.

Remote procedure call *n.* In programming, a call by one programme to a second programme on a remote system. The second programme generally performs a task and returns the results of that task to the first programme. Acronym: RPC.

Remote system *n.* The computer or network that a remote user is accessing via a modem. See also remote access.

Remote terminal *n.* A terminal that is located at a site removed from the computer to which it is attached. Remote terminals rely on modems and telephone lines to communicate with the host computer. See also remote access.

Removable disk *n.* A disk that can be removed from a disk drive. Floppy disks are removable; hard disks usually are not. Also called: exchangeable disk.

REM statement *n.* Short for remark statement. A statement in the Basic programming language and the MS-DOS and OS/2 batch file languages that is used to add comments to a programme or batch file. Any statement beginning with the word REM is ignored by the interpreter or compiler or the command processor. See also comment.

Rename *n.* A command in most file transfer protocol (FTP) clients and in many other systems that allows the user to assign a new name to a file or files.

Render *vb.* To produce a graphic image from a data file on an output device such as a video display or printer.

Rendering *n.* The creation of an image containing geometric models, using colour and shading to give the image a realistic look. Usually part of a geometric modeling package such as a CAD programme, rendering uses mathematics to describe the location of a light source in relation to the object and to calculate the way in which the light would create highlights, shading, and variations in colour. The degree of realism can range from opaque, shaded polygons to images approximating photographs in their complexity. See also ray tracing.

RenderMan Shading Language *n.* A C-like graphics and rendering language developed by Pixar.

Repaginate *vb.* To recalculate the page breaks in a document.

Repeat *n.* A command in Microsoft Word that causes all information contained in either the last command dialog box or the last uninterrupted editing session to be repeated.

Repeat counter *n.* A loop counter; typically, a register that holds a number representing how many times a repetitive process has been or is to be executed.

Repeat delay *n.* A delay for the amount of time that elapses before a character begins repeating when you hold down a key.

Repeater *n.* A device used on communications circuits that decreases distortion by amplifying or regenerating a signal so that it can be transmitted onward in its original strength and form. On a network, a repeater connects two networks or two network segments at the physical layer of the ISO/OSI reference model and regenerates the signal.

Repeating Ethernet *n.* See repeater.

Repeat key *n.* On some keyboards, a key that must be held down at the same time as a character key to cause the character key's key code to be sent repeatedly. On most computer keyboards, however, a repeat key is not needed because a key automatically repeats if held down for longer than a brief delay.

RepeatKeys *n.* A feature of Windows 9x and Windows NT that allows a user to adjust or disable the typematic keyboard feature so as to accommodate users with restricted mobility, who may activate typematic by accident because they have trouble lifting their fingers from the keys. See also typematic.

Repetitive strain injury *n.* An occupational disorder of the tendons, ligaments, and nerves caused by the cumulative effects of prolonged repetitious movements. Repetitive strain injuries are appearing with increasing frequency among office workers who spend long hours typing at computerised workstations that are not equipped with safeguards such as wrist supports. Acronym: RSI. See also carpal tunnel syndrome, ergonomic keyboard, wrist support.

Replace *vb.* To put new data in the place of other data, usually after conducting a search for the data to be replaced. Text-based applications such as word processors typically include search-and-replace commands. In such operations, both old and new data must be specified, and search-and-replace procedures may or may not be sensitive to uppercase and lowercase, depending on the application programme. See also search1, search and replace.

Replay attack *n.* An attack in which a valid message is intercepted and then repeatedly retransmitted, either for fraudulent purposes or as part of a larger attack scheme.

Replication *n.* In a distributed database management system, the process of copying the database (or parts of it) to the other parts of the network. Replication allows distributed database systems to remain synchronised. See also distributed database, distributed database management system.

Report *n.* The presentation of information about a given topic, typically in printed form. Reports prepared with computers and appropriate software can include text, graphics, and charts. Database programmes can include special software for creating report forms and generating reports. Desktop publishing software and laser printers or typesetting equipment can be used to produce publication-quality output.

Report generator *n.* An application, commonly part of a database management programme, that uses a report "form" created by the user to lay out and print the contents of a database. A report generator is used to select specific record fields or ranges of records, to make the output attractive by including such features as headings, running heads, page numbers, and fonts.

Report writer *n.* See report generator.

Repository *n.* 1. A collection of information about a computing system. 2. A superset of a data dictionary. See also data dictionary.

Requested permissions *n.* Optionally specified permissions in an assembly that represent the minimum required, optionally desired, and always refused permissions for all code in the assembly. If there is no request, the code is granted the maximum that policy allows.

Request for Comments *n.* See RFC.

Request for Discussion *n.* A formal proposal for a discussion concerning the addition of a newsgroup to the Usenet hierarchy, the first step in a process that ends with a call for votes. Acronym: RFD. See also traditional newsgroup hierarchy, Usenet.

Research Libraries Information Network *n.* The combined online catalog of the Research Libraries Group, which includes many of the major research libraries in the United States. Acronym: RLIN.

Reserve *n.* A command that allocates contiguous disk space for the device instance's workspace. Digital video devices recognise this command.

Reserve accumulator *n.* An auxiliary storage register generally used to store the intermediate results of an extended calculation.

Reserved character *n.* A keyboard character that has a special meaning to a programme and, as a result, normally cannot be used in assigning names to files, documents, and other user-generated tools, such as macros. Characters commonly reserved for special uses include the asterisk (*), forward slash (/), backslash (\), question mark (?), and vertical bar (%).

Reserved date *n.* A date with a special meaning, rather than the date on the calendar. For example, some programmes use 9999 to indicate an account or a database listing that does not expire. See also magic dates.

Reserved memory *n.* See UMA.

Reserved word *n.* A word that has special meaning to a programme or in a programming language. Reserved words usually include those used for control statements (IF, FOR, END), data declarations, and the like. A reserved word can be used only in certain predefined circumstances; it cannot be used in naming documents, files, labels, variables, or user-generated tools such as macros.

Reset button *n.* A device that restarts a computer without turning off its power.

Resident font *n.* See internal font.

Resident programme *n.* See TSR.

Resistance *n.* The ability to impede (resist) the flow of electric current. With the exception of superconductors, all substances have a greater or lesser degree of resistance. Substances with very low resistance, such as metals, conduct electricity well and are called conductors. Substances with very high resistance, such as glass and rubber, conduct electricity poorly and are called nonconductors or insulators.

Resistor *n.* A circuit component designed to provide a specific amount of resistance to current flow.

Resize *vb.* To make an object or space larger or smaller. Also called: scale.

Resolution *n.* 1. The fineness of detail attained by a printer or a monitor in producing an image. For printers that form characters from small, closely spaced dots, resolution is measured in dots per inch, or dpi, and ranges from about 125 dpi for low-quality dot-matrix printers to about 600 dpi for some laser and ink-jet printers (typesetting equipment can print at resolutions of over 1000 dpi). For a video display, the number of pixels is determined by the graphics mode and video adapter, but the size of the display depends on the size and adjustment of the monitor; hence the resolution of a video display is taken as the total number of pixels displayed horizontally and vertically. See also high resolution, low resolution. 2. The process of translation between a domain name address and an IP address. See also DNS, IP address.

Resolve *vb.* 1. To match one piece of information to another in a database or lookup table. 2. To find a setting in which no hardware conflicts occur. 3. To convert a logical address to a physical address or vice versa. 4. To convert an Internet domain name to its corresponding IP address. See also DNS, IP address.

Resource *n.* 1. Any part of a computer system or a network, such as a disk drive, printer, or memory, that can be allotted to a programme or a process while it is running. 2. An item of data or code that can be used by more than one programme or in more than one place in a programme, such as a dialog box, a sound effect, or a font in a windowing environment. Many features in a programme can be altered by adding or replacing resources without the necessity of recompiling the programme from source code. Resources can also be copied and pasted from one programme into another, typically by a specialised utility programme called a resource editor. 3. Any nonexecutable data that is logically deployed with an application. A resource might be displayed in an application as error messages or as part of the user interface. Resources can contain data in a number of forms, including strings, images, and persisted objects.

Resource allocation *n.* The process of distributing a computer system's facilities to different components of a job in order to perform the job.

Resource data *n.* The data structures, templates, definition procedures, management routines, icon maps, and so forth associated with a particular resource, such as a menu, window, or dialog box. See also resource (definition 2), resource fork.

Resource Description Framework *n.* A specification developed by the World Wide Web Consortium (W3C) to define a flexible infrastructure for organising and managing metadata (data about data) across the Web and the Internet. The Resource Description Framework is intended to provide a framework based on XML (eXtensible Markup Language) that can standardise the way applications exchange metadata (or metacontent). Possible uses include search engines, content rating systems, and other areas in which exchange of information about data is valuable. Acronym: RDF. See also XML.

Resource file *n.* A file that consists of resource data and the resource map that indexes it. See also resource (definition 2), resource fork.

Resource fork *n.* One of the two forks of an Apple Macintosh file (the other being the data fork). The resource fork of a programme file contains reusable items of information that the programme can use during the course of execution, such as fonts, icons, windows, dialog boxes, menus, and the programme code itself. A user-created document typically stores its data in the data fork, but it can also use its resource fork for storing items that might be used more than once in the document. For example, in a HyperCard stack, the data that constitutes each card, or record, in the stack is stored in the data fork; digitised sounds and icons that might be used more than once are stored in the resource fork. The use of such resources makes programme development easier because resources can be developed and altered independently of the programme code. See also HyperCard, resource (definition 2).

Resource ID *n.* A number that identifies a particular resource within a given resource type on the Apple Macintosh—for example, a particular menu among many resources of type MENU that a programme might use. See also resource (definition 2).

Resource Reservation Setup Protocol *n.* A communications protocol designed to allow for "bandwidth on demand." A remote receiver requests that a certain amount of bandwidth be reserved by the server for a data stream; the server sends back a message (similar to the RSVP sent in reply to an invitation) indicating whether or not the request has been granted. Acronym: RSVP (Resourceeeration Setuprotocol).

Resource sharing *n.* The act of making files, printers, and other network resources available for use by others.

Resource type *n.* One of numerous classes of structural and procedural resources in the Macintosh operating system, such as code, fonts, windows, dialog boxes, templates, icons, patterns, strings, drivers, cursors, colour tables, and menus. Resource types have characteristic identifying labels, such as CODE for blocks of programme instructions, FONT for fonts, and CURS for mouse cursors. See also resource (definition 2), resource fork.

Response time *n.* 1. The time, often an average, that elapses between the issuance of a request and the provision of the data requested (or notification of inability to provide it). 2. The time required for a memory circuit or storage device to furnish data requested by the central processing unit (CPU).

Restart *vb.* See reboot.

Restore 1 *n.* The act of restoring a file or files. See also backup, recovery.

Restore 2 *vb.* To copy files from a backup storage device to their normal location, especially if the files are being copied to replace files that were accidentally lost or deleted.

Restricted function *n.* A function or an operation that can be executed only under certain circumstances, especially when the central processing unit (CPU) is in privileged mode. See also privileged mode.

Restructured Extended Executor *n.* See REXX.

Retrace *n.* The path followed by the electron beam in a raster-scan computer monitor as it returns either from the right to the left edge of the screen or from the bottom to the top of the screen. The retrace positions the electron beam for its next sweep across or down the screen; during this interval, the beam is briefly turned off to avoid drawing an unwanted line on the screen. Retracing occurs many times each second and uses tightly synchronised signals to ensure that the electron beam is turned off and on during the retrace. See also blanking, horizontal retrace, raster display, vertical retrace.

Retrieve *vb.* To obtain a specific requested item or set of data by locating it and returning it to a programme or to the user.

Computers can retrieve information from any source of storage—disks, tapes, or memory.

Retro virus *n.* A type of virus that avoids detection by attacking or disabling antivirus programmes. Also called: anti-anti-virus.

Return *vb.* 1. To transfer control of the system from a called routine or programme back to the calling routine or programme. Some languages support an explicit return or exit statement; others allow return only at the end (last statement) of the called routine or programme. See also call(definition 2). 2. To report the outcome of a called routine to the calling routine or programme.

Return code *n.* In programming, a code that is used to report the outcome of a procedure or to influence subsequent events when a routine or process terminates (returns) and passes control of the system to another routine. Return codes can, for example, indicate whether an operation was successful or not and can thus be used to determine what is to be done next.

Return from the dead *vb.* To regain access to the Internet after having been disconnected.

Return key *n.* A key on a keyboard that is used to terminate input of a field or record or to execute the default action of a dialog box. On IBM PCs and compatibles, this key is called ENTER. The corresponding key on a typewriter causes the carriage holding the paper to return to the starting position to begin a new line; hence the name. See also Enter key.

Return to zero *n.* A method of recording on magnetic media in which the reference condition, or "neutral state," is the absence of magnetisation. Abbreviation: RZ.

Reusability *n.* The ability of code or a design to be usable again in another application or system.

Reverse Address Resolution Protocol *n.* See RARP.

Reverse ARP *n.* See RARP.

Reverse byte ordering *n.* See little endian.

Reverse engineering *n.* A method of analysing a product in which the finished item is studied to determine its makeup or component parts—for example, studying a completed ROM chip to determine its programming or studying a new computer system to learn about its design. For computer software, reverse engineering typically involves decompilation of a substantial portion of the object code and studying the resulting decompiled code.

Reverse path forwarding *n.* A technique that makes routing decisions through a TCP/IP network by using the source address of a datagram rather than the destination address. Reverse path forwarding is used in broadcast and multicast applications because it reduces redundant transmissions to multiple recipients. Acronym: RPF. See also datagram, TCP/IP.

Reverse Polish notation *n.* See postfix notation.

Reverse video *n.* The reversal of light and dark in the display of selected characters on a video screen. For example, if text is normally displayed as white characters on a black background, reverse video presents text as black letters on a white background. Programmers commonly use reverse video as a means of highlighting text or special items (such as menu choices or the cursor) on the screen.

Revert *vb.* To return to the last saved version of a document. Choosing this command tells the application to abandon all changes made in a document since the last time it was saved.

Revisable-Form-Text DCA *n.* A standard within Document Content Architecture (DCA) for storing documents in such a way that the formatting can be changed by the receiver. A related standard is Final-Form-Text DCA. Acronym: RFTDCA. See also DCA.

Revision mark *n.* A mark that shows where a deletion, insertion, or other editing change has been made in a document.

Rewind *vb.* To wind a magnetic tape spool or cassette to its beginning.

Rewritable digital video disc *n.* Technology for recording data on disks that have the same storage capacity as digital video discs (DVDs) but can be rewritten like the compact disc–

rewritable (CD-RW) devices. See also digital video disc, PD-CD drive.

Rewrite *vb.* To write again, especially in situations where information is not permanently recorded, such as RAM or a video display. Also called: refresh, regenerate. See also dynamic RAM.

REXX *n.* Acronym for Restructured Extended Executor. A structured programming language used on IBM mainframes and with OS/2 Version 2.0. REXX programmes invoke application programmes and operating system commands.

RF *n.* See radio frequency.

RFC *n.* Acronym for Request for Comments. A document in which a standard, a protocol, or other information pertaining to the operation of the Internet is published. The RFC is actually issued, under the control of the IAB, after discussion and serves as the standard. RFCs can be obtained from sources such as InterNIC.

RFD *n.* See Request for Discussion.

RFI *n.* Acronym for radio frequency interference. Noise introduced into an electronic circuit, such as a radio or television, by electromagnetic radiation produced by another circuit, such as a computer.

RF shielding *n.* A structure, generally sheet metal or metallic foil, designed to prevent the passage of radio frequency (RF) electromagnetic radiation. RF shielding is intended to keep RF radiation either inside a device or out of a device. Without proper RF shielding, devices that use or emit RF radiation can interfere with each other; for example, running an electric mixer might cause interference on a television. Computers generate RF radiation and, to meet Federal Communications Commission (FCC) standards, must be properly shielded to prevent this RF radiation from leaking out. The metal case of a PC provides most of the needed RF shielding. Devices meeting FCC type A standards are suitable for business use. Devices meeting the more stringent FCC type B standards are suitable for home use. See also radio frequency, RFI.

RFTDCA *n.* See Revisable-Form-Text DCA.

RGB *n.* Acronym for red-green-blue. A model for describing colours that are produced by emitting light, as on a video monitor, rather than by absorbing it, as with ink on paper. The three kinds of cone cells in the eye respond to red, green, and blue light, respectively, so percentages of these additive primary colours can be mixed to get the appearance of any desired colour. Adding no colour produces black; adding 100 per cent of all three colours results in white. See also CMYK, RGB monitor.

RGB display *n.* See RGB monitor.

RGB monitor *n.* A colour monitor that receives its signals for red, green, and blue levels over separate lines. An RGB monitor generally produces sharper and cleaner images than those produced by a composite monitor, which receives levels for all three colours over a single line. See also RGB.

Ribbon cable *n.* A flat cable containing up to 100 parallel wires for data and control lines. For example, ribbon cables are used inside a computer's case to connect the disk drives to their controllers.

Ribbon cartridge *n.* A disposable module containing an inked fabric ribbon or a carbon-coated plastic film ribbon. Many impact printers use ribbon cartridges to make ribbon changing easier and cleaner.

Rich Text Format *n.* An adaptation of DCA (Document Content Architecture) that is used for transferring formatted text documents between applications, even those applications running on different platforms, such as between IBM and compatibles and Macintoshes. Acronym: RTF. See also DCA.

RIFF *n.* Acronym for Resource Interchange File Format. Developed jointly by IBM and Microsoft, RIFF is a broad-based specification designed to be used in defining standard formats for different types of multimedia files. A tagged-file specification, RIFF relies on headers that "tag" individual data elements in a file, identifying them by type and length. Because tags identify data elements, the RIFF specification can be extended to cover new types of elements while continuing to support older applications, which can simply ignore new, unrecognised elements they encounter in a file. See also AVI, MCI.

Right click *vb.* To make a selection using the button on the right side of a mouse or other pointing device. Doing so in Windows 9x and Windows NT 4.0 and later typically brings up a pop-up menu with options applicable to the object over which the cursor is positioned. See also mouse, pointing device.

Right click disabler *n.* A programme or script that prevents a user from employing any functions controlled by clicking the right mouse button. A right click disabler script may be run when a user visits a Web site to control the user's actions and options.

Right justification *n.* In typesetting, word processing, and desktop publishing, the process of aligning text evenly along the right margins of a column or page. The left edge of the text is ragged. See also justify (definition 1), rag.

Right-justify *vb.* To align lines of text and other display elements so that the right edges form a smooth line. See also align (definition 1), rag.

Rigid disk *n.* See hard disk.

RIMM *n.* A plug-in module jointly developed by Rambus and Intel for the high-bandwidth computer memory known as Direct RDRAM. A RIMM is comparable to a DIMM in size and shape, but the two are not pin-compatible. See also DIMM, RDRAM.

Ring network *n.* A LAN (local area network) in which devices (nodes) are connected in a closed loop, or ring. Messages in a ring network pass around the ring from node to node in one direction. When a node receives a message, it examines the destination address attached to the message. If the address is the same as the node's, the node accepts the message; otherwise, it regenerates the signal and passes the message along to the next node in the ring. Such regeneration allows a ring network to cover larger distances than star and bus networks. The ring can also be designed to bypass any malfunctioning or failed node. Because of the closed loop, however, adding new nodes can be difficult. See the illustration. Also called: ring topology. See also token passing, token ring network.

Ring topology *n.* See ring network.

Rip *vb.* To convert audio data from a compact disc into a WAV file or other digital format, typically in preparation for further encoding as an MP3 file. See also MP3.

RIP *n.* 1. Acronym for Routing Information Protocol. An Internet protocol, defined in RFC 1058, that defines the exchange of routing table information. Through RIP, each router on a network sends its routing table to its nearest neighbor every 30 seconds. Under RIP, routing is determined by the number of hops between source and destination. RIP is an interior gateway protocol (a protocol used by gateways for exchanging routing information). Because it is not the most efficient of routing protocols, it is being replaced by the more efficient Open Shortest Path First (OSPF) protocol. See also Bellman-Ford distance-vector routing algorithm, communications protocol, interior gateway protocol, OSPF. 2. See raster image processor.

RIPE *n.* Acronym for Reseaux IP Européens. A voluntary organisation of ISPs (Internet service providers) dedicated to the goal of a smoothly functioning, pan-European Internet network. Most of the work performed by RIPE is handled by discrete working groups that deal with issues such as management of the RIPE database and technical networking questions. RIPE also provides services that include registering domain names within top-level Internet domains and assigning IP (Internet Protocol) addresses. Member organisations of RIPE are supported by the RIPE NCC (Network Coordination Centre), based in Amsterdam, The Netherlands. See also American Registry for Internet Numbers.

Ripper *n.* Digital audio technology that converts audio data from a compact disc into a WAV file or other digital format. An encoder then converts this file into a file (typically an MP3 file) that can be played back by software known as a player. See also encoder, MP3.

RIPX *n.* A protocol used by routers to exchange information between routers on an IPX network and by hosts to determine the best routers to use when forwarding IPX traffic to a remote IPX network. Also called: RIP for IPX. See also communications protocol, IPX, NWLink, router.

RIS *n.* See Remote Installation Services.

RISC *n.* Acronym for Reduced Instruction Set Computing. A microprocessor design that focuses on rapid and efficient processing of a relatively small set of simple instructions that comprises most of the instructions a computer decodes and executes. RISC architecture optimises each of these instructions so that it can be carried out very rapidly—usually within a single clock cycle. RISC chips thus execute simple instructions more quickly than general-purpose CISC (Complex Instruction Set Computing) microprocessors, which are designed to handle a much wider array of instructions. They are, however, slower than CISC chips at executing complex instructions, which must be broken down into many machine instructions that RISC microprocessors can perform. Families of RISC chips include Sun Microsystems' SPARC, Motorola's 88000, Intel's i860, and the PowerPC developed by Apple, IBM, and Motorola. See also architecture, SPARC.

RISC86 *n.* A "hybrid" microprocessor technology in which CISC (Complex Instruction Set Computing) instructions are translated into RISC (Reduced Instruction Set Computing) instructions for processing. RISC86 is designed to support the 80x86 CISC architecture while providing the speed gains characteristic of RISC technology. RISC86 was developed by NexGen and is implemented in AMD's K6 microprocessor.

RJ-45 connector *n.* Short for Registered Jack-45 connector. An eight-wire connector used to attach devices to cables. The eight wires are encased in a plastic sheath and colour-coded to match corresponding slots in jacks. RJ-45 jacks are used to connect computers to LANs (local area networks) and to link ISDN (Integrated Services Digital Network) devices to NT-1

(Network Terminator 1) devices. Also called: RJ-45 jack. See also ISDN.

RJ-45 jack *n.* See RJ-45 connector.

RLE *n.* Short for Run Length Encoding. A data compression format in which only the first of a series of consecutive identical pixels is saved, along with the total number of pixels in the run. When the file is decompressed, each representative pixel is copied the correct number of times to replace those not saved. RLE compression works best with simple black and white or flat colour graphics.

RLIN *n.* See Research Libraries Information Network.

RLL encoding *n.* See run-length limited encoding.

Rlogin 1 *n.* 1. A protocol used to log in to a networked computer in which the local system automatically supplies the user's login name. See also communications protocol, logon. 2. A UNIX command in BSD UNIX that enables a user to log in to a remote computer on a network using the rlogin protocol. See also BSD UNIX.

Rlogin 2 *vb.* To connect to a networked computer using the rlogin protocol.

RLSD *n.* Acronym for Received Line Signal Detect. See DCD.

RMI-IIOP *n.* Acronym for Remote Method Invocation over Internet Inter-ORB Protocol. A subsystem of the Java 2 Platform, Enterprise Edition (J2EE). It provides the ability to write CORBA applications for the Java platform without learning the CORBA Interface Definition Language (IDL). RMI-IIOP includes the full functionality of a CORBA Object Request Broker and allows the programming of CORBA servers and applications via the RMI application programming interface (API). RMI-IIOP is useful for developers using Enterprise Java Beans (EJBs), since the remote object model for an EJB is RMI-based. Also called: RMI over IIOP. See also CORBA, Enterprise JavaBeans, J2EE.

RMM *n.* See real-mode mapper.

RMON *n.* Acronym for remote monitoring or remote network monitoring. A protocol that enables network information to be monitored and analysed at a central site. The nine management information bases (MIBs) defined by RMON provide statistics about network traffic. See also MIB.

Roaming user profile *n.* A server-based user profile that is downloaded to the local computer when a user logs on; it is updated both locally and on the server when the user logs off. A roaming user profile is available from the server when logging on to a workstation or server computer. When logging on, the user can use the local user profile if it is more current than the copy on the server. See also local user profile, mandatory user profile, user profile.

Robopost *vb.* To post articles to newsgroups automatically, usually by means of a bot. See also bot (definition 3), newsgroup, post.

Robot *n.* 1. A machine that can sense and react to input and cause changes in its surroundings with some degree of intelligence, ideally without human supervision. Although robots are often designed to mimic human movements in carrying out their work, they are seldom humanlike in appearance. Robots are commonly used in manufacturing products such as automobiles and computers. See also robotics. 2. See bot, spider.

Robotics *n.* The branch of engineering devoted to the creation and training of robots. Roboticists work within a wide range of fields, such as mechanical and electronic engineering, cybernetics, bionics, and artificial intelligence, all toward the end of endowing their creations with as much sensory awareness, physical dexterity, independence, and flexibility as possible. See also artificial intelligence, bionics, cybernetics.

Robust *adj.* Able to function or to continue functioning well in unexpected situations.

ROFL *n.* Acronym for rolling on the floor, laughing. An expression, used mostly in newsgroups and online conferences, to indicate one's appreciation of a joke or other humourous circumstance. Also called: ROTFL.

Role-playing game *n.* A game that is played on line, such as MUD, in which participants take on the identities of characters who interact with each other. These games often have a fantasy or science fiction setting and a set of rules that all players need to follow. Role-playing games may be similar to adventure games in terms of story line, but also feature management and decision making for the character assumed during the course of the game. Acronym: RPG. See also MUD.

Rollback *n.* 1. A return to a previous stable condition, as when the contents of a hard disk are restored from a backup after a destructive hard disk error. 2. The point in an online transaction when all updates to any databases involved in the transaction are reversed.

Rollover *n.* See Year 2000 rollover.

ROM *n.* 1. Acronym for read-only memory. A semiconductor circuit into which code or data is permanently installed by the manufacturing process. The use of this technology is economically viable only if the chips are produced in large quantities; experimental designs or small volumes are best handled using PROM or EPROM. 2. Acronym for read-only memory. Any semiconductor circuit serving as a memory that contains instructions or data that can be read but not modified (whether placed there by manufacturing or by a programming process, as in PROM and EPROM). See also EEPROM, EPROM, PROM.

Roman *adj.* Having upright rather than slanted characters in a typeface. See also font family.

ROM Basic *n.* Short for Read-Only Memory Beginner's All-purpose Symbolic Instruction Code. A Basic interpreter stored in ROM (read-only memory) so that the user can start programming after simply turning on the machine, without having to load Basic from a disk or tape. ROM Basic was a feature of many early home computers.

ROM BIOS *n.* Acronym for read-only memory basic input/output system. See BIOS.

ROM card *n.* Short for read-only memory card. A plug-in module that contains one or more printer fonts, programmes, or games or other information stored in ROM (read-only memory). A typical ROM card is about the size of a credit card and several times thicker. It stores information directly in integrated circuit boards. Also called: font card, game card. See also ROM (definition 1), ROM cartridge.

ROM cartridge *n.* Short for read-only memory cartridge. A plug-in module that contains one or more printer fonts, programmes, games, or other information stored in ROM (read-only memory) chips on a board enclosed in a plastic case with a connector exposed at one end so that it can easily plug into a printer, computer, game system, or other device. For example, a cartridge that plugs into a game system is a ROM cartridge. Also called: game cartridge. See also ROM (definition 1), ROM card.

ROM emulator *n.* Short for read-only memory emulator. A special circuit containing RAM memory that is connected to a target computer in place of the target computer's ROM chips. A separate computer writes the contents into the RAM, and then the target computer reads the RAM as if it were ROM. ROM emulators are used to debug ROM-resident software without the high cost and delay of manufacturing chips. Even though the use of a ROM emulator is more expensive than programming an EPROM, it is often preferred today because its contents can be changed much more quickly than those of an EPROM. Also called: ROM simulator. See also EEPROM, EPROM, ROM (definition 1).

ROM simulator *n.* See ROM emulator.

Root *n.* The main or uppermost level in a hierarchically organised set of information. The root is the point from which subsets branch in a logical sequence that moves from a broad focus to narrower perspectives. See also leaf, tree.

Root account *n.* On UNIX systems, the account having control over the operation of a computer. The system administrator uses this account for system maintenance. Also called: superuser. See also system administrator.

Root directory *n.* The point of entry into the directory tree in a disk-based hierarchical directory structure. Branching from this root are various directories and subdirectories, each of which can contain one or more files and subdirectories of its own. For example, in the MS-DOS operating system the root directory is identified by a name consisting of a single backslash character (\). Beneath the root are other directories, which may contain further directories, and so on. See the illustration.

Root folder *n.* The folder on a drive from which all other folders branch. The root folder's name consists of a single backslash character (\). For example, on drive C, this folder would be represented in the file system as C:\.

Rootless *n.* A mode in which an application belonging to a different user interface can run on top of a computer's underlying operating system without affecting that desktop or applications it may be running. For example, programmes belonging to a rootless version of the X Window System can be run on a Mac OS X computer without disturbing the Aqua desktop. See also Mac OS X, X Window System.

Root name *n.* In MS-DOS and Windows, the first part of a filename. In MS-DOS and earlier versions of Windows, the maximum length of the root name was eight characters; in Windows NT and later versions of Windows, the root name may be as long as 255 characters. See also 8.3, extension (definition 1), filename, long filenames.

Root name server *n.* See root server.

Root server *n.* A computer with the ability to locate DNS servers containing information about top-level Internet domains, such as com, org, uk, it, jp, and other country domains, in the Internet's Domain Name System (DNS) hierarchy. Beginning with the root server and continuing through referrals to name servers at lower levels of the hierarchy, the DNS is able to match a "friendly" Internet address, such as microsoft.com, with its numerical counterpart, the IP address. Root servers thus contain the data needed for referrals to name servers at the highest level of the hierarchy. There are 13 root servers in the world, located in the United States, the United Kingdom, Sweden, and Japan. Also called: root name server. See also DNS (definition 1), DNS server, top-level domain.

Root web *n.* The default, top-level web provided by a Web server. To access the root web, you supply the URL of the server without specifying a page name or subweb.

ROT13 encryption *n.* A simple encryption method in which each letter is replaced with the letter of the alphabet 13 letters after the original letter, so that A is replaced by N, and so forth; N, in turn, is replaced by A, and Z is replaced by M. ROT13 encryption is not used to protect messages against unauthorised readers; rather, it is used in newsgroups to encode messages that a user may not want to read, such as sexual jokes or spoilers. Some newsreaders can automatically perform ROT13 encryption and decryption at the touch of a key.

Rotary dialing *n.* The signaling system used in telephones with rotary dials, in which each digit is associated with a set number of pulses. During dialing, these pulses, which are audible as series of clicks, momentarily turn the current in the telephone wires on and off. Also called: pulse dialing.

Rotate *vb.* 1. To turn a model or other graphical image so that it is viewed at a different angle. 2. To move bits in a register to the left or to the right. The bit that moves out of the end position rotates to the newly vacated position at the opposite end of the register.

Rotational delay *n.* The time required for a desired disk sector to rotate to the read/write head. Also called: rotational latency.

Rotational latency *n.* See rotational delay.

RO terminal *n.* Short for read-only terminal. A terminal that can receive data but cannot send data. Nearly all printers can be classified as RO terminals.

ROTFL *n.* See ROFL.

Round *vb.* To shorten the fractional part of a number, increasing the last remaining (rightmost) digit or not, according to whether the deleted portion was over or under five. For example, 0.3333 rounded to two decimal places is 0.33, and 0.6666 is 0.67. Computer programmes often round numbers, sometimes causing confusion when the resulting values do not add up "correctly." Percentages in a spreadsheet can thus total 99 per cent or 101 per cent because of rounding.

Round robin *n.* A sequential, cyclical allocation of resources to more than one process or device.

Roundtripping *n.* The process of converting files from one format to another for viewing or editing and then converting the files back to the original format again. In some cases, roundtripping can involve repeated conversions of the file from one format to another and back. Frequent roundtripping may be a concern because each conversion has the potential to introduce unwanted changes to the file.

Routable protocol *n.* A communications protocol that is used to route data from one network to another by means of a network address and a device address. TCP/IP is an example of a routable protocol.

Router *n.* An intermediary device on a communications network that expedites message delivery. On a single network linking many computers through a mesh of possible connections, a router receives transmitted messages and forwards them to their correct destinations over the most efficient available route. On an interconnected set of LANs (local area networks)—including those based on differing architectures and protocols—using the same communications protocols, a router serves the somewhat different function of acting as a link between LANs, enabling messages to be sent from one to another. See also bridge, gateway.

Routine *n.* Any section of code that can be invoked (executed) within a programme. A routine usually has a name (identifier) associated with it and is executed by referencing that name. Related terms (which may or may not be exact synonyms, depending on the context) are function, procedure, and subroutine. See also function (definition 3), procedure, subroutine.

Routing *n.* The process of forwarding packets between networks from source to destination. See also dynamic routing, static routing.

Routing Information Protocol *n.* See RIP (definition 1).

Routing table *n.* In data communications, a table of information that provides network hardware (bridges and routers) with the directions needed to forward packets of data to locations on other networks. The information contained in a routing table differs according to whether it is used by a bridge or a router. A bridge relies on both the source (originating) and destination addresses to determine where and how to forward a packet. A router relies on the destination address and on information in the table that gives the possible routes—in hops or in number of jumps—between itself, intervening routers, and the destination. Routing tables are updated frequently as new or more current information becomes available. See also bridge, hop, internetwork, router.

Row *n.* A series of items arranged horizontally within some type of framework—for example, a continuous series of cells running from left to right in a spreadsheet; a horizontal line of pixels on a video screen; or a set of data values aligned horizontally in a table.

Royalty-free *n.* The absence of a requirement to pay the original owner of music, images, software, or other content for the right to use, edit, or distribute their content.

RPC *n.* See remote procedure call.

RPF *n.* See reverse path forwarding.

RPG *n.* 1. See role-playing game. 2. Acronym for Report Programme Generator. An IBM programming platform introduced in 1964. The earliest version of RPG was not a language but a programme generator intended to aid in producing business reports. Versions of RPG have been developed for various platforms, including IBM's AS/400 server, UNIX, MS-DOS, and Windows.

RPN *n.* Acronym for reverse Polish notation. See postfix notation.

RPROM *n.* Short for reprogrammable PROM. See EPROM.

RS-232-C standard *n.* An accepted industry standard for serial communications connections. Adopted by the Electrical Industries Association, this Recommended Standard (RS) defines the specific lines and signal characteristics used by serial communications controllers to standardise the transmission of serial data between devices. The letter C denotes that the current version of the standard is the third in a series. See also CTS, DSR, DTR, RTS, RXD, TXD.

RS-422/423/449 *n.* Standards for serial communications with transmission distances over 50 feet. RS-449 incorporates RS-422 and RS-423. Macintosh serial ports are RS-422 ports. See also RS-232-C standard.

RSA *n.* A widely used public/private key algorithm. It is the default cryptographic service provider (CSP) for Microsoft Windows. It was patented by RSA Data Security, Inc., in 1977. See also cryptographic service provider.

RSAC *n.* See Recreational Software Advisory Council.

RSA encryption *n.* Short for Rivest-Shamir-Adleman encryption. The public key encryption algorithm, introduced by Ronald Rivest, Adi Shamir, and Leonard Adleman in 1978, on which the PGP (Pretty Good Privacy) encryption programme is based. See also PGP, public key encryption.

RSI *n.* See repetitive strain injury.

RSN *adv.* See Real Soon Now.

R-squared value *n.* An indicator from 0 to 1 that reveals how closely the estimated values for the trendline correspond to your actual data. A trendline is most reliable when its R-squared value is at or near 1. Also called: the coefficient of determination.

RTF *n.* See Rich Text Format.

RTFM *n.* Acronym for read the flaming (or friendly) manual. A common answer to a question in an Internet newsgroup or product support conference that is adequately explained in the instruction manual. (The F in this acronym is not necessarily assumed to represent polite language.) Also called: RTM.

RTM *n.* Acronym for read the manual. See RTFM.

RTOS *n.* See real-time operating system.

RTP *n.* See Real-Time Protocol.

RTS *n.* Acronym for Request to Send. A signal sent, as from a computer to its modem, to request permission to transmit; the signal is often used in serial communications. RTS is a hardware signal sent over pin 4 in RS-232-C connections. See also RS-232-C standard.

RTSP *n.* See Real-Time Streaming Protocol.

Rubber banding *n.* In computer graphics, changing the shape of an object made up of connected lines by "grabbing" a point on an anchored line and "pulling" it to the new location.

Ruby *n.* An interpreted open source scripting language for object-oriented programming. Its simple syntax is partially based on the syntax of Eiffel and Ada. Considered to be similar to Perl, it has many features to process text files and perform system management tasks.

Rudder control *n.* A device, consisting of a pair of pedals, that enables a user to input rudder movements in a flight simulation programme. The rudder control is used along with a joystick (which controls the simulated ailerons and elevators) and possibly a throttle control.

Rule *n.* 1. A line printed above, below, or to the side of some element, either to set that item off from the remainder of the page or to improve the look of the page. Footnotes, for example, often appear below a short rule that sets them off from the main text on the page. The thickness of a rule is typically measured in points. (A point is approximately 1/72 inch.) See also point1 (definition 1). 2. In expert systems, a statement that can be used to verify premises and to enable a conclusion to be drawn. See also expert system.

Rule-based system *n.* See expert system, production system.

Ruler *n.* In some application programmes, such as word processors, an onscreen scale marked off in inches or other units of measure and used to show line widths, tab settings, paragraph indents, and so on. In programmes in which the ruler is "live," the onscreen ruler can be used with the mouse or with the keyboard to set, adjust, or remove tab stops and other settings.

Run *vb.* To execute a programme.

Run around *vb.* In page composition, to position text so that it flows around an illustration or other display.

Run-length encoding *n.* A simple compression method that replaces a contiguous series (run) of identical values in a data stream with a pair of values that represent the length of the series and the value itself. For example, a data stream that contains 57 consecutive entries with the value 10 could replace them all with the much shorter pair of values 57, 10. Acronym: RLE.

Run Length Encoding *n.* See RLE.

Run-length limited encoding *n.* A fast and highly efficient method of storing data on a disk (usually a hard disk) in which patterns in the bits representing information are translated into codes rather than being stored literally bit by bit and character by character. In RLL encoding, changes in magnetic flux are based on the number of zeros that occur in sequence. This scheme allows data to be stored with fewer changes in magnetic flux than would otherwise be needed for the number of data bits involved and results in considerably higher storage capacity than is possible with older technologies, such as frequency modulation (FM) and modified frequency modulation (MFM) encoding. Abbreviation: RLL encoding.

Running foot *n.* One or more lines of text in the bottom margin area of a page, composed of one or more elements such as the page number, the name of the chapter, and the date. Also called: footer.

Running head *n.* One or more lines of text in the top margin area of a page, composed of one or more elements such as the page number, the name of the chapter, and the date. Also called: header.

RUNOFF *n.* A very early text editor/text formatting programme, developed by J. E. Saltzer at M.I.T. for the CTSS (Compatible Time-Sharing System) operating system in the mid-1960s, in order to format his Ph.D. thesis. RUNOFF was the ancestor of many other text processors, including TeX, and the UNIX programmes roff, nroff, and troff.

Run-time *adj.* Occurring after a programme has begun to be executed, such as evaluation of variable expressions and dynamic allocation of memory.

Run time *n.* 1. The time period during which a programme is running. See also compile time, dynamic allocation, dynamic binding, link time. 2. The amount of time needed to execute a given programme.

Runtime *n.* See common language runtime.

Run-time binding *n.* Assignment of a meaning to an identifier (such as a variable) in a programme at the time the programme is executed rather than at the time the programme is compiled.

Run-time error *n.* A software error that occurs while a programme is being executed, as detected by a compiler or other supervisory programme.

Run-time library *n.* A file containing one or more prewritten routines to perform specific, commonly used functions. A run-time library, used primarily in high-level languages such as C, saves the programmer from having to rewrite those routines.

Run-time version *n.* 1. Programme code that is ready to be executed. Generally, this code has been compiled and can operate without error under most user command sequences and over most ranges of data sets. 2. A special release that provides the computer user with some, but not all, of the capabilities available in the full-fledged software package.

R/W *adj.* See read/write.

RXD *n.* Short for Receive (rx) Data. A line used to carry received serial data from one device to another, such as from a modem to a computer. Pin 3 is the RXD line in RS-232-C connections. See also RS-232-C standard.

RZ *n.* See return to zero.

S

S-100 bus *n.* A 100-pin bus specification used in the design of computers built around the Intel 8080 and Zilog Z-80 microprocessors. System designs using the Motorola 6800, 68000, and Intel iAPx86 family of microprocessors have also been built around the S-100 bus. S-100 computers were extremely popular with early computer enthusiasts. They had an open architecture, which permitted the configuration of systems with a wide range of add-on expansion boards.

SA *n.* Identifier for Intel's line of RISC-based microprocessors for portable and embedded devices. See also StrongARM.

SAA *n.* Acronym for Systems Application Architecture. An IBM-developed standard for the appearance and operation of application software that will give programmes written for all IBM computers—mainframe computers, minicomputers, and personal computers—a similar look and feel. SAA defines how an application interfaces with both the user and the supporting operating system. True SAA-compliant applications are compatible at the source level (before being compiled) with any SAA-compliant operating system—provided the system is capable of furnishing all the services required by the application.

Sad Mac *n.* An error indication that occurs on Apple Macintosh computers when the system fails the initial diagnostic test. A Sad Mac is a picture of a Macintosh with a frowning face and X's for eyes, with an error code beneath the picture.

Safe mode *n.* In some versions of Windows, such as Windows 95, a boot mode that bypasses startup files and loads only the most basic drivers. Safe mode allows the user to correct some problem with the system—for example, if the system fails to boot or the registry has become corrupted. See also boot1.

Salt *n.* Random data used to supplement encryption schemes. A salt value allows two identical packets of data to be encrypted into two different packets of ciphertext using the same key by changing the salt value with each packet. Also called: salt string, salt value.

Samba *n.* A popular freeware programme that provides file and print services, authentication and authorisation, name resolution, and service announcement (browsing). As a file server, Samba enables the sharing of files, printers, and other resources on a UNIX Samba server with Windows clients over a network. Based on the Server Message Block (SMB) protocol, Samba originally was developed as a Network File System (NFS) for UNIX by Andrew Tridgell. See also NFS, SMB.

Sampling *vb.* 1. In statistics, gathering data from a representative subset of a larger group (called a population)—for example, determining a country's presumed voting pattern by polling a demographic cross section of voters. Other uses of this type of sampling might include checking the accuracy and efficiency of computerised transactions by reviewing every hundredth transaction or predicting traffic volumes by measuring traffic flow in a few strategic streets. There are many statistical procedures for estimating how accurately a given sample reflects the behaviour of a group as a whole. 2. The conversion of analog signals to a digital format; samples are taken at periodic intervals to measure and record some parameter, such as a signal from a temperature sensor or a microphone. Analog-to-digital converters are used in computers to sample analog signals as voltages and convert them to the binary form a computer can process. The two primary characteristics of this type of sampling are the sampling rate (usually express

Sampling rate *n.* The frequency with which samples of a physical variable, such as sound, are taken. The higher the sampling rate (that is, the more samples taken per unit of time), the more closely the digitised result resembles the original. See also sampling (definition 2).

Sampling synthesizer *n.* A device designed to reproduce sounds, at differing frequencies, based on a digitised sound stored in read-only memory. For example, a recorded piano note, digitised and stored in memory, is used by the synthesizer to create other piano-like notes.

Samurai *n.* A hacker employed by a company or organisation to manage network security or conduct legal cracking operations. A samurai uses the skills of a hacker to meet the legitimate needs of an employer.

SAN *n.* See storage area network.

Sandbox *n.* 1. Java Virtual Machine security area for downloaded (remote or untrusted) applets, an area in which such applets are confined and prevented from accessing system resources. Confinement to the sandbox prevents downloaded applets from carrying out potentially dangerous operations, maliciously or otherwise. They have to "play" inside the sandbox, and any attempt to "escape" is thwarted by the Java Security Manager. 2. Slang for the research and development department at many software and computer companies. See also applet, Java Virtual Machine.

Sans serif *adj.* Literally, "without stroke"; describes any typeface in which the characters have no serifs (the short lines or ornaments at the upper and lower ends of the strokes). A sans serif typeface usually possesses a more straightforward, geometric appearance than a typeface with serifs and typically lacks the contrast between thick and thin strokes found in serif faces. Sans serif typefaces are used more frequently in display type, such as headlines, than in blocks of text.

SAOL *n.* Acronym for Structured Audio Orchestra Language. Part of the MPEG-4 standard, SAOL describes a set of tools for producing computer music, audio for computer games, streaming Internet sound or music, and other multimedia applications. SAOL is a flexible computer language for describing music synthesis and integrating synthetic sound with recorded sound in an MPEG-4 bit stream. See also bit stream, MPEG-4, streaming (definition 1).

SAP *n.* See Service Advertising Protocol.

SAPI *n.* Acronym for Speech Application Programming Interface. A feature in Windows 9x and Windows NT that allows applications to include speech recognition or convert text to speech. Also called: Speech API. See also voice recognition.

SAS *n.* See single attachment station.

SASL *n.* Acronym for Simple Authentication and Security Layer. An authentication support mechanism for use with connection-based protocols. SASL allows a client to request identification from a server and negotiate use of an added security layer for authentication during subsequent client/ server interaction.

Satellite *n.* See communications satellite.

Satellite computer *n.* A computer that is connected to another computer, with which it interacts over a communications link. As its name indicates, a satellite computer is of lesser "stature" than the main, or host, computer; the host controls either the satellite itself or the tasks the satellite performs. See also remote communications.

Satellite dish *n.* A parabolic (dish-shaped) reflector and antenna that is used for transmitting and receiving signals between the ground and earth satellites. Satellite dishes are commonly used for receiving television transmissions.

Saturated mode *n.* The state in which a switching device or amplifier is passing the maximum possible current. A device is in saturated mode when increasing the control signal does not result in output of additional current.

Saturation *n.* 1. In a switching device or amplifier, the fully conducting state. At saturation, the device is passing the maximum possible current. The term is most commonly used with reference to circuits containing bipolar or field-effect transistors. 2. In colour graphics and printing, the amount of colour in a specified hue, often specified as a percentage. See also HSB.

Save *vb.* To write data (typically a file) to a storage medium, such as a disk or tape.

SAX *n.* Acronym for Simple API for XML. An event-driven application programme interface (API) used to interpret an XML file. SAX works with an XML parser, providing an interface between the parser and an XML application. SAX is used as an alternative to the more complex object-based Document Object Model (DOM) interface. See also DOM.

Scalability *n.* A measure of how well a computer, service, or application can grow to meet increasing performance demands. For server clusters, it is the ability to incrementally add one or more systems to an existing cluster when the overall load of the cluster exceeds its capabilities. See also server cluster.

Scalable *adj.* Of or relating to the characteristic of a piece of hardware or software or a network that makes it possible for it to expand—or shrink—to meet future needs and circumstances. For example, a scalable network allows the network administrator to add many additional nodes without the need to redesign the basic system.

Scalable font *n.* Any font that can be scaled to produce characters in varying sizes. Examples of scalable fonts are screen fonts in a graphical user interface, stroke fonts (such as Courier) and outline fonts common to most PostScript printers, TrueType fonts, and the method for screen font definition used in Macintosh System 7. In contrast, most text-based interfaces and printing devices (such as daisy-wheel printers) offer text in only one size. See also outline font, PostScript font, screen font, stroke font, TrueType.

Scalable parallel processing *n.* Multiprocessing architectures in which additional processors and additional users can easily be added without excessive increases in complexity and loss of performance. Acronym: SPP.

Scalable Processor Architecture *n.* See SPARC.

Scalable Vector Graphics *n.* See SVG.

scalar *n.* A factor, coefficient, or variable consisting of a single value (as opposed to a record, an array, or some other complex data structure).

Scalar data type *n.* A data type defined as having a predictable and enumerable sequence of values that can be compared for greater-than/less-than relationships. Scalar data types include integers, characters, user-defined enumerated data types, and (in most implementations) Boolean values. Some debate exists as to whether or not floating-point numbers can be considered a scalar data type; although they can be ordered, enumeration is often questionable because of rounding and conversion errors. See also Boolean expression, enumerated data type, floating-point number.

Scalar processor *n.* A processor designed for high-speed computation of scalar values. A scalar value can be represented by a single number.

Scalar variable *n.* See scalar.

scale 1 *n.* A horizontal or vertical line on a graph that shows minimum, maximum, and interval values for the data plotted.

Scale 2 *vb.* 1. To enlarge or reduce a graphic display, such as a drawing or a proportional character font, by adjusting its size proportionally. 2. To alter the way in which values are represented so as to bring them into a different range—for example, to change linear feet to quarter inches on a blueprint drawing of a house. 3. In programming, to determine the number of digits occupied by fixed-point or floating-point numbers. See also fixed-point notation, floating-point number.

Scaling *n.* In computer graphics, the process of enlarging or reducing a graphical image—scaling a font to a desired size or scaling a model created with a CAD programme, for example. See also CAD.

Scan *vb.* 1. In television and computer display technologies, to move an electron beam across the inner surface of the screen, one line at a time, to light the phosphors that create a displayed image. 2. In facsimile and other optical technologies, to move a light-sensitive device across an image-bearing surface such as a page of text, converting the light and dark areas on the surface to binary digits that can be interpreted by a computer.

Scan code *n.* A code number transmitted to an IBM or compatible computer whenever a key is pressed or released. Each key on the keyboard has a unique scan code. This code is not the same as the ASCII code for the letter, number, or symbol shown on the key; it is a special identifier for the key itself and is always the same for a particular key. When a key is pressed, the scan code is transmitted to the computer, where a portion of the ROM BIOS (read-only memory basic input/ output system) dedicated to the keyboard translates the scan code into its ASCII equivalent. Because a single key can generate more than one character (lowercase a and uppercase A, for example), the ROM BIOS also keeps track of the status of keys that change the keyboard state, such as the Shift key, and takes them into account when translating a scan code.

Scan head *n.* An optical device found in scanners and fax machines that moves across the subject being scanned, converts light and dark areas to electrical signals, and sends those signals to the scanning system for processing.

Scan line *n.* 1. One of many horizontal lines of a graphics display screen, such as a television or raster-scan monitor. 2. A single row of pixels read by a scanning device.

Scanner *n.* An optical input device that uses light-sensing equipment to capture an image on paper or some other subject. The image is translated into a digital signal that can then be manipulated by optical character recognition (OCR) software or graphics software. Scanners come in a number of types, including flatbed (scan head passes over a stationary subject), feed (subject is pulled across a stationary scan head), drum (subject is rotated around a stationary scan head), and handheld (user passes device over a stationary subject).

Scan rate *n.* See refresh rate.

Scatter diagram *n.* A graph consisting of points whose coordinates represent values of data, often used to illustrate a correlation between one or more variables and a test group.

Schedule *vb.* To programme a computer to perform a specified action at a specified time and date.

Scheduler *n.* An operating-system process that starts and ends tasks (programmes), manages concurrently running processes, and allocates system resources. Also called: -dispatcher.

Scheduling algorithm *n.* An algorithm that governs the proper timing of a sequence of events in an operating system or application. For example, an effective motion graphics scheduling algorithm would be able to retrieve the graphic objects, process them, and display them without causing stutter or disruptions. See also algorithm.

Schema *n.* A description of a database to a database management system (DBMS) in the language provided by the DBMS. A schema defines aspects of the database, such as attributes (fields) and domains and parameters of the attributes.

Schematic *n.* A diagram that shows a circuit's components and the connections between them using lines and a set of standard symbols to represent various electronic components.

Schottky diode *n.* A type of diode (device that passes current in one direction) in which a semiconductor layer and a metal layer are brought into contact. It is characterised by very fast switching speeds. Also called: hot carrier diode, Schottky barrier diode.

Scientific notation *n.* A floating-point method of representing a number, especially a very large or very small one, in which numbers are expressed as products consisting of a number between 1 and 10 multiplied by a power of 10. Scientific notation commonly uses the letter E in place of "times 10," as in 5.0E3, meaning 5.0 times 10 to the third power, or 103. See also floating-point notation.

Sci. newsgroups *n.* Usenet newsgroups that are part of the sci. hierarchy and begin with "sci." These newsgroups are devoted to discussions of scientific research and applications, except for computer science, which is discussed in the comp. newsgroups. See also newsgroup, traditional newsgroup hierarchy, Usenet.

Scissoring *n.* See clip.

Scope *n.* 1. In programming, the extent to which an identifier, such as a constant, data type, variable, or routine, can be referenced within a programme. Scope can be global or local. Scope can also be affected by redefining identifiers, such as by giving the same name to both a global variable and a local variable. See also block(definition 3), global, local. 2. In electronics, slang for oscilloscope. See also oscilloscope.

Score *n.* When referring to a spelling checker, a score is a number that indicates how much a replacement word differs from the original misspelled word. A low score indicates that the misspelled word was changed slightly, while a high score indicates that the word was changed a great deal.

SCP *n.* Acronym for Simple Control Protocol. A lightweight peer-to-peer networking protocol for devices that have limited processing and memory resources and operate over limited-bandwidth networks such as powerline carrier (PLC) systems. Products using SCP can interoperate with products using the Universal Plug and Play (UPnP), CEBus, and Home Plug & Play (HPnP) standards. Developed by a team of companies including Microsoft and General Electric, SCP enables the interaction between UPnP devices, devices based on Internet Protocol (IP), and non-IP-capable devices such as coffeemakers and alarm clocks. SCP, which was designed as a stand-alone protocol, can be used in residential, commercial, industrial, and utility applications. See also UPnP networking.

SCR *n.* See silicon-controlled rectifier.

Scrambler *n.* A device or programme that reorders a signal sequence in order to render it indecipherable. See also encryption.

Scrap *n.* An application or system file maintained for storing data that has been marked for movement, copying, or deletion. See also clipboard (definition 1).

Scrapbook *n.* 1. A file in which a series of text and graphical images can be saved for subsequent use. 2. A Macintosh system file that can hold a number of text and graphical images for later use.

Scratch 1 *n.* A memory region or file used by a programme or operating system to hold work in progress temporarily. Created and maintained usually without the end user's knowledge, the scratch is needed only until the current session is terminated, at which time the data is saved or discarded. Also called: scratch file. See also temporary file.

Scratch 2 *vb.* To erase or discard data.

Scratch file *n.* See scratch1.

Scratchpad *n.* 1. A temporary storage area used by a programme or operating system for calculations, data, and other work in progress. See also scratch1, temporary file. 2. A high-speed memory circuit used to hold small items of data for rapid retrieval. See also cache.

Scratchpad memory *n.* See cache.

Scratchpad RAM *n.* Memory used by a central processing unit (CPU) for temporary data storage. Also called: scratchpad, scratchpad memory. See also central processing unit, register.

Scream *vb.* To operate at very high speed. For example, a modem that can transfer data several times faster than the one it replaced or a computer with a very high clock speed could be said to "scream."

Screamer *n.* Slang for a piece of computer equipment that operates at a very high speed. Generally, "screamers" are the newest versions of a particular piece of equipment, such as a PC with the latest, fastest microprocessor, or are comprised of multiple components that increase the operating speed over standard models, such as a PC that has a huge amount of RAM (Random Access Memory), a high-performance video board, a superfast CD-ROM drive, and the latest microprocessor. However, as technology evolves and new, faster devices are introduced, yesterday's screamer rapidly becomes today's snail.

Screen angle *n.* The angle at which the dots in a halftone screen are printed. A correct angle will minimise blur and other undesirable effects, such as moiré patterns. See also colour separation (definition 1), halftone, moiré.

Screen buffer *n.* See video buffer.

Screen dump *n.* A duplicate of a screen image; essentially, a snapshot of the screen that is either sent to a printer or saved as a file.

Screen flicker *n.* See flicker.

Screen font *n.* A typeface designed for display on a computer monitor screen. Screen fonts often have accompanying PostScript fonts for printing to PostScript-compatible printers. See also derived font, intrinsic font.

Screen frequency *n.* See halftone.

Screen grabber *n.* See grabber (definition 3).

Screen name *n.* A name under which an America Online user is known. The screen name may be the same as the user's real name. See also America Online.

Screen phone *n.* A type of Internet appliance combining a telephone with an LCD display screen, a digital fax modem, and a computer keyboard, with ports for a mouse, printer, and other peripheral devices. Screen phones can be used as regular telephones for voice communications and can also be used as terminals to gain access to the Internet and other online services.

Screen pitch *n.* A measurement of a computer monitor's screen density, representing the distance between phosphors on the display. The lower the number, the more detail can be displayed clearly. For example, a .28-dot-pitch screen has better resolution than one with .32.

Screen saver *n.* A utility that causes a monitor to blank out or display a certain image after a specified amount of time passes without the keyboard being touched or the mouse being moved. Touching a key or moving the mouse deactivates the screen saver. Screen savers were originally used to prevent images from becoming permanently etched on a monitor's screen. Although modern monitors are not susceptible to this problem, screen savers remain popular for their decorative and entertainment value.

Screen shot *n.* An image that shows all or part of a computer display.

ScreenTips *n.* Notes that appear on the screen to provide information about a toolbar button, tracked change, or comment or to display a footnote or an endnote. ScreenTips also display the text that will appear if you choose to insert a date or AutoText entry.

Script *n.* A programme consisting of a set of instructions to an application or a utility programme. The instructions usually use the rules and syntax of the application or utility. On the World Wide Web, scripts are commonly used to customise or add interactivity to Web pages. See also macro.

Scripting language *n.* A simple programming language designed to perform special or limited tasks, sometimes associated with a particular application or function. An example of a scripting language is Perl. See also Perl, script.

Script kiddie *n.* A would-be hacker who does not have the technical skills or knowledge needed for traditional hacking methods; one who relies on easy-to-use kiddie scripts. See also hacker, kiddie script.

Scriptlet *n.* A reusable Web page based on the features of Dynamic HTML (DHTML) that can be created with HTML text and a scripting language and then inserted as a control in another Web page or in an application. Developed by Microsoft and introduced in Internet Explorer version 4, scriptlets are implemented as .htm files that give developers a relatively easy, object-based means of creating components that reflect the Web metaphor and that can be used to add interactivity and functionality—for example, animation, colour changes, pop-up menus, or drag-and-drop capability—to Web pages without requiring repeated trips to the server. Also called: Microsoft Scripting Component. See also dynamic HTML.

Scroll *vb.* To move a document or other data in a window in order to view a particular portion of the document. Scrolling may be controlled by the mouse, arrow keys, or other keys on the keyboard. See also scroll bar.

Scroll arrow *n.* See scroll bar.

Scroll bar *n.* In some graphical user interfaces, a vertical or horizontal bar at the side or bottom of a display area that can be used with a mouse for moving around in that area. Scroll bars often have four active areas: two scroll arrows for moving line by line, a sliding scroll box for moving to an arbitrary location in the display area, and gray areas for moving in increments of one window at a time.

Scroll box *n.* See elevator.

Scroll Lock key *n.* On the IBM PC/XT and AT and compatible keyboards, a key on the top row of the numeric keypad that controls the effect of the cursor control keys and sometimes prevents the screen from scrolling. On the enhanced and Macintosh keyboards, this key is to the right of the function keys on the top row. Many modern applications ignore the Scroll Lock setting.

Scroll wheel *n.* A thumbwheel on a mouse that, when turned, enables the user to scroll or zoom without clicking the scroll bar or using the keyboard. Depending on the mouse, a scroll wheel can also double as a third mouse button. See also scroll bar.

SCSI *n.* Acronym for Small Computer System Interface, a standard high-speed parallel interface defined by the X3T9.2 committee of the American National Standards Institute (ANSI). A SCSI (pronounced "scuzzy") interface is used to connect microcomputers to SCSI peripheral devices, such as many hard disks and printers, and to other computers and local area networks. Also called: SCSI-1, SCSI I.

SCSI-1 *n.* See SCSI.

SCSI-2 *n.* An enhanced ANSI standard for SCSI (Small Computer System Interface) buses. Compared with the original SCSI standard (now called SCSI-1), which can transfer data 8 bits at a time at up to 5 MB per second, SCSI-2 offers increased data width, increased speed, or both. A SCSI-2 disk drive or host adapter can work with SCSI-1 equipment at the older equipment's maximum speed. Also called: SCSI II. See also Fast SCSI, Fast/Wide SCSI, SCSI, Wide SCSI.

SCSI bus *n.* A parallel bus that carries data and control signals from SCSI devices to a SCSI controller. See also bus, controller, SCSI device.

SCSI chain *n.* A set of devices on a SCSI bus. Each device (except the host adapter and the last device) is connected to two other devices by two cables, forming a daisy chain. See also daisy chain, SCSI.

SCSI connector *n.* A cable connector used to connect a SCSI device to a SCSI bus.

SCSI device *n.* A peripheral device that uses the SCSI standard to exchange data and control signals with a computer's CPU. See also peripheral, SCSI.

SCSI I *n.* See SCSI.

SCSI II *n.* See SCSI-2.

SCSI ID *n.* The unique identity of a SCSI device. Each device connected to a SCSI bus must have a different SCSI ID. A maximum of eight SCSI IDs can be used on the same SCSI bus. See also bus, SCSI device.

SCSI network *n.* A set of devices on a SCSI bus, which acts like a local area network. See also SCSI.

SCSI port *n.* 1. A SCSI host adapter within a computer, which provides a logical connection between the computer and all of the devices on the SCSI bus. See also SCSI. 2. A connector on a device for a SCSI bus cable. See also SCSI.

SDH *n.* See Synchronous Digital Hierarchy.

SDK *n.* Acronym for software development kit. See developer's toolkit.

SDLC *n.* Acronym for Synchronous Data Link Control, the data transmission protocol most widely used by networks conforming to IBM's Systems Network Architecture (SNA). SDLC is similar to the HDLC (High-level Data Link Control) protocol developed by the International Organisation for Standardisation (ISO). See also HDLC.

SDM *n.* See space-division multiplexing.

SDMI *n.* See Secure Digital Music Initiative.

SDRAM *n.* Acronym for synchronous DRAM. A form of dynamic random access memory (DRAM) that can run at higher clock speeds than conventional DRAM by employing a bursting technique in which the DRAM predicts the address of the next memory location to be accessed. See also dynamic RAM.

SDSL *n.* Acronym for symmetric (or single-line) digital subscriber line, a digital telecommunications technology that is a variation of HDSL. SDSL uses one pair of copper wires rather than two pairs of wires and transmits at 1.544 Mbps.

.sea *n.* A file extension for a self-extracting Macintosh archive compressed with StuffIt. See also self-extracting file.

Seamless integration *n.* The favourable result that occurs when a new hardware component or programme blends smoothly into the overall operation of the system. It is usually the result of thoughtful design and programming.

Search 1 *n.* The process of seeking a particular file or specific data. A search is carried out by a programme through comparison or calculation to determine whether a match to some pattern exists or whether some other criteria have been met. See also binary search, hash search, linear search, search and replace, wildcard character.

Search 2 *vb.* 1. To look for the location of a file. 2. To seek specific data within a file or data structure. See also replace.

Search algorithm *n.* An algorithm designed to locate a certain element, called the target, in a data structure. See also algorithm, binary search, hash search, linear search.

Search and replace *n.* A common process in applications such as word processors in which the user specifies two strings of characters. The process finds instances of the first string and replaces them with the second string.

Search criteria *n.* The terms or conditions that a search engine uses to find items in a database. See also search engine.

Search engine *n.* 1. A programme that searches for keywords in documents or in a database. 2. On the Internet, a programme that searches for keywords in files and documents found on the World Wide Web, newsgroups, Gopher menus, and FTP archives. Some search engines are used for a single Internet site, such as a dedicated search engine for a Web site. Others search across many sites, using such agents as spiders to gather lists of available files and documents and store these lists in databases that users can search by keyword. Examples of the latter type of search engine are Lycos and Excite. Most search engines reside on a server. See also agent (definition 2), FTP, Gopher or gopher, newsgroup, spider, World Wide Web.

Search key *n.* 1. The particular field (or column) of the records to be searched in a database. See also primary key, secondary key. 2. The value that is to be searched for in a document or any collection of data.

Search path *n.* The route followed by an operating system to find the location of a stored file. The search path begins with a drive or volume (disk) designator or a network share, continues through a chain of directories and subdirectories, if any, and ends with the file name. C:\books\diction\start.exe is an example of a search path. Also called: access path.

Search string *n.* The string of characters to be matched in a search—typically (but not necessarily) a text string.

Seat 1 *n.* One workstation or computer, in the context of software licensing on a per-seat basis. See also license agreement, workstation (definition 1).

Seat 2 *vb.* To insert a piece of hardware fully and position it correctly in a computer or affiliated equipment, as in seating a single inline memory module (SIMM) in its socket.

Secondary channel *n.* A transmission channel in a communications system that carries testing and diagnostic information rather than actual data.

Secondary key *n.* A field that is to be sorted or searched within a subset of the records having identical primary key values. See also alternate key (definition 1), candidate key.

Secondary service provider *n.* An Internet service provider that provides a Web presence but not direct connectivity. See also ISP.

Secondary storage *n.* Any data storage medium other than a computer's random access memory (RAM)—typically tape or disk.

Second-level domain *n.* The level immediately beneath the top-level domain in the Internet's DNS hierarchy. See also domain (definition 3).

Second normal form *n.* See normal form (definition 1).

Secret channel *n.* See private channel.

Section *n.* A length of fiberoptic cable in a SONET network. See also line, path.

Sector *n.* A portion of the data storage area on a disk. A disk is divided into sides (top and bottom), tracks (rings on each surface), and sectors (sections of each ring). Sectors are the smallest physical storage units on a disk and are of fixed size; typically, they are capable of holding 512 bytes of information apiece.

Sector interleave *n.* See interleave.

Sector map *n.* 1. A map that indicates the unusable sectors on a disk. 2. A table used to translate the sector numbers that are requested by the operating system into physical sector numbers. The sector map represents a different method of performing sector interleaving. When a sector map is used, the sectors are formatted on the disk in sequential order. The mapping enables the system to read sectors in a nonsequential order. For example, using a 3-to-1 sector interleaving map, a system request for sectors 1 through 4 will result in the disk driver reading physical sectors 1, 4, 7, and 10. See also interleave.

Secure channel *n.* A communications link that has been protected against unauthorised access, operation, or use by means of isolation from the public network, encryption, or other forms of control. See also encryption.

Secure Digital Music Initiative *n.* A coalition of companies from the recording, electronics, and information technology industries founded in February 1999 for the purpose of developing an open standard for the secure distribution of music in digital form. The Secure Digital Music Initiative specification is designed to provide consumers with flexibility and convenient access to electronically distributed music (that is, over the Internet) while also protecting the rights of artists. Acronym: SDMI. See also MP3, Windows Media Technologies.

Secure Electronics Transactions protocol *n.* Protocol for conducting secure transactions over the Internet, the result of a joint effort by GTE, IBM, MasterCard, Microsoft, Netscape, SAIC, Terisa Systems, VeriSign, and Visa. Acronym: SET.

Secure/Multipurpose Internet Mail Extensions *n.* See S/MIME.

Secure Password Authentication *n.* A feature that allows a server to confirm the identity of the person logging on. Acronym: SPA.

Secure site *n.* A Web site having the capability of providing secure transactions, ensuring that credit card numbers and other personal information will not be accessible to unauthorised parties.

Secure Sockets Layer *n.* See SSL.

Secure Transaction Technology *n.* The use of the SSL (Secure Sockets Layer), S-HTTP (Secure HTTP), or both in online transactions, such as form transmission or credit card purchases. Acronym: STT. See also S-HTTP, SSL.

Secure wide area network *n.* A set of computers that communicate over a public network, such as the Internet, but use security measures, such as encryption, authentication, and authorisation, to prevent their communications from being intercepted and understood by unauthorised users. Acronym: S/WAN. See also authentication, authorisation, encryption, virtual private network (definition 1).

Security *n.* The technologies used to make a service resistant to unauthorised access to the data that it holds or for which it is responsible. A major focus of computer security, especially on systems that are accessed by many people or through communications lines, is the prevention of system access by unauthorised individuals.

Security kernel *n.* An operating-system kernel that is protected from unauthorised use. See also kernel.

Security log *n.* A log, generated by a firewall or other security device, that lists events that could affect security, such as access attempts or commands, and the names of the users involved. See also firewall, log (definition 1).

Seed *n.* A starting value used in generating a sequence of random or pseudorandom numbers. See also random number generation.

Seek *n.* The process of moving the read/write head in a disk drive to the proper site, typically for a read or write operation.

Seek time *n.* The time required to move a disk drive's read/write head to a specific location on a disk. See also access time (definition 2).

Segment *n.* A section of a programme that, when compiled, occupies a contiguous address space and that is usually position independent; that is, it can be loaded anywhere in memory. With Intel-based microcomputers, a native-mode segment is a logical reference to a 64-KB contiguous portion of RAM in which the individual bytes are accessed by means of an offset value. Collectively, the segment:offset values reference a single physical location in RAM. See also overlay1 (definition 1), real mode, segmentation.

Segmentation *n.* The act of breaking up a programme into several sections, or segments. See also segment.

Segmented addressing architecture *n.* A memory-access technique typified by Intel 80x86 processors. Memory is divided into 64-KB segments in this architecture for addressing locations under the 16-bit address scheme; 32-bit schemes can address memory in segments as large as 4 GB. Also called: segmented instruction addressing, segmented memory architecture.

Segmented address space *n.* An address space that is logically divided into chunks called segments. To address a given location, a programme must specify both a segment and an offset within that segment. (The offset is a value that references a specific point within the segment, based on the beginning of the segment.) Because segments may overlap, addresses are not unique; there are many logical ways to access a given physical location. The Intel 80x86 real-mode architecture is segmented; most other microprocessor architectures are flat. See also segment.

Select *vb.* 1. In general computer use, to specify a block of data or text on screen by highlighting it or otherwise marking it with the intent of performing some operation on it. 2. In database management, to choose records according to a specified set of criteria. See also sort. 3. In information processing, to choose from a number of options or alternatives, such as subroutines or input/output channels.

Selected cell *n.* See active cell.

Selection *n.* 1. In applications, the highlighted portion of an onscreen document. 2. In communications, the initial contact made between a computer and a remote station receiving a message. 3. In programming, a conditional branch. See also conditional branch.

Selective calling *n.* The capability of a station on a communications line to designate the station that is to receive a transmission.

Selector channel *n.* An input/output data transfer line used by one high-speed device at a time.

Selector pen *n.* See light pen.

Select query *n.* A query that asks a question about the data stored in your tables and returns a result set in the form of a datasheet, all without changing the data.

Self-adapting *adj.* The ability of systems, devices, or processes to adjust their operational behaviour to environmental conditions.

Self-checking digit *n.* A digit, appended to a number during its encoding, whose function is to confirm the accuracy of the encoding. See also checksum, parity bit.

Self-clocking *n.* A process in which timing signals are inserted into a data stream rather than being provided by an external source, such as in phase encoding.

Self-documenting code *n.* Programme source code that, through its use of a high-level language and descriptive identifiers, can be understood by other programmers without the need for additional comments.

Self-extracting archive *n.* See self-extracting file.

Self-extracting file *n.* An executable programme file that contains one or more compressed text or data files. When a user runs the programme, it uncompresses the compressed files and stores them on the user's hard drive.

Self-modifying code *n.* Programme code, usually object code generated by a compiler or an assembler, that modifies itself during instruction by writing new operation codes, addresses, or data values over existing instructions. See also pure procedure.

Self-monitoring analysis and reporting technology system *n.* See SMART system.

Self-organising map *n.* See SOM (definition 2).

Self-test *n.* A set of one or more diagnostic tests that a computer or peripheral device (such as a printer) performs on itself. See also power-on self test.

Self-validating code *n.* Programme code that can test itself to verify that it behaves correctly, usually by feeding itself a set of standard input values and testing the results against a set of expected output values.

Semantic error *n.* An error in meaning; a statement in a programme that is syntactically correct (legal) but functionally incorrect. See also logic, semantics (definition 1), syntax.

Semantics *n.* 1. In programming, the relationship between words or symbols and their intended meanings. Programming languages are subject to certain semantic rules; thus, a programme statement can be syntactically correct but semantically incorrect; that is, a statement can be written in an acceptable form and still convey the wrong meaning. 2. In artificial-intelligence research, the capacity of a network to represent relationships among objects, ideas, or situations in a humanlike way.

Semaphore *n.* In programming, a signal—a flag variable—used to govern access to shared system resources. A semaphore indicates to other potential users that a file or other resource is in use and prevents access by more than one user. See also flag (definition 1).

Semicon *n.* Short for Semiconductors Equipment and Material International Conference. A series of international conferences sponsored by the Semiconductors Equipment and Material International (SEMI), a trade group for the international semiconductor industry. The conference provides members with up-to-date information on issues affecting the semiconductor industry and provides SEMI members with a forum for showcasing products and services.

Semiconductor *n.* A substance, commonly silicon or germanium, whose ability to conduct electricity falls between that of a conductor and that of a nonconductor (insulator). The term is used loosely to refer to electronic components made from semiconductor materials.

Send *vb.* To transmit a message or file through a communications channel.

Sendmail *n.* A popular open-source UNIX-based implementation of the Simple Mail Transfer Protocol (SMTP) for delivering e-mail. Written in 1981 by Eric Allman at the University of California at Berkeley, sendmail was the first Internet message transfer agent (MTA).

Send statement *n.* In SLIP and PPP scripting languages, a statement that tells the programme that dials an Internet service provider's number (a dialer programme) to send certain characters. See also ISP, PPP, scripting language, SLIP.

Sensor *n.* A device that detects or measures something by converting nonelectrical energy to electrical energy. A photocell, for example, detects or measures light by converting it to electrical energy. See also transducer.

Sensor glove *n.* A hand-worn computer input device for virtual-reality environments. The glove translates finger movements by the user to commands for manipulating objects in the environment. Also called: data glove. See also virtual reality.

SEPP *n.* Acronym for Software Engineering for Parallel Processing. A project of nine European universities and research institutions to develop tools for the development of parallel application programmes for distributed memory multiprocessors.

Sequence *n.* An ordered arrangement, as in a set of numbers, such as the Fibonacci sequence. See also Fibonacci numbers.

Sequence check *n.* A process that verifies that data or records conform to a particular order.

Sequenced Packet Exchange *n.* See SPX (definition 1).

Sequential access *n.* A method of storing or retrieving information that requires the programme to start reading at the beginning and continue until it finds the desired data. Sequential access is best used for files in which each piece of information is related to the information that comes before it, such as mailing list files and word processing documents. Also called: serial access. See also indexed sequential access method.

Sequential algorithm *n.* An algorithm in which each step must occur in a particular order. See also algorithm.

Sequential execution *n.* The act of executing routines or programmes in a linear sequence.

Sequential logic element *n.* A logic circuit element that has at least one input and one output and in which the output signal depends on the present and past states of the input signal or signals.

Sequential processing *n.* 1. The processing of items of information in the order in which they are stored or input. 2. The execution of one instruction, routine, or task followed by the execution of the next in line.

Sequential search *n.* See linear search.

Serial *adj.* One by one. For example, in serial transmission, information is transferred one bit at a time; a serial computer has only one arithmetic logic unit, which must execute the whole programme one step at a time.

Serial access *n.* See sequential access.

Serial adder *n.* A circuit that adds two numbers one bit position (one digit place) at a time.

Serial communication *n.* The exchange of information between computers or between computers and peripheral devices one bit at a time over a single channel. Serial communications can be synchronous or asynchronous. Both sender and receiver must use the same baud rate, parity, and control information. See also baud rate, parity, start bit, stop bit.

Serial Infrared *n.* A system developed by Hewlett-Packard for transmitting data between two devices up to 1 meter apart using an infrared light beam. Infrared ports on the receiving and the sending devices must be aligned. Generally, Serial Infrared is used with laptops and many notebook computers, as well as with peripherals such as printers. Acronym: SIR. See also infrared port.

Serial interface *n.* A data transmission scheme in which data and control bits are sent sequentially over a single channel. In reference to a serial input/output connection, the term usually implies the use of an RS-232 or RS-422 interface. See also RS-232-C standard, RS-422/423/449.

Serialize *vb.* To change from parallel transmission (byte by byte) to serial transmission (bit by bit).

SerialKey device *n.* Enables you to attach an alternative input device (also called an augmentative communication device) to your computer's serial port. This feature is designed for people who are unable to use the computer's standard keyboard and mouse.

SerialKeys *n.* A feature of Windows 9x, Windows NT, Windows 2000, and Windows XP that, in conjunction with a communications aid interface device, allows keystrokes and mouse controls to be accepted through a computer's serial port.

Serial Line Internet Protocol *n.* See SLIP.

Serial mouse *n.* A pointing device that attaches to the computer through a standard serial port. See also mouse.

Serial port *n.* An input/output location (channel) that sends and receives data to and from a computer's central processing unit or a communications device one bit at a time. Serial ports are used for serial data communication and as interfaces with some peripheral devices, such as mice and printers.

Serial port adapter *n.* An interface card or device that either provides a serial port or converts a serial port to another use. See also adapter, serial port.

Serial printer *n.* A printer connected to the computer via a serial interface (commonly RS-232-C or compatible). Connectors for this type of printer vary widely, which is one reason they are less popular than parallel printers among those who use IBM and IBM-compatible PCs. Serial printers are standard for Apple computers. See also DB connector, serial, serial transmission.

Serial processing *n.* See sequential processing (definition 2).

Serial Storage Architecture *n.* See SSA.

Serial transmission *n.* The transfer of discrete signals one after another. In communications and data transfer, serial transmission involves sending information over a single line one bit at a time, as in modem-to-modem connections.

Series circuit *n.* A circuit in which two or more components are linked in series. All the current passes through each component in a series circuit, but the voltage is divided among the components.

Serif 1 *adj.* Marked by the use of serifs. For example, Goudy is a serif typeface, whereas Helvetica is a sans serif typeface.

Serif 2 *n.* Any of the short lines or ornaments at the ends of the strokes that form a typeface character.

Server *n.* 1. On a local area network (LAN), a computer running administrative software that controls access to the network and its resources, such as printers and disk drives, and provides resources to computers functioning as workstations on the network. 2. On the Internet or other network, a computer or programme that responds to commands from a client. For example, a file server may contain an archive of data or programme files; when a client submits a request for a file, the server transfers a copy of the file to the client. See also application server (definitions 1 and 2), client/server architecture.

Server appliance *n.* A device designed to deliver one or more specific network services in a single turnkey package that includes both hardware and software. All necessary programmes are preinstalled on a server appliance, which has minimal, simplified options and controls. Server appliances can be used to complement or replace traditional servers on a network and can provide such services as file and printer sharing and Internet connectivity. Also called: appliance. See also information appliance.

Server-based application *n.* A programme that is shared over a network. The programme is stored on the network server and can be used at more than one client machine at a time.

Server cluster *n.* A group of independent computer systems, known as nodes, working together as a single system to ensure that mission-critical applications and resources remain available to clients. A server cluster is the type of cluster that Cluster service implements. See also cluster.

Server control *n.* See ASP.NET server control.

Server error *n.* A failure to complete a request for information through HTTP that results from an error at the server rather than an error by the client or the user. Server errors are indicated by HTTP status codes beginning with 5. See also HTTP, HTTP status codes.

Server farm *n.* A centralised grouping of network servers maintained by an enterprise or, often, an Internet service provider (ISP). A server farm provides a network with load balancing, scalability, and fault tolerance. Individual servers may be connected in such a way that they appear to represent a single resource.

Serverlet *n.* See servlet.

Server Message Block *n.* See SMB.

Server push-pull *n.* A combination of Web client/server techniques individually called "server push" and "client pull."

In server push, the server loads data to the client, but the data connection stays open. This allows the server to continue sending data to the browser as necessary. In client pull, the server loads data to the client, but the data connection does not stay open. The server sends an HTML directive to the browser telling it to reopen the connection after a certain interval to get more data or possibly to open a new URL.

Server-side include *n.* A mechanism for including dynamic text in World Wide Web documents. Server-side includes are special command codes that are recognised and interpreted by the server; their output is placed in the document body before the document is sent to the browser. Server-side includes can be used, for example, to include the date/time stamp in the text of the file. Acronym: SSI. See also server (definition 2).

Service *n.* 1. A customer-based or user-oriented function, such as technical support or network provision. 2. In reference to programming and software, a programme or routine that provides support to other programmes, particularly at a low (close to the hardware) level. 3. In networking, specialised, software-based functionality provided by network servers—for example, directory services that provide the network equivalent of "phone books" needed for locating users and resources. See also utility.

Service Advertising Protocol *n.* A method used by a service-providing node in a network (such as a file server or application server) to notify other nodes on the network that it is available for access. When a server boots, it uses the protocol to advertise its service; when the same server goes off line, it uses the protocol to announce that it is no longer available. Acronym: SAP. See also server (definition 1).

Service bureau *n.* 1. A company that provides various services related to publishing, such as prepress production, desktop publishing, typesetting, imagesetting, and optical scanning of graphics. 2. An organisation that provides data processing services and access to software packages for a fee.

Service provider *n.* See ISP.

Servlet or servelet *n.* A small Java programme that runs on a server. The term is a companion to applet, a Java programme that usually runs on the client. Servlets perform lightweight Web services, such as redirecting a Web user from an outdated address to the correct page—tasks traditionally handled by CGI (Common Gateway Interface) applications. Because servlets are automatically threaded and highly responsive, they execute quickly, thereby reducing system overhead. Also called: serverlet. See also applet, CGI.

Servlet container *n.* In Sun Microsystems's J2EE network platform, a container that decodes requests, formats responses, and provides the network services over which requests and responses are sent. All servlet containers must support HTTP as a protocol for requests and responses, but they may also support additional request-response protocols such as HTTPS. See also container, HTTP, HTTPS, J2EE.

Servo *n.* The part of a servomechanism, controlled by the servomechanism's feedback circuit, that produces the final mechanical output. Also called: servomotor. See also servomechanism.

Servomechanism *n.* A control system in which the final output is mechanical movement. A servomechanism uses feedback to control the position, velocity, or acceleration of a mechanical component. Also called: servo system.

Servomotor *n.* See servo.

Servo system *n.* See servomechanism.

Session *n.* 1. The time during which a programme is running. In most interactive programmes, a session is the time during which the programme accepts input and processes information. 2. In communications, the time during which two computers maintain a connection. 3. A specific protocol layer in the ISO/OSI reference model that manages communication between remote users or processes. See also ISO/OSI reference model, session layer.

Session bean *n.* In the Java programming language and J2EE network platform, an enterprise bean that is created by a client and usually exists only for the duration of a single client/server session. It performs operations, such as calculations or accessing a database, for the client. While a session bean may be transactional, it is not recoverable should a system crash occur. Session bean objects can either be stateless or can maintain conversational state across methods and transactions. If a session bean maintains state, the Enterprise JavaBean (EJB) container manages this state if the object must be removed from memory. However, the session bean object itself must manage its own persistent data. See also EJB, stateless.

Session layer *n.* The fifth of seven layers in the ISO/OSI reference model. The session layer handles the details that must be agreed on by the two communicating devices.

Set 1 *n.* In printing and display, a group of related characters, such as a character set. See also character set.

Set 2 *vb.* 1. To change the value of a bit to 1. 2. To establish a particular condition, such as setting tab stops, setting a counter to 0, or setting a breakpoint. See also breakpoint.

SET protocol *n.* See Secure Electronics Transactions protocol.

Settling time *n.* The time required for a disk drive's read/write head to stabilise over a new location on the disk after being moved.

Set-top box *n.* A device that converts a cable TV signal to an input signal to the TV set. Set-top boxes can be used to access the World Wide Web and are a type of information appliance. See also information appliance.

Setup *n.* 1. A computer along with all its devices. 2. The procedures involved in preparing a software programme or application to operate within a computer.

Setup programme *n.* 1. A built-in BIOS programme for reconfiguring system parameters to accommodate a new disk drive. See also BIOS. 2. See installation programme.

Setup string *n.* See control code.

Setup wizard *n.* In Windows, a utility that asks users a structured series of questions and gives them options to aid the process of installing a new programme.

Seven-segment display *n.* A light-emitting diode (LED) display or liquid crystal display (LCD) that can show any of the 10 decimal digits. The seven segments are the seven bars that form a numeral 8 as in a calculator display.

Sex changer *n.* See gender changer.

Sfx *n.* A computer language used to generate digital audio effects and synthesizer instrument audio. It is a superset of the MPEG-4 standard SAOL audio compiler language. Sfx provides professional-quality audio synthesis, real-time MIDI and audio generation, and fully customizable instruments and effects. Because the sfx compiler is a C++ front-end compiler, code is converted to C++ and then compiled into executable orchestras that are used to generate real-time audio. As a result, the current release of sfx requires that Microsoft Visual C++ be installed on the system on which sfx is running. See also C++, compiler, MIDI, MPEG-4, SAOL, Visual C++.

.sgm *n.* The MS-DOS/Windows 3.x file extension that identifies files encoded in Standard Generalised Markup Language (SGML). Because MS-DOS and Windows 3.x cannot recognise file extensions longer than three letters, the .sgml extension is truncated to three letters in those environments. See also SGML.

.sgml *n.* The file extension that identifies files encoded in Standard Generalised Markup Language. See also SGML.

SGML *n.* Acronym for Standard Generalised Markup Language. An information management standard adopted by the International Organisation for Standardisation (ISO) in 1986 as a means of providing platform- and application-independent documents that retain formatting, indexing, and linked information. SGML provides a grammarlike mechanism for users to define the structure of their documents and the tags they will use to denote the structure in individual documents. See also ISO.

SGRAM *n.* See synchronous graphics RAM.

sh *n.* See Bourne shell.

SHA *n.* Acronym for Secure Hash Algorithm. A technique that computes a 160-bit condensed representation of a message or data file, called a message digest. The SHA is used by the sender and the receiver of a message in computing and verifying a digital signature, for security purposes. See also algorithm, digital signature.

Shade 1 *n.* A particular colour variation produced by mixing black with a pure colour. See also brightness, IRGB.

Shade 2 *vb.* To give added dimension to an image by including changes in appearance caused by light and shadow. See also colour model.

Shadow mask *n.* A type of mask used in cathode ray tube (CRT) monitors in which an opaque sheet perforated by tiny pinholes ensures that the electron beam for a particular colour strikes only the phosphor it is supposed to illuminate. Like the aperture grill, which relies on vertical stripes, and the slot mask, which is based on elliptical openings, a shadow mask helps create a clear, sharp image by narrowly focusing the electron beam. See also CRT, mask (definition 2).

Shadow memory *n.* A technique employed by the BIOS in some 80x86-based computers to copy the system's ROM BIOS routines into an unused section of RAM during the computer's startup process. This helps boost system performance by diverting system requests for the BIOS routines to their "shadow" copies. Also called: shadow RAM, shadow ROM.

Shadow print *n.* A style applied to text in which a duplicate of each character is shifted, typically down and to the right, to create a shadow effect.

Shadow RAM *n.* See shadow memory.

Shadow ROM *n.* See shadow memory.

Share *vb.* To make files, directories, or folders accessible to other users over a network.

Shared assembly *n.* An assembly that can be referenced by more than one application. An assembly must be explicitly built to be shared by giving it a cryptographically strong name. See also private assembly, strong name.

Shared directory *n.* See network directory.

Shared folder *n.* On a Macintosh computer connected to a network and running System 6.0 or higher, a folder that a user has made available to others on the network. A shared folder is analogous to a network directory on a PC. See also network directory.

Shared logic *n.* The use, by multiple circuits or software routines, of common circuits or routines to implement an operation.

Shared medium *n.* The communications medium shared by network nodes; essentially, the network bandwidth.

Shared memory *n.* 1. Memory accessed by more than one programme in a multitasking environment. 2. A portion of memory used by parallel-processor computer systems to exchange information. See also parallel processing.

Shared name *n.* See strong name.

Shared network directory *n.* See network directory.

Shared printer *n.* A printer that receives input from more than one computer.

Shared resource *n.* 1. Any device, data, or programme used by more than one device or programme. 2. On a network, any resource made available to network users, such as directories, files, and printers.

SharePoint team Web site *n.* A customizable Web site with features that help a team work together. The default site has pages for document libraries, announcements, and team events. Only members, specified by the site creator, can use the site.

Shareware *n.* Copyrighted software that is distributed on a try-before-you-buy basis. Users who want to continue using the programme after the trial period are encouraged to send a payment to the program's author.

Sharpness *n.* See resolution (definition 1).

Sheet *n.* A feature for handling dialog boxes included in the Mac OS X Aqua interface. When the user chooses to save or print a document, a translucent sheet emerges from the window title bar and remains attached to that window even if it is moved to the background. The sheet allows the user to continue working in the window, or in other windows, without closing the sheet.

Sheet-fed scanner *n.* A scanner with a single-sheet feed mechanism, in which sheets of paper are pulled in by the scanner and scanned as they pass over a stationary scanning mechanism. Sheet-fed scanners allow for automatic scanning of multiple-sheet documents. See also scanner.

Sheet feeder *n.* A device that accepts a stack of paper and feeds it to a printer one page at a time.

Shelfware *n.* Software that has been unsold or unused for a long time, and so has remained on a retailer's or user's shelf.

Shell 1 *n.* A piece of software, usually a separate programme, that provides direct communication between the user and the operating system. Examples of shells are Macintosh Finder and the MS-DOS command interface programme COMMAND.COM. See also Bourne shell, C shell, Finder, Korn shell.

Shell 2 *vb.* See shell out.

Shell account *n.* A computer service that permits a user to enter operating-system commands on the service provider's system through a command-line interface (usually one of the UNIX shells) rather than having to access the Internet through a graphical user interface. Shell accounts can provide Internet access through character-based tools such as Lynx for browsing the World Wide Web. See also shell1.

Shell archive *n.* In UNIX and GNU, a collection of compressed files that has been prepared for transmission by an e-mail service using the shar command.

Shell out *vb.* To obtain temporary access to the operating-system shell without having to shut down the current application and return to that application after performing the desired shell function. Many UNIX programmes allow the user to shell out; the user can do the same in windowing environments by switching to the main system window.

Shell script *n.* A script executed by the command interpreter (shell) of an operating system. The term generally refers to scripts executed by the Bourne, C, and Korn shells on UNIX platforms. Also called: batch file. See also batch file, script, shell1.

Shell sort *n.* A programming algorithm used for ordering data in which data are sorted in subsets so that the process works its way from unsorted to progressively more sorted. Named after its inventor, Donald Shell, it is faster than the bubble sort and the insertion sort. See also algorithm.

Sherlock *n.* An advanced search mechanism included with the Macintosh OS. Sherlock provides the ability to search multiple Internet search engines simultaneously and incorporates the Macintosh Find File interface for searches of local volumes. Additional plug-ins can expand the number of search engines available for access and increase search options.

Shielded twisted-pair wiring *n.* See twisted-pair wiring.

Shift *vb.* In programming, to move the bit values one position to the left or right in a register or memory location. See also end-around shift.

Shift+click or Shift click *vb.* To click the mouse button while holding down the Shift key. Shift+clicking performs different operations in different applications, but its most common use in Windows is to allow users to select multiple items in a list, for example, to select a number of files for deletion or copying.

Shift key *n.* A keyboard key that, when pressed in combination with another key, gives that key an alternative meaning; for example, producing an uppercase character when a letter key is pressed. The Shift key is also used in various key combinations to create nonstandard characters or to perform special operations. The term is adapted from usage in relation to manual typewriters, in which the key physically shifted the carriage to print an alternative character. See also Caps Lock key.

Shift-PrtSc *n.* See Print Screen key.

Shift register *n.* A circuit in which all bits are shifted one position at each clock cycle. It can be either linear (a bit is inserted at one end and "lost" at the other during each cycle) or it can be cyclic or looped (the "lost" bit is inserted back at the beginning). See also register, shift.

Shockwave *n.* A format for multimedia audio and video files within HTML documents, created by Macromedia, which markets a family of Shockwave servers and plug-in programmes for Web browsers. See also HTML.

Shopping cart *n.* In e-commerce programmes, a file in which an online customer stores information on potential purchases until ready to order. Usually represented on screen with a drawing of a shopping cart, the virtual shopping cart provides a recognizable point of reference to users new to the e-commerce experience. See also e-commerce.

Short card *n.* A printed circuit board that is half as long as a standard-size circuit board. Also called: half-card. See also printed circuit board.

Short-circuit evaluation *n.* A form of expression evaluation that guarantees that Boolean expressions will be evaluated only far enough to determine their value. See also AND, Boolean operator, OR.

Shortcut *n.* In Windows 9x, Windows XP, Windows NT 4, and Windows 2000, an icon on the desktop that a user can double-click to immediately access a programme, a text or data file, or a Web page. See also symbolic link.

Shortcut key *n.* See accelerator.

Short-haul *adj.* Of or pertaining to a communications device that transmits a signal over a communications line for a distance less than approximately 20 miles.

Short message service *n.* Service for wireless phones that allows users to send and receive brief messages consisting of text and numbers. Acronym: SMS.

Shout *vb.* To use ALL CAPITAL LETTERS for emphasis in e-mail or a newsgroup article. Excessive shouting is considered a violation of netiquette. A word can be more acceptably emphasised by placing it between *asterisks* or _underscores_. See also netiquette.

Shovelware *n.* A commercially sold CD-ROM containing a miscellaneous assortment of software, graphic images, text, or other data that could otherwise be obtained at little or no cost, such as freeware or shareware from the Internet and BBSs or public-domain clip art. See also BBS (definition 1), freeware, shareware.

ShowSounds *n.* In Windows 9x and Windows NT 4, a global flag that instructs application programmes to provide some kind of visual indication that the programme is generating a sound in order to alert users with hearing impairments or those in a noisy location such as a factory floor.

Shredder *n.* An application designed to completely destroy digital data so it cannot be reconstructed with file recovery software.

Shrinkwrap agreement *n.* A contract or license in or on a software box or package that sets forth conditions for use of the software. Typically, a shrinkwrap agreement states that a user accepts the terms of the agreement when he or she opens the box. A shrinkwrap agreement is a print version of an End-User License Agreement. Also called: box-top license. See also End-User License Agreement.

Shrink-wrapped *adj.* Boxed and sealed in clear plastic film for commercial distribution. Use of the term implies a final version of a product as opposed to a beta version. See also beta1.

SHS virus *n.* Any of a class of viruses that infect a user's system by hiding in files with an .shs extension. These viruses typically spread through e-mail attachments. A widely distributed e-mail warning cautions readers to beware of the "SHS virus," but no one specific virus by that name exists.

SHTML *n.* Short for server-parsed HTML. Hypertext Markup Language (HTML) text that contains embedded server-side include commands. SHTML documents are fully read, parsed, and modified by the server before being passed to the browser. See also HTML, server-side include.

S-HTTP or SHTTP *n.* Acronym for Secure Hypertext Transfer Protocol. An extension to HTTP that supports various encryption and authentication measures to keep all transactions secure from end to end. S-HTTP is designed to ensure the security of individual transmissions over the Internet and has been approved as a standard by the Internet Engineering Task Force (IETF). S-HTTP should not be confused with HTTPS, a Netscape-developed technology based on SSL (Secure Sockets Layer). HTTPS is also designed to ensure secure transmissions, but does so between communicating computers rather than on a message-by-message basis. Also called: Secure HTTP. See also SSL.

Shut down *vb.* To close a programme or an operating system in a manner ensuring that no data is lost.

Sibling *n.* A process or node in a data tree that is descended from the same immediate ancestor(s) as other processes or nodes. See also generation (definition 2), node (definition 3).

Sideband *n.* The upper or lower portion of a modulated carrier wave. One portion can be processed while the other is used to carry separate data, a technique that doubles the amount of information that can be carried over a single line.

Sidebar *n.* A block of text placed to the side of the main body of text in a document, often set off by a border or other graphic element.

Side-by-side execution *n.* The ability to install and use multiple versions of an assembly in isolation at the same time. This can occur on the same machine, or in the same process or application domain. Side-by-side execution can apply to applications and components as well as the components of the .NET Framework. Allowing assemblies to run side-by-side is essential to support robust versioning in the common language runtime.

Side effect *n.* Any change of state caused by a subroutine, such as a routine that reads a value from a file and advances the current file position.

Side head *n.* A heading placed in the margin of a printed document and top-aligned with the body text, rather than being vertically aligned with text, as is a normal head.

Sieve of Eratosthenes *n.* An algorithm for finding prime numbers. It is often used as a benchmark in testing the speed of a computer or programming language. See also benchmark.

.sig *n.* A file extension for a signature file for e-mail or Internet newsgroup use. The contents of this file are automatically appended to e-mail correspondence or newsgroup articles by their respective client software. See also signature file (definition 1).

SIG *n.* Acronym for special interest group. An e-mail online discussion group or a group of users who meet and share information, especially one of the groups supported by the Association for Computing Machinery (ACM), such as SIGGRAPH for computer graphics.

SIGGRAPH *n.* Short for Special Interest Group on Computer Graphics, a part of the Association for Computing Machinery (ACM).

Sigmoid function *n.* A kind of S-shaped mathematical function arising in many dynamical systems, including neural networks, because it is the solution to a first-order differential equation. It typically maps a real value, which may be arbitrarily large in magnitude (positive or negative), to another real value, which lies within some narrow range. The sigmoid function, in neural network computation literature, is also sometimes referred to as the logistic function. The reason for its prevalence is that it is thought to resemble the probability that a true neuron generates as an action potential in response to particular input and output. See also artificial intelligence, neural network.

Sign *n.* The character used to indicate a positive or negative number. In assembly-level programming, the sign is indicated by the sign bit accompanying the number. See also sign bit.

Signal *n.* 1. Any electrical quantity, such as voltage, current, or frequency, that can be used to transmit information. 2. A beep or tone from a computer's speaker or a prompt displayed on screen that tells a user that the computer is ready to receive input.

Signal converter *n.* A device or circuit that converts a signal from one form to another, such as analog to digital, or pulse code modulation to frequency modulation.

Signal-to-noise ratio *n.* The amount of power, measured in decibels, by which the signal exceeds the amount of channel noise at the same point in transmission. Abbreviation: S/N. See also noise (definition 2).

Signature *n.* 1. A sequence of data used for identification, such as text appended to an e-mail message or a fax. 2. A unique number built into hardware or software for authentication purposes.

Signature block *n.* A block of text that an e-mail client or a newsreader automatically places at the end of every message or article before the message or article is transmitted. Signature blocks typically contain the name, e-mail address, and affiliation of the person who created the message or article.

Signature file *n.* 1. A file that contains information inserted by a user and automatically appended to e-mail correspondence or newsgroup articles by client software. A signature file typically contains the name or nickname of the user and might include such information as the user's e-mail address, Web page, company, or job title. 2. A file that updates an antivirus programme so that the programme recognises signatures of new viruses and removes the viruses from the user's computer. See also antivirus programme, virus signature.

Sign bit *n.* The most significant, or leftmost, bit of a number field, usually set to 1 if the number is negative.

Sign extension *n.* See sign bit.

Significand *n.* See mantissa.

Significant digits *n.* The sequence from the first nonzero digit to the last digit in a number (the last nonzero digit in an integer), used to express the number's precision (for example, 12,300 has three significant digits, and 0.000120300 has six). See also floating-point notation.

Sign off *vb.* See log off.

Sign on *vb.* See log on.

Sign propagation *n.* See sign bit.

SIIA *n.* Acronym for Software & Information Industry Association. A nonprofit trade association representing over

1200 high-tech companies worldwide and charged with watching over the interests of the software and digital content industry. The SIIA was formed in 1999 when the Software Publishers Association (SPA) merged with the Information Industry Association (IIA). The SIIA focuses on three areas: providing information and forums in which to distribute information to the high-tech industry; protection in the form of an antipiracy programme geared to help members enforce their copyrights; and promotion and education.

Silica gel *n.* A desiccant (moisture-absorbing substance) often packaged with optical or electronic equipment.

Silicon *n.* A semiconductor used in many devices, especially microchips. Silicon, with atomic number 14 and atomic weight 28, is the second most common element in nature.

Silicon Alley *n.* The Manhattan, New York, metropolitan area. Originally the term referred to the area of Manhattan below 41st Street, which had a heavy concentration of technology companies, but it now includes the entire island, reflecting the number of businesses involved in computer technology in that area. The name was inspired by Silicon Valley, the area of northern California that is home to many technology firms. See also Silicon Valley.

Silicon chip *n.* An integrated circuit that uses silicon as its semiconductor material.

Silicon-controlled rectifier *n.* A semiconductor rectifier whose conductance can be controlled by a gate signal. Acronym: SCR. See also gate (definition 1), rectifier.

Silicon dioxide *n.* An insulator used to form thin insulating layers in some types of semiconductors; also the primary component of glass.

Silicone *n.* A polymer in which silicon and oxygen are major components. Silicone is an excellent electrical insulator and conducts heat well.

Silicon foundry *n.* A factory or machine used to create wafers of crystalline silicon.

Silicon on insulator *n.* See SOI.

Silicon-on-sapphire *n.* A method of fabricating semiconductors in which the semiconductor devices are formed in a thin single layer of silicon that has been grown on an insulating substrate of synthetic sapphire. Acronym: SOS.

Silicon Valley *n.* The region of California south of San Francisco Bay, otherwise known as the Santa Clara Valley, roughly extending from Palo Alto to San Jose. Silicon Valley is a major center of electronics and computer research, development, and manufacturing.

Silicorn Valley *n.* Clusters of high-tech companies headquartered in small cities in the Midwestern United States, particularly in areas of rural Iowa.

SIM *n.* See Society for Information Management.

SIM card *n.* Short for Subscriber Identity Module card. A smart card designed for use with GSM (Global System for Mobile Communications) mobile phones. SIM cards contain chips that store a subscriber's personal identifier (SIM PIN), billing information, and data (names, phone numbers). See also Global System for Mobile Communications, smart card (definition 2).

SIMD *n.* Acronym for single-instruction, multiple-data stream processing. A category of parallel-processor computer architecture in which one instruction processor fetches instructions and distributes orders to several other processors.

SIMM *n.* Acronym for single inline memory module. A small circuit board designed to accommodate surface-mount memory chips.

Simple API for XML *n.* See SAX.

Simple Authentication and Security Layer *n.* See SASL.

Simple Control Protocol *n.* See SCP.

Simple Mail Transfer Protocol *n.* A TCP/IP protocol for sending messages from one computer to another on a network. This protocol is used on the Internet to route e-mail. Acronym: SMTP. See also communications protocol, TCP/IP.

Simple Network Management Protocol *n.* See SNMP.

Simple Object Access Protocol *n.* See SOAP.

Simplex *n.* Communication that takes place only from sender to receiver.

Simplex transmission *n.* See simplex.

SIMULA *n.* Short for simulation language. A general-purpose programming language based on ALGOL 60, with special features designed to aid the description and simulation of active processes. Visual C++ is based on aspects of this language.

Simulation *n.* The imitation of a physical process or an object by a programme that causes a computer to respond mathematically to data and changing conditions as though it were the process or object itself. See also emulator, modeling (definition 1).

Simultaneous access *n.* See parallel access.

Simultaneous processing *n.* 1. True multiple-processor operation in which more than one task can be processed at a time. See also multiprocessing, parallel processing. 2. Loosely, concurrent operation in which more than one task is processed by dividing processor time among the tasks. See also concurrent, multitasking.

Sine wave *n.* A uniform, periodic wave often generated by an object that vibrates at a single frequency.

Single attachment station *n.* An FDDI node that connects to the primary ring through a concentrator.

Single-board *adj.* Of or pertaining to a computer that occupies only one circuit board, usually with no capacity for additional boards.

Single-density *adj.* Of or pertaining to a disk that is certified only for use with frequency modulation (FM) recording. A single-density disk can store much less data than a disk using modified FM encoding or run-length limited encoding. See also modified frequency modulation encoding, run-length limited encoding.

Single Image Random Dot Stereogram *n.* See auto-stereogram.

Single Image Stereograms *n.* See autostereogram.

Single inline memory module *n.* See SIMM.

Single inline package *n.* See SIP.

Single inline pinned package *n.* See SIP.

Single-instruction, multiple-data stream processing *n.* See SIMD.

Single-line digital subscriber line *n.* See SDSL.

Single-precision *adj.* Of or pertaining to a floating-point number having the least precision among two or more options commonly offered by a programming language, such as single-precision versus double-precision. See also floating-point notation, precision (definition 2).

Single-sided *adj.* Of or pertaining to a floppy disk in which data can be stored on only one side.

Single sign-on *n.* A system enabling a user to enter one name and password to log on to different computer systems or Web sites. Single sign-on is also available for enterprise systems so a user with a domain account can log on to a network once, using a password or smart card, and thereby gain access to any computer in the domain. See also domain, smart card (definition 1).

Single step *vb.* To execute a programme one step at a time, usually within the context of a debugger. See also debugger.

Single switch device *n.* An assistive computer technology for people with mobility impairments. A single switch device allows users to interact with a computer by using slight body movements.

Single threading *n.* 1. Within a programme, the running of a single process at a time. 2. A condition in which each leaf node of a tree data structure contains a pointer to its parent. See also node (definition 3), pointer (definition 1), threading.

Single-user computer *n.* A computer designed for use by a single individual; a personal computer.

Sink *n.* A device or part of a device that receives something from another device. See also data sink, heat sink.

SIP *n.* Acronym for single inline package. A type of housing for an electronic component in which all leads (connections) protrude from one side of the package. Also called: single inline pinned package.

SIPP *n.* Acronym for single inline pinned package. See SIP.

SIR *n.* See Serial Infrared.

SirCam worm *n.* A malicious worm that combines fast infection with the potential to deliver multiple malicious payloads. SirCam spreads through multiple means, both by mailing infected personal files from a compromised disk to other potential victims and through Windows network shares on unprotected machines. One time in 20 SirCam deletes the contents of the infected drive, and one time in 50 it fills all free space on the disk with trash data. SirCam was discovered in mid-2001 and has reappeared regularly since that time.

SIRDS *n.* Acronym for Single Image Random Dot Stereogram. See autostereogram.

SIS *n.* Acronym for Single Image Stereogram. See autostereogram.

.sit *n.* The file extension for a Macintosh file compressed with StuffIt. See also StuffIt.

Site *n.* See Web site.

Site license *n.* A purchase agreement for using multiple copies of the same software at a business or an institution, usually at a volume discount.

Size box *n.* A control in the upper right corner of the frame of a window on the Macintosh screen. When the user clicks the size box, the window toggles between the size the user has set for it by dragging and the maximum size.

Skew *n.* The difference between what is and what should be—for example, the misalignment of a page that prevents accurate reproduction, or the difference between input and output when circuits do not respond evenly to a propagated signal.

Skin *n.* An alternative graphical interface for an operating system (OS) or a software programme. A skin customises the look of the OS or programme but does not affect its functionality.

Programmes that allow the use of skins usually make standards available for the creation and distribution of new skins. See also graphical user interface.

Skin mode *n.* An operational state of various media players, including RealPlayer, Winamp, and Windows Media Player, in which the user interface is customised and displayed as a skin. Often some features of the player are not accessible in skin mode. Skin mode was called compact mode in Windows Media Player 7. See also full mode.

Skutch box *n.* A slang term for a device manufactured by Skutch Electronics, Inc., that simulates the functioning of a telephone line with a good connection. Telephone line simulators are used to test telecommunications systems and devices.

Skyscraper *n.* One of several larger formats for online ads developed to replace traditional banner ads on the Internet. See avalanche ad.

Slave *n.* Any device, including a computer, that is controlled by another computer, referred to as the master. See also master/slave arrangement.

Sleep 1 *n.* 1. In a multiprocessing environment, a temporary state of suspension during which a process remains in memory so that some event, such as an interrupt or a call from another process, can "awaken" it. 2. In programming, a state of suspension caused by a loop statement that creates an intentional delay.

Sleep 2 *vb.* To suspend operation without terminating.

Sleep mode *n.* A power management mode that shuts down all unnecessary computer operations to save energy after it has received no input or other activity for a specified period of time. A computer in sleep mode usually awakens when it receives an input signal from a user or a network, such as a keyboard entry or an incoming call through a modem. Many battery-powered devices, including portable computers, support sleep mode. See also green PC, sleep1 (definition 1), Suspend command.

Sleeve *n.* See disk envelope.

Slice *n.* See time slice.

SLIP *n.* Acronym for Serial Line Internet Protocol. A data link protocol that allows transmission of TCP/IP data packets over dial-up telephone connections, thus enabling a computer or a LAN (local area network) to be connected to the Internet or some other network. It is an older, less secure protocol than the PPP (Point-to-Point Protocol) and does not support dynamic allocation of IP addresses. A newer form of SLIP, known as CSLIP (Compressed SLIP), optimises transmission of long documents by compressing header information. See also data link, IP.

SLIP emulator *n.* Software that mimics a SLIP connection in UNIX shell accounts that do not offer a direct SLIP connection. Many Internet service providers (ISPs) are UNIX based and offer shell accounts to users for Internet access. Like a SLIP connection, the SLIP emulator allows the user to avoid dealing with the ISP's UNIX environment directly when accessing the Internet and to use Internet applications such as graphical Web browsers. See also ISP, shell account, SLIP.

Slot *n.* 1. See expansion slot. 2. An integrated circuit mounting connector designed to connect a microprocessor with a PC's data bus. Currently, only newer models of Intel's Pentium family employ this. See also Pentium, Slot 1, Slot 2.

Slot 1 *n.* A receptacle on a PC motherboard designed to hold a Pentium II microprocessor. The microprocessor, which is encased in Intel's Single Edge Contact (SEC) packaging, slides into the slot on the motherboard. Slot 1 includes 242 electrical contact points and communicates with the chip's L2 cache at half of the PC's clock speed. Slot 1 replaced socket 7 and socket 8 in Intel architectures, but has been superceded by Slot 2 in newer model Pentiums. See also L2 cache, motherboard, Pentium.

Slot 2 *n.* A receptacle on a PC motherboard designed to hold Intel microprocessors beginning with the Pentium II Xeon and including the Pentium III microprocessor. Like Slot 1, Slot 2 is encased in Intel's Single Edge Contact packaging, so it slides easily into the slot on the motherboard. It includes

330 electrical contact points and is slightly wider than Slot 1. It also supports communication between the CPU and the L2 cache at the full clock speed of the PC. See also L2 cache, motherboard, Pentium.

Slot mask *n.* A type of mask used in cathode ray tube (CRT) monitors in which a thin sheet of metal perforated with elliptical holes is used to ensure that the electron beam for a particular colour (red, green, or blue) strikes only the phosphor (of the corresponding colour) that it is intended to illuminate. The elliptical—lozenge-shaped—holes in a slot mask place it between a shadow mask, which is based on round openings, and an aperture grill, which is based on vertical strips of metal. Slot masks were introduced by NEC in its CromaClear technology. See also CRT, mask (definition 2).

Slot pitch *n.* The distance, measured horizontally, between phosphor dots of the same colour on a cathode ray tube (CRT) display based on slot mask technology. Although the measurements are based on different methods of applying phosphor to the screen surface, slot pitch is comparable to dot pitch, the measurement used with CRTs based on shadow mask technology. See also CRT, mask (definition 2), slot mask.

Slotted-ring network *n.* A ring network allowing data to be transmitted between data stations in one direction. A slotted-ring network transfers data in predefined time slots (fixed-length portions of a data frame) in the transmission stream over one transmission medium. See also data frame, ring network.

SlowKeys *n.* An accessibility feature built into Macintosh computers and available for DOS and Windows that allows the user to add a delay to the keyboard so that a key must be held down for a certain amount of time before it is accepted. This feature facilitates the use of the keyboard by individuals with poor motor control who might accidentally bump keys when moving around the keyboard.

SLSI *n.* See super-large-scale integration.

Small Business Server *n.* A software application developed by Microsoft Corporation to increase the efficiency of Web-based services for small businesses with 50 or fewer personal computers. Small Business Server provides shared Internet access, features for building Web-based customer management and customer communications tools, and additional features that increase productivity by streamlining employee access to files and applications over the Web.

Small caps *n.* A font of capital letters that are smaller than the standard capital letters in that typeface.

Small Computer System Interface *n.* See SCSI.

small model *n.* A memory model of the Intel 80x86 processor family that allows only 64 kilobytes (KB) for code and 64 KB for data. See also memory model.

Small Office/Home Office *n.* See SOHO.

Small-scale integration *n.* A concentration of fewer than 10 components on a single chip. Acronym: SSI. See also integrated circuit.

Smalltalk *n.* An object-oriented language and development system developed at Xerox Palo Alto Research Center (PARC) in 1980. Smalltalk pioneered many language and user interface concepts that are now widely used in other environments, such as the concept of an object that contains data and routines and onscreen icons that the user can choose to make the computer perform certain tasks. See also object-oriented programming.

Smart *adj.* A synonym for intelligent. See intelligence.

Smart cable *n.* See intelligent cable.

Smart card *n.* 1. In computers and electronics, a circuit board with built-in logic or firmware that gives it some kind of independent decision-making ability. 2. In banking and finance, a credit card that contains an integrated circuit that gives it a limited amount of intelligence and memory.

Smart card reader *n.* A device that is installed in computers to enable the use of smart cards for enhanced security features. See also smart card (definition 2).

Smart device *n.* An electronic device capable of being networked and remotely controlled in a smart home. Smart devices can include appliances, lighting, heating and cooling systems, entertainment systems, and security systems. See also home automation, home network (definition 1), smart home.

Smart home *n.* A home or building wired for networking and home automation. In a smart home, occupants control smart devices programmatically or on command using a home-networking communications protocol. Also called: automated home, digital home, e-home, Internet home, networked home, smart house, wired home. See also home automation, home network (definition 1).

Smart house *n.* See smart home.

Smart linkage *n.* A feature of programming languages that guarantees that routines will always be called with correct parameter types. See also link (definition 1).

Smartphone *n.* A hybrid between a wireless telephone and a personal digital assistant (PDA). Smartphones integrate wireless telephones with many of the personal organisational functions of PDAs, such as calendar, calculator, database, e-mail, wireless Web access, note taking, and other programmes common to lightweight palm-style computers. Smartphones may rely on a stylus, keypad, or both for data entry or may use voice recognition technology. See also cell, palmtop, PDA, pen computer, wireless phone.

Smart quotes *n.* In word processors, a function that automatically converts the ditto marks (") produced by most computer keyboards to the inverted commas (" and ") used in typeset text.

SmartSuite *n.* A suite of business application programmes sold by Lotus Development. Lotus SmartSuite includes six programmes: Lotus 1-2-3 spreadsheet, Lotus WordPro word processor, Lotus Approach database, Lotus Freelance Graphics presentation software, Lotus Organizer time-management software, and Lotus FastSite Internet/intranet publishing tool. SmartSuite Millennium Edition 9.7 supports collaboration, Web publishing, use of Internet/intranet resources, and customizable document and project organizers. SmartSuite competes with Microsoft Office and WordPerfect Office.

SMART system *n.* Short for Self-Monitoring Analysis and Reporting Technology system. A system by which technology is used to monitor and predict device performance and reliability. A SMART system employs various diagnostic tests to detect problems with devices, with the object of increasing productivity and protecting data.

Smart terminal *n.* A terminal that contains a microprocessor and random access memory (RAM) and that does some rudimentary processing without intervention from the host computer.

SMB *n.* Acronym for Server Message Block. A file-sharing protocol designed to allow networked computers to transparently access files that reside on remote systems over a variety of networks. The SMB protocol defines a series of commands that pass information between computers. SMB uses four message types: session control, file, printer, and message. See also LAN Manager, NetBIOS, Samba.

SMDS *n.* Acronym for Switched Multimegabit Data Services. A very high-speed, connectionless, packet-switched data transport service that connects LANs (local area networks) and WANs (wide area networks).

SMIL *n.* Acronym for Synchronised Multimedia Integration Language. A markup language that enables separate elements, including audio, video, text, and still images, to be accessed separately and then integrated and played back as a synchronised multimedia presentation. Based on XML (eXtensible Markup Language), SMIL allows Web authors to define the objects in the presentation, describe their locations onscreen, and determine when they will be played back. The language is based on statements that can be entered with a text editor and was developed under the auspices of the World Wide Web Consortium (W3C). See also markup language, XML.

Smiley *n.* See emoticon.

S/MIME *n.* Acronym for Secure/Multipurpose Internet Mail Extensions. An Internet e-mail security-oriented protocol that adds public key encryption and support for digital signatures to the widely used MIME e-mail protocol. See also public key encryption.

SMIS *n.* Acronym for Society for Management Information Systems. See Society for Information Management.

Smoke test *n.* The testing of a piece of hardware after assembly or repairs by turning it on. The device fails the test if it produces smoke, explodes, or has some other unexpected violent or dramatic reaction, even if it appears to work.

Smooth *vb.* 1. To eliminate irregularities in statistical data by some process such as continuous averaging or by removing random (irrelevant) values. 2. In graphics, to remove jagged edges from a figure or line. See also anti-aliasing.

SMP *n.* Acronym for symmetric multiprocessing. A computer architecture in which multiple processors share the same memory, which contains one copy of the operating system, one copy of any applications that are in use, and one copy of the data. Because the operating system divides the workload into tasks and assigns those tasks to whichever processors are free, SMP reduces transaction time. See also architecture, multiprocessing.

SMP server *n.* Short for symmetric multiprocessing server. A computer that is designed with the SMP architecture to improve its performance as a server in client/server applications. See also SMP.

SMS *n.* See Systems Management Server.

SMS *n.* See short message service.

SMT *n.* See surface-mount technology.

SMTP *n.* See Simple Mail Transfer Protocol.

Smurf attack *n.* A form of denial-of-service attack on an Internet server that sends simultaneous echo request packets ("ping" packets) to one or more broadcast IP addresses (such as an IRC server), each of which in turn relays the request to as many as 255 individual host computers, with the address of the attack's victim as the forged (spoofed) source address.

When the hosts return echo packets to the apparent source of the request, the volume of the responses is enough to disable the network. See also denial of service attack, spoofing.

SNA *n.* Acronym for Systems Network Architecture. A network model devised by IBM to enable IBM products, including mainframes, terminals, and peripherals, to communicate and exchange data. SNA started out as a five-layer model and was later extended with two additional layers to correspond more closely to the ISO/OSI reference model. More recently, the SNA model was modified to include minicomputers and microcomputers in a specification known as APPC (Advanced Programme to Programme Communications).

Snail mail *n.* A popular phrase on the Internet for referring to mail services provided by the U.S. Postal Service and similar agencies in other countries. The term has its origins in the fact that regular postal mail is slow compared with e-mail.

Snap-in *n.* 1. See plug-in. 2. A software component that provides system administration and system management capability within the framework of the Microsoft Management Console (MMC) for Windows NT, Windows 2000, and Windows XP. A snap-in (also capitalised as Snap-In) is a COM object that represents one unit of management behaviour, the smallest extension available through the MMC. There are two types of snap-ins: stand-alone (not reliant on any other snap-in) and extension (invoked by a parent snap-in). Multiple snap-ins can be combined to create larger management tools.

Snapshot *n.* A copy of main memory or video memory at a given instant, sent to the printer or hard disk. Also called: snapshot dump. See also screen dump.

Snapshot programme *n.* A programme that performs a trace by taking a snapshot of certain chunks of memory at specified times.

.snd *n.* A file extension for a type of interchangeable sound file format used on Sun, NeXT, and Silicon Graphics computers, consisting of raw audio data preceded by a text identifier.

Sneaker *n.* An individual employed by a company or organisation to test their security by breaking into the employer's network.

Information gathered by the sneaker can be used to repair network security weaknesses. See also tiger team.

Sneakernet *n.* Transfer of data between computers that are not networked together. The files must be written onto floppy disks on the source machine, and a person must physically transport the disks to the destination machine.

Sniffer *n.* See packet sniffer.

SNMP *n.* Acronym for Simple Network Management Protocol. The network management protocol of TCP/IP. In SNMP, agents, which can be hardware as well as software, monitor the activity in the various devices on the network and report to the network console workstation. Control information about each device is maintained in a structure known as a management information block. See also agent (definition 4), TCP/IP.

SNOBOL *n.* Acronym for String-Oriented Symbolic Language. A string- and text-processing language developed between 1962 and 1967 by Ralph Griswold, David Farber, and I. Polonsky at AT&T Bell Laboratories. See also string.

Snow *n.* 1. In television, temporary distortion of a displayed image caused by interference, usually in a weak signal, that takes the form of random white spots. 2. In computer displays, a specific type of distortion characterised by the blinking on and off of random pixels that occurs when the microprocessor and the display hardware interfere with each other by attempting to use the computer's video memory at the same time.

SOAP *n.* Acronym for Simple Object Access Protocol. A simple, XML-based protocol for exchanging structured and type information on the Web. The protocol contains no application or transport semantics, which makes it highly modular and extensible.

SOC *n.* Acronym for system on a chip. A chip integrating computer, microprocessors, and all necessary support components in a single unit. SOC technology is used in firewalls, gateways, specialised servers, and interactive devices like Web pads and vending machines.

Social engineering *n.* The practice of penetrating system security by tricking individuals into divulging passwords and information about network vulnerabilities. Often done by calling the individual on phone and pretending to be another employee of company with a computer-related question.

Society for Information Management *n.* A professional society based in Chicago for information systems executives, formerly the Society for Management Information Systems. Acronym: SIM.

Society for Management Information Systems *n.* See Society for Information Management.

Socket *n.* 1. An identifier for a particular service on a particular node on a network. The socket consists of a node address and a port number, which identifies the service. For example, port 80 on an Internet node indicates a Web server. See also port number, sockets API. 2. The receptacle part of a connector, which receives a plug. See also female connector. 3. A receptacle on a PC motherboard into which a microprocessor is plugged. A socket-mounted microprocessor, such as the Pentium, connects to the motherboard through numerous pins on the underside. Newer Intel microprocessors, such as the Pentium II and later, plug into the motherboard through an edge connector along the side of the chip. See also socket 4, socket 5, socket 7, socket 8.

Socket 4 *n.* A 5-volt mounting socket on a PC motherboard designed to hold a Pentium microprocessor operating at 60 MHz or 66 MHz. Socket 4 includes openings for 273 pins. See also Pentium, socket (definition 3).

Socket 5 *n.* A 3.3-volt mounting socket on a PC motherboard designed to hold a Pentium microprocessor operating at the following speeds: 75, 90, 100, 120, 133, 150, 166, 180, and 200 MHz. Socket 5 includes openings for 320 pins. It has been superceded by socket 7, socket 8, slot 1, and slot 2. See also Pentium, socket (definition 3).

Socket 7 *n.* A mounting socket on a PC motherboard designed to hold a microprocessor operating at the following speeds: 150, 166, 180, 200, 210, and 233 MHz. Socket 7 includes openings for 321 pins and operates at two voltages, 2.5 volts at the core and 3.3 volts input/output. It is used with the Pentium MMX chip and competitive microprocessor chips from other manufacturers, such as AMD and Cyrix. See also MMX, Pentium, socket (definition 3).

Socket 8 *n.* A 2.5-volt mounting socket on a PC motherboard designed to hold a Pentium Pro microprocessor. Socket 8 has openings for 387 pins. See also Pentium, socket (definition 3).

Sockets API *n.* An application programming interface implemented to create and use sockets in client/server networking. The most common sockets API is the University of California at Berkeley UNIX/BSD implementation (Berkeley Sockets API), which is the basis for Winsock. See also socket (definition 1).

Soc. newsgroups *n.* Usenet newsgroups that are part of the soc. hierarchy and have the prefix soc. These newsgroups are devoted to discussions of current events and social issues. Soc. newsgroups are one of the seven original Usenet newsgroup hierarchies. The other six are comp., misc., news., rec., sci., and talk. See also newsgroup, traditional newsgroup hierarchy, Usenet.

Soft *adj.* 1. In computing, temporary or changeable. For example, a soft error is a problem from which the system can recover, and a soft patch is a temporary programme fix that holds only while the programme is running. 2. In electronics, characterised by magnetic materials that do not retain their magnetism when a magnetic field is removed.

Soft boot *n.* See warm boot.

Soft copy *n.* The temporary images presented on a computer display screen.

Soft error *n.* An error from which a programme or operating system is able to recover.

Soft patch *n.* A fix or modification performed only while the code being patched is loaded into memory, so that the executable or object file is not modified in any way. See also patch1.

Soft return *n.* A line break inserted in a document by a word processor when the next word in the current line of text would cause the line to overflow into the margin—a movable line break. See also wordwrap.

Soft-sectored disk *n.* A disk, especially a floppy disk, whose sectors have been marked with recorded data marks rather than punched holes. See also index hole.

Software *n.* Computer programmes; instructions that make hardware work. Two main types of software are system software (operating systems), which controls the workings of the computer, and applications, such as word processing programmes, spreadsheets, and databases, which perform the tasks for which people use computers. Two additional categories, which are neither system nor application software but contain elements of both, are network software, which enables groups of computers to communicate, and language software, which provides programmers with the tools they need to write programmes. In addition to these task-based categories, several types of software are described based on their method of distribution. These include packaged software (canned programmes), sold primarily through retail outlets; freeware and public domain software, which are distributed free of charge; shareware, which is also distributed free of charge, although users are requested to pay a small registration fee for continued use of the programme.

Software & Information Industry Association *n.* See SIIA.

Software-based modem *n.* A modem that uses a general-purpose, reprogrammable digital signal processor chip and RAM-based programme memory rather than a dedicated chip with the modem functions burned into the silicon. A software-based modem can be reconfigured to update and change the modem's features and functions.

Software bloat *n.* A software condition caused by the addition of excessive number of possibly unnecessary features and functions as new versions of the software are released. Software bloat is generally assumed to result in long loading times and inordinate resource (memory and storage) requirements. See also bloatware, creeping featurism.

Software conversion *n.* Changing or moving a programme designed to run on one computer to run on another. Usually this involves detailed (professional) work on the programme itself.

Software-dependent *adj.* Of, pertaining to, or being a computer or device that is tied to a particular programme or set of programmes developed for it.

Software development kit *n.* See developer's kit.

Software engineer *n.* 1. In general, one who works at the code level with software. Although such engineering can be considered to encompass everything from software design to management and testing, the term is generally considered more or less synonymous with programmer—one who actually writes the code. 2. See developer.

Software engineering *n.* The design and development of software. See also programming.

Software handshake *n.* A handshake that consists of signals transmitted over the same wires used to transfer the data, as in modem-to-modem communications over telephone lines, rather than signals transmitted over special wires. See also handshake.

Software house *n.* An organisation that develops and supports software for its customers.

Software IC *n.* See software integrated circuit.

Software integrated circuit *n.* An existing software module that can be designed into a programme, much as an integrated circuit can be designed into a logic board. Abbreviation: software IC. See also abstract data type, module (definition 1), object-oriented programming.

Software interrupt *n.* A programme-generated interrupt that stops current processing in order to request a service provided by an interrupt handler (a separate set of instructions designed to perform the task required). Also called: trap.

Software package *n.* A programme sold to the public, ready to run and containing all necessary components and documentation.

Software tools *n.* Programmes, utilities, libraries, and other aids, such as editors, compilers, and debuggers, that can be used to develop programmes.

SOHO *n.* Acronym for Small Office/Home Office, a term used for home-based and small businesses. The fast-growing SOHO market has sparked a concomitant expansion in computer software and hardware products designed specifically to meet the needs of self-employed individuals or small businesses. See also distributed workplace, telecommuter.

SOI *n.* Acronym for silicon on insulator. A method used in the construction of microprocessors in which the chip's transistors—the tiny circuits that conduct electrical charges—are built on a layer of silicon placed on top of a layer of insulating material, such as glass. SOI construction improves speed at the same time it reduces the amount of power required by the microprocessor.

Solar cell *n.* A photoelectric device that produces electrical power when exposed to light. Also called: photovoltaic cell.

Solaris *n.* A distributed UNIX-based computing environment created by Sun Microsystems, Inc., widely used as a server operating system. Versions of Solaris exist for SPARC computers, 386 and higher Intel platforms, and the PowerPC.

Solenoid *n.* An electromagnetic device that converts electrical energy to mechanical movement, typically consisting of an electromagnet with a movable rod through the center.

Solid ink *n.* Ink manufactured in the form of solid sticks resembling crayons, for use in solid-ink printers. See also solid-ink printer.

Solid-ink printer *n.* A computer printer using solid ink sticks. The ink sticks are heated until they melt, and the molten ink is sprayed onto the page, where it cools and solidifies. See also solid ink.

Solid model *n.* A geometric shape or construction that has continuity in length, width, and depth and is treated by a programme as if it had both surface and internal substance.

Solid-state device *n.* A circuit component whose properties depend on the electrical or magnetic characteristics of a solid substance (as opposed to a gas or vacuum). Transistors, diodes, and integrated circuits are solid-state devices.

Solid-state disk drive *n.* A mass storage device that holds data in RAM rather than in magnetic storage. See also magnetic storage, RAM.

Solid-state memory *n.* Computer memory that stores information in solid-state devices.

Solid-state relay *n.* A relay that depends on solid-state components, rather than mechanical components, to open and close a circuit.

SOM *n.* 1. Acronym for System Object Model. A language-independent architecture from IBM that implements the CORBA standard. See also CORBA, OMA. 2. Acronym for self-organising map. A form of neural network in which neurons and their connections are added automatically as needed to develop the desired mapping from input to output.

SONET *n.* Acronym for Synchronous Optical Network. A high-speed network that provides a standard interface for communications carriers to connect networks based on fiberoptic cable. SONET is designed to handle multiple data types (voice, video, and so on). It transmits at a base rate of 51.84 Mbps, but multiples of this base rate go as high as 2.488 Gbps (gigabits per second).

Sort *vb.* To organise data, typically a set of records, in a particular order. Programmes and programming algorithms for sorting vary in performance and application. See also bubble sort, distributive sort, insertion sort, merge sort, quicksort, Shell sort.

Sort algorithm *n.* An algorithm that puts a collection of data elements into some sequenced order, sometimes based on one or more key values in each element. See also algorithm, bubble sort, distributive sort, insertion sort, merge sort, quicksort, Shell sort.

Sorter *n.* A programme or routine that sorts data. See also sort.

Sort field *n.* See sort key.

Sort key *n.* A field (commonly called a key) whose entries are sorted to produce a desired arrangement of the records containing the field. See also field (definition 1), primary key, secondary key.

SOS *n.* See silicon-on-sapphire.

Sound Blaster *n.* 1. A family of sound cards manufactured by Creative Technology or its subsidiary, Creative Labs. See also sound card. 2. A de facto standard set by the family of sound cards developed by Creative Technologies and its subsidiaries. Many other manufacturers also make Sound Blaster–compatible products.

Sound board *n.* See sound card.

Sound buffer *n.* A region of memory used to store the bit image of a sequence of sounds to be sent to a computer's speaker(s).

Sound card *n.* A type of expansion board on PC-compatible computers that allows the playback and recording of sound, such as from a WAV or MIDI file or a music CD-ROM. Most PCs sold at retail include a sound card. Also called: sound board. See also expansion board, MIDI, WAV.

Sound clip *n.* A file that contains a short audio item, usually an excerpt from a longer recording.

Sound editor *n.* A programme that allows the user to create and manipulate sound files.

Sound generator *n.* A chip or chip-level circuit that can produce electronic signals that can drive a speaker and synthesize sound.

Sound hood *n.* A five-sided box, lined with soundproofing material, that is placed over a loud printer to muffle its noise.

SoundSentry *n.* An optional Windows feature that instructs Windows to produce a visual cue such as a screen flash or a blinking title bar whenever a system beep occurs. SoundSentry is designed for users with hearing impairments or users who operate a computer in a noisy environment.

Source *n.* 1. In information processing, a disk, file, document, or other collection of information from which data is taken or moved. 2. In a FET, the electrode toward which charge carriers (electrons or holes) move from the source under control of the gate. See also CMOS (definition 1), drain (definition 1), FET, gate (definition 2), MOSFET, NMOS, PMOS.

Source code *n.* Human-readable programme statements written by a programmer or developer in a high-level or assembly language that are not directly readable by a computer. Source code needs to be compiled into object code before it can be executed by a computer.

Source code control system *n.* A tool designed to track changes made to source code files. Changes are documented in such a way that previous versions of the files can be retrieved. Source code control is used in software development, particularly in situations involving concurrent development and multiple user access to source code files.

Source computer *n.* 1. A computer on which a programme is compiled. 2. A computer from which data is transferred to another computer.

Source data *n.* The original data on which a computer application is based.

Source data acquisition *n.* The process of sensing, as with a bar code reader or other scanning device, or receiving source data. See also source data.

Source data capture *n.* See source data acquisition.

Source directory *n.* During a file copy operation, the directory in which the original versions of the files are located.

Source disk *n.* Any disk from which data will be read, as during a copy operation or when an application is loaded from a disk into memory.

Source document *n.* The original document from which data is taken.

Source drive *n.* The disk drive from which files are being copied during a copy operation.

Source file *n.* 1. A file that contains source code. See also source code. 2. A file that contains the data that a programme will process and store in a destination file. 3. In MS-DOS and Windows commands that involve the copying of data or programme instructions, the file containing the data or instructions that are copied.

Source language *n.* The programming language in which the source code for a programme is written. See also programming language, source code.

Source programme *n.* The source code version of a programme. See also source code.

Source statement *n.* A single statement in the source code of a programme. See also source code, statement.

SPA *n.* See SIIA.

Spacebar *n.* The long key occupying much of the bottom row of most keyboards that sends a space character to the computer.

Space character *n.* A character that is entered by pressing the Spacebar on the keyboard and that typically appears on the screen as a blank space.

Space-division multiplexing *n.* The first automated form of communications multiplexing, which replaced the human-operated switchboard. Space-division multiplexing was replaced by frequency-division multiplexing (FDM), which was in turn replaced by time-division multiplexing (TDM). Acronym: SDM. See also FDM, multiplexing, time-division multiplexing.

Spaghetti code *n.* Code that results in convoluted programme flow, usually because of excessive or inappropriate use of GOTO or JUMP statements. See also GOTO statement, jump instruction.

Spam 1 *vb.* To distribute unwanted, unrequested mail widely on the Internet by posting a message to too many recipients or too many newsgroups. The act of distributing such mail, known as spamming, angers most Internet users and has been known to invite retaliation, often in the form of return spamming that can flood and possibly disable the electronic mailbox of the original spammer.

Spam 2 *n.* 1. An unsolicited e-mail message sent to many recipients at one time, or a news article posted simultaneously to many newsgroups. Spam is the electronic equivalent of junk mail. In most cases, the content of a spam message or article is not relevant to the topic of the newsgroup or the interests of the recipient; spam is an abuse of the Internet in order to distribute a message to a huge number of people at minimal cost. 2. An unsolicited e-mail message from a business or individual that seeks to sell the recipient something. Also called: UCE, unsolicited commercial e-mail.

Spam blocking *n.* See address munging.

Spambot *n.* A programme or device that automatically posts large amounts of repetitive or otherwise inappropriate material to newsgroups on the Internet. See also bot (definition 3), robopost, spam1.

Spamdexter *n.* An individual who lures users to spam-related Web sites by loading the site with hundreds of hidden copies of popular keywords, even if those words have no relation to the Web site. Because the keywords appear so many times, the spamdexter's site will appear near the top of search result and indexing lists. The term spamdexter was created by combining the words spam and index. Also called: keyword stuffing.

Span *n.* See range.

SPARC *n.* Short for Scalable Processor Architecture. A RISC (reduced instruction set computing) microprocessor specification from Sun Microsystems, Inc. See also RISC.

Sparse array *n.* An array (arrangement of items) in which many of the entries are identical, commonly zero. It is not possible to define precisely when an array is sparse, but it is clear that at some point, usually when about one-third of the array consists of identical entries, it becomes worthwhile to redefine the array. See also array.

Sparse infector *n.* A type of virus or other malicious code that delivers its payload only when certain predetermined conditions are met. A sparse infector might hide on an infected computer until a certain date or until a certain number of files or applications have been run. By restricting their active phases to only certain situations, sparse infectors are more likely to avoid detection.

Spatial data management *n.* The representation of data as a collection of objects in space, particularly as icons on a screen, in order to make the data easier to comprehend and manipulate.

Spatial digitizer *n.* A three-dimensional scanner most often used in medical and geographical work.

Speaker dependent recognition *n.* A type of automatic speech recognition (ASR) in which the computer system becomes accustomed to the voice and accent of a specific speaker, allowing a larger vocabulary can be recognised. See also ASR, speaker independent recognition.

Speaker independent recognition *n.* A type of automatic speech recognition (ASR) in which the computer system will respond to commands from any speaker. Because the system does not adjust to the nuances of a specific voice, only a limited vocabulary is possible. See also ASR, speaker dependent recognition.

Spec *n.* See specification.

Special character *n.* Any character that is not alphabetic, numeric, or the space character (for example, a punctuation character). See also reserved character, wildcard character.

Special interest group *n.* See SIG.

Special-purpose language *n.* A programming language whose syntax and semantics are best suited for a given field or approach. See also Prolog.

Specification *n.* 1. A detailed description of something. 2. In relation to computer hardware, an item of information about the computer's components, capabilities, and features. 3. In relation to software, a description of the operating environment and proposed features of a new programme. 4. In information processing, a description of the data records, programmes, and procedures involved in a particular task. Also called: spec.

Spectral colour *n.* In video, the hue represented by a single wavelength in the visible spectrum. See also colour model.

Spectral response *n.* In relation to sensing devices, the relationship between the device's sensitivity and the frequency of the detected energy.

Spectrum *n.* The range of frequencies of a particular type of radiation. See also electromagnetic spectrum.

Speech Recognition Application Programming Interface *n.* See SRAPI.

Speech synthesis *n.* The ability of a computer to produce "spoken" words. Speech synthesis is produced either by splicing together prerecorded words or by programming the computer to produce the sounds that make up spoken words. See also artificial intelligence, neural network, synthesizer.

Spelling checker *n.* An application that employs a disk-based dictionary to check for misspellings in a document. Also called: spell checker.

Spew *vb.* On the Internet, to post an excessive number of e-mail messages or newsgroup articles.

Spider *n.* An automated programme that searches the Internet for new Web documents and indexes their addresses and content-related information in a database, which can be examined for matches by a search engine. Spiders are generally considered to be a type of bot, or Internet robot. Also called: crawler. See also bot (definition 3), search engine (definition 2).

Spike *n.* A transient electrical signal of very short duration and usually high amplitude.

Spindle *n.* 1. An axle for mounting a disk or reel of magnetic tape. 2. Any drive included within the chassis of a laptop or other portable computer. A laptop including a floppy disk drive and a hard drive would be considered a two-spindle machine.

Spintronics *n.* An emerging field of study in electronics and physics that is based on the ability to detect and control the spin of electrons in magnetic materials. Using spintronics, it might eventually be possible to produce small, fast electronic devices, including transistors, memory devices, and quantum computers.

Spirale virus *n.* See Hybris virus.

Splash screen *n.* A screen containing graphics, animation, or other attention-getting elements that appears while a programme is loading or as an introductory page to a Web site. A splash screen used with an application typically contains a logo, version information, author credits, or a copyright notice, and it appears when a user opens a programme and disappears when loading is complete. A splash screen used on a Web site serves as a front door, typically loading before any content-related pages.

Spline *n.* In computer graphics, a curve calculated by a mathematical function that connects separate points with a high degree of smoothness.

Split screen *n.* A display method in which a programme can divide the display area into two or more sections, which can contain different files or show different parts of the same file.

Spoiler *n.* A post to a newsgroup or mailing list that reveals what is intended to be a surprise, such as a plot twist in a film or television episode or the solution to a game. The subject line should contain the word spoiler, but netiquette requires that the sender further protect readers who do not or cannot scan posts for subject lines in advance by encrypting the post, putting one or more screenfuls of white space above the text, or both. See also netiquette.

Spoofing *n.* The practice of making a transmission appear to come from an authorised user. For example, in IP spoofing, a transmission is given the IP address of an authorised user in order to obtain access to a computer or network. See also IP address.

Spool *vb.* To store a data document in a queue, where it awaits its turn to be printed. See also print spooler.

Spot *n.* A "composite dot" produced through the halftone creation process on a PostScript printer that consists of a group of dots arranged in a pattern reflecting the gray level of a particular pixel. See also gray scale, halftone.

Spot colour *n.* A method of handling colour in a document in which a particular colour of ink is specified and each page having elements in that colour is printed as a separate layer. The printer then prints one layer for each spot colour in the document. See also colour model, colour separation (definition 1), Pantone Matching System.

Spot function *n.* The PostScript procedure used to create a given type of screen in a halftone. See also halftone, PostScript, spot.

SPP *n.* See scalable parallel processing.

Spraycan *n.* An artist's tool in Paintbrush or another graphics application for applying a pattern of dots to an image.

Spreadsheet programme *n.* An application commonly used for budgets, forecasting, and other finance-related tasks that organises data values using cells, where the relationships between cells are defined by formulas. A change to one cell produces changes to related cells. Spreadsheet programmes usually provide graphing capabilities for output and a variety of formatting options for text, numeric values, and graph features. See also cell (definition 1).

Spread spectrum *adj.* Of or pertaining to a system of secure radio communication in which the content of a transmission is broken into split-second pieces, which are transmitted over separate frequencies. When a receiver identifies a spread spectrum signal, it reassembles it to its original form. Spread spectrum was invented by the actress Hedy Lamarr in 1940, but it was not used until 1962.

Springboard *n.* Handspring Inc.'s expansion platform for its line of Visor handheld personal digital assistants. The term describes both the 68-pin Springboard socket incorporated into the Visor, as well as a series of add-on Springboard modules that fit into the socket. Add-on modules include features such as multimedia, games, e-books, additional memory storage, and a wireless phone module. See also Visor.

Sprite *n.* In computer graphics, a small image that can be moved on the screen independently of other images in the background. Sprites are widely used in animation sequences and video games. See also object (definition 3).

Sprocket feed *n.* A paper feed in which pins engage holes in the paper to move it through a printer. Pin feed and tractor feed are both sprocket feeds. See also paper feed, pin feed, tractor feed.

SPX *n.* 1. Acronym for Sequenced Packet Exchange. The transport level (ISO/OSI level 4) protocol used by Novell NetWare. SPX uses IPX to transfer the packets, but SPX ensures that messages are complete. See also ISO/OSI reference model. 2. Acronym for simplex. See simplex.

SQL *n.* See structured query language.

Square wave *n.* A blocklike waveform that is generated by a source that changes instantly between alternate states, usually at a single frequency.

SRAM *n.* See static RAM.

SRAPI *n.* Acronym for Speech Recognition Application Programming Interface. A cross-platform application programming interface for speech recognition and text-to-speech functions supported by a consortium of developers including Novell, IBM, Intel, and Philips Dictation Systems. See also application programming interface, speech recognition.

SSA *n.* Acronym for Serial Storage Architecture. An interface specification from IBM in which devices are arranged in a ring topology. In SSA, which is compatible with SCSI devices, data can be transferred at up to 20 megabytes per second in each direction. See also SCSI device.

SSD *n.* Acronym for solid-state disk. See solid-state disk drive.

SSE *n.* Short for Streaming SIMD Extensions. A set of 70 new instructions implemented in Intel's Pentium III microprocessor.

SSE, more formally called Internet SSE (ISSE), uses SIMD (single-instruction, multiple-data) operations to accelerate floating point calculations. Designed to improve performance in visual areas such as real-time 3-D and graphics rendering, SSE also provides support for development of such applications as real-time video and speech recognition. See also SIMD.

SSI *n.* 1. See small-scale integration. 2. See server-side include.

SSL *n.* Acronym for Secure Sockets Layer. A protocol developed by Netscape Communications Corporation for ensuring security and privacy in Internet communications. SSL supports authentication of client, server, or both, as well as encryption during a communications session. While primary purpose of SSL is to enable secure electronic financial transactions on the World Wide Web, it is designed to work with other Internet services as well. This technology, which uses public key encryption, is incorporated into the Netscape Navigator Web browser and Netscape's commerce servers. See also commerce server, open standard, public key encryption, PCT.

SSO *n.* See single sign-on.

ST506 interface *n.* The hardware signal specification developed by Seagate Technologies for hard-disk-drive controllers and connectors. The ST506/412 version of this interface has become a de facto standard.

Stack *n.* A region of reserved memory in which programmes store status data such as procedure and function call addresses, passed parameters, and sometimes local variables. See also pop, push (definition 1).

Stacking order *n.* The order in which layers in a digital graphic file are arranged. Foreground elements are typically stacked on top of background elements. Changes in stacking order can affect the way the final graphic is seen by the viewer. See also layering.

Stack pointer *n.* A register that contains the current address of the top element of the stack. See also pointer (definition 1), stack.

Stackware *n.* A HyperCard application consisting of a HyperCard data stack and HyperCard programming. See also HyperCard.

Staging web *n.* A local Web site maintained on a file system or local Web server that currently cannot be browsed by site visitors. These Web sites allow authors and workgroups to make changes or updates to Web sites before they are published.

Staging Web server *n.* A Web server where you publish and test your Web site before putting it on a production server. A staging Web server cannot be browsed by an Internet or intranet audience.

Stairstepping *n.* A rough outline like the steps of a stair in a graphic line or curve that should be smooth. Also called: aliasing, jaggies.

Stale link *n.* A hyperlink to an HTML document that has been deleted or moved, rendering the hyperlink useless. See also HTML document, hyperlink.

Stale pointer bug *n.* See aliasing bug.

Stand-alone or standalone *adj.* Of, pertaining to, or being a device that does not require support from another device or system, for example, a computer that is not connected to a network.

Standard *n.* 1. A de jure technical guideline advocated by a recognised noncommercial or government organisation that is used to establish uniformity in an area of hardware or software development. The standard is the result of a formal process, based on specifications drafted by a cooperative group or committee after an intensive study of existing methods, approaches, and technological trends and developments. The proposed standard is later ratified or approved by a recognised organisation and adopted over time by consensus as products based on the standard become increasingly prevalent in the market. Standards of this type are numerous, including the ASCII character set, the RS-232-C standard, the SCSI interface, and ANSI-standard programming languages, such as C and FORTRAN. See also ANSI, convention, RS-232-C standard, SCSI. 2. A de facto technical guideline for hardware or software development that occurs when a product or philosophy is developed by a single company and, through success and imitation, becomes so w

Standard ASCII *n.* The set of characters assigned to ASCII (American Standard Code for Information Interchange) values between decimal 0 and 127 (hexadecimal 00 through 7F). These characters include most found on a standard keyboard, including the letters A–Z (uppercase and lowercase), numerals (0 through 9), and some special characters, such as colons and parentheses. Standard ASCII has for years been used as a near-universal "common language" in the PC environment for enabling different programmes to exchange information reliably. See also ASCII.

Standard deviation *n.* In statistics, a measure of the dispersion of a group of measurements relative to the mean (average) of that group. Each score's difference from the mean is squared, and the standard deviation is defined as the square root of the average of these squared values.

Standard disclaimer *n.* A phrase placed in an e-mail message or news article that is intended to replace the statement required by some businesses and institutions that the contents of the message or article do not necessarily represent the opinions or policies of the organisation from whose e-mail system the message originated.

Standard function *n.* A function that is always available within a particular programming language. See also function (definition 1).

Standard Generalised Markup Language *n.* See SGML.

Standby *n.* A state in which your computer consumes less power when it is idle but remains available for immediate use. While your computer is on standby, information in computer memory is not saved on your hard disk. If there is an interruption in power, the information in memory is lost.

Star bus *n.* A network topology in which nodes connect to hubs in a star pattern, but the hubs are connected by a bus trunk. Star bus is a combination of star and bus topologies.

Star-dot-star or star dot star *n.* A file specification (*.*) using the asterisk wildcard, which means "any combination of file name and extension" in operating systems such as MS-DOS. See also *.*, asterisk, wildcard character.

Star network *n.* A LAN (local area network) in which each device (node) is connected to a central computer in a star-shaped configuration (topology); commonly, a network consisting of a central computer (the hub) surrounded by terminals.

Start bit *n.* In asynchronous transmission, the bit (actually, a timing signal) that represents the beginning of a character. See also asynchronous transmission.

Start button *n.* In Microsoft Windows 9x and Windows NT 4 and later, the control on the desktop task bar that opens the main menu.

Starting point *n.* A World Wide Web document designed to help users begin navigating the Web. A starting point often contains tools such as search engines and hyperlinks to selected Web sites. See also hyperlink, search engine (definition 2), World Wide Web.

Star topology *n.* A network configuration based on a central hub, from which nodes radiate in a star-shaped pattern. See also topology.

Start page *n.* See home page (definition 2).

Start/stop transmission *n.* See asynchronous transmission.

Startup *n.* See boot1.

Startup application *n.* On the Macintosh, the application that takes control of the system when the computer is turned on.

STARTUP.CMD *n.* A special-purpose batch file stored in the root directory of the startup disk in OS/2—the OS/2 equivalent of an MS-DOS AUTOEXEC.BAT file.

Startup disk *n.* See system disk.

Startup ROM *n.* The bootstrap instructions coded into a computer's ROM (read-only memory) and executed at startup. The startup ROM routines enable a computer to check itself and its devices (such as the keyboard and disk drives), prepare itself for operation, and run a short programme to load an operating-system loader programme. See also boot1, power-on self test.

Startup screen *n.* A text or graphics display that appears on the screen when a programme is started (run). Startup screens usually contain information about the software's version and often contain a product or corporate logo.

Star-wired ring *n.* A network topology in which hubs and nodes connect to a central hub in typical star fashion, but the connections within the central hub form a ring. Star-wired ring is a combination of star and ring topologies.

State *n.* See status.

Stateful *adj.* Of or pertaining to a system or process that monitors all details of the state of an activity in which it participates. For example, stateful handling of messages takes account of their content.

Stateless *adj.* Of or pertaining to a system or process that participates in an activity without monitoring all details of its state. For example, stateless handling of messages might take account of only their sources and destinations but not their content.

Statement *n.* The smallest executable entity within a programming language.

State-of-the-art *adj.* Up to date; at the forefront of current hardware or software technology.

Static 1 *adj.* In information processing, fixed or predetermined. For example, a static memory buffer remains invariant in size throughout programme execution. The opposite condition is dynamic, or ever-changing.

Static 2 *n.* In communications, a crackling noise caused by electrical interference with a transmitted signal. See also noise (definition 2).

Static allocation *n.* Apportionment of memory that occurs once, usually when the programme starts. The memory remains allocated during the program's execution and is not deallocated until the programme is finished. See also allocate, deallocate.

Static binding *n.* Binding (converting symbolic addresses in the programme to storage-related addresses) that occurs during programme compilation or linkage. Also called: early binding.

Static buffer *n.* A secondary sound buffer that contains an entire sound; these buffers are convenient because the entire sound can be written once to the buffer. See also streaming buffer.

Static electricity *n.* An electrical charge accumulated in an object. Although generally harmless to humans, the discharge of static electricity through an electronic circuit can cause severe damage to the circuit.

Static RAM *n.* A form of semiconductor memory (RAM) based on the logic circuit known as a flip-flop, which retains information as long as there is enough power to run the device. Static RAMs are usually reserved for use in caches. Acronym: SRAM. See also cache, RAM, synchronous burst static RAM.

Static routing *n.* Routing based on a fixed forwarding path. Unlike dynamic routing, static routing does not adjust to changing network conditions.

Static Web page *n.* Web page that displays the same content to all viewers. Usually written in hypertext markup language (HTML), a static Web page displays content that changes only if the HTML code is altered. See also dynamic Web page.

Station *n.* 1. In the IEEE 802.11 wireless LAN specification, a single, often mobile, node. 2. See workstation.

Stationery 1 *adj.* Describing a type of document that, when opened by the user, is duplicated by the system; the copy is opened for the user's modification while the original document remains intact. Stationery documents can be used as document templates or boilerplates. See also boilerplate, template (definition 5).

Stationery 2 *n.* A stationery document. See also stationery1.

Statistical multiplexer *n.* A multiplexing device that adds intelligence to time-division multiplexing by using buffering (temporary storage) and a microprocessor to combine transmission streams into a single signal and to allocate available bandwidth dynamically. Also called: stat mux. See also dynamic allocation, multiplexing, time-division multiplexing.

Statistics *n.* The branch of mathematics that deals with the relationships among groups of measurements and with the relevance of similarities and differences in those relationships. See also binomial distribution, Monte Carlo method, probability, regression analysis, standard deviation, stochastic.

Stat mux *n.* See statistical multiplexer.

Status *n.* The condition at a particular time of any of numerous elements of computing—a device, a communications channel, a network station, a programme, a bit, or other element—used to report on or to control computer operations.

Status bar *n.* In Windows 9x and Windows NT 4 and later, a space at the bottom of many programme windows that contains a short text message about the current condition of the programme. Some programmes also display an explanation of the currently selected menu command in the status bar.

Status codes *n.* Strings of digits or other characters that indicate the success or failure of some attempted action. Status codes were commonly used to report the results of early computer programmes, but most software today uses words or graphics. Internet users, especially those with UNIX shell accounts, are likely to encounter status codes while using the Web or FTP. See also HTTP status codes.

Steganography *n.* A "hide-in-plain-sight" technique for concealing information by embedding a message within an innocuous cover message. In steganography, bits of unnecessary data within an image, sound, text, or even a blank file are replaced with bits of invisible information. The term steganography comes from the Greek for "covered writing" and has traditionally included any method of secret communication that conceals the existence of the message.

Because steganography cannot be detected by decryption software, it is often used to replace or supplement encryption.

Step-frame *n.* The process of capturing video images one frame at a time. This process is used by computers that are too slow to capture analog video images in real time.

Stepper motor *n.* A mechanical device that rotates only a fixed distance each time it receives an electrical pulse. A stepper motor is part of a disk drive.

Step-rate time *n.* The time required to move a disk actuator arm from one track to the next. See also actuator, stepper motor.

Stereogram *n.* See autostereogram.

Sticky *adj.* In reference to a Web site, properties such as targeted content or services that increase the amount of time users choose to spend at the site and increase user's desire to return to the site repeatedly.

StickyKeys *n.* An accessibility feature built into Macintosh and Windows computers that causes modifier keys such as Shift, Control, or Alt to "stay on" after they are pressed, eliminating the need to press multiple keys simultaneously. This feature facilitates the use of modifier keys by users who are unable to hold down one key while pressing another.

Stochastic *adj.* Based on random occurrences. For example, a stochastic model describes a system by taking into account chance events as well as planned events.

Stop bit *n.* In asynchronous transmission, a bit that signals the end of a character. In early electromechanical teleprinters, the stop bit provided time for the receiving mechanism to coast back to the idle position and, depending on the mechanism, had a duration of 1, 1.5, or 2 data bits. See also asynchronous transmission.

Stop error *n.* A serious error that affects the operating system and that could place data at risk. The operating system generates an obvious message, a screen with the Stop error, rather than continuing on and possibly corrupting data. Also called: blue screen error, fatal system error. See also Blue Screen of Death.

Storage *n.* In computing, any device in or on which information can be kept. Microcomputers have two main types of storage: random access memory (RAM) and disk drives and other external storage media. Other types of storage include read-only memory (ROM) and buffers.

Storage area network *n.* A high-speed network that provides a direct connection between servers and storage, including shared storage, clusters, and disaster-recovery devices. A storage area network, or SAN, includes components such as hubs and routers that are also used in local area networks (LANs), but it differs in being something of a "subnetwork" dedicated to providing a high-speed connection between storage elements and servers. Most SANs rely on fiber-channel connections that deliver speeds up to 1000 Mbps and can support up to 128 devices. SANs are implemented to provide the scalability, speed, and manageability required in environments that demand high data availability. Acronym: SAN. Also called: system area network.

Storage device *n.* An apparatus for recording computer data in permanent or semipermanent form. When a distinction is made between primary (main) storage devices and secondary (auxiliary) storage devices, the former refers to random access memory (RAM) and the latter refers to disk drives and other external devices.

Storage location *n.* The position at which a particular item can be found—either an addressed location or a uniquely identified location on a disk, tape, or similar medium.

Storage media *n.* The various types of physical material on which data bits are written and stored, such as floppy disks, hard disks, tape, and optical discs.

Storage tube *n.* See direct view storage tube.

Store-and-forward *n.* A method of delivering transmissions in which messages are held temporarily by an intermediary before being sent on to their destination. Store and forward is used by some switches in delivering packets to their destinations.

Stored procedure *n.* A precompiled collection of SQL statements and optional control-of-flow statements stored under a name and processed as a unit. They are stored in an SQL database and can be run with one call from an application.

Stored programme concept *n.* A system architecture scheme, credited largely to the mathematician John von Neumann, in which both programmes and data are in direct-access storage (random access memory, or RAM), thereby allowing code and data to be treated interchangeably. See also von Neumann architecture.

Storefront *n.* See virtual storefront.

Storm *n.* On a network, a sudden, excessive burst of traffic. Storms are often responsible for network outages.

STP *n.* Acronym for shielded twisted pair. A cable consisting of one or more twisted pairs of wires and a sheath of foil and copper braid. The twists protect the pairs from interference by each other, and the shielding protects the pairs from interference from outside. Therefore, STP cable can be used for high-speed transmission over long distances. See also twisted-pair cable.

Straight-line code *n.* Programme code that follows a direct sequence of statements rather than skipping ahead or jumping back via transfer statements such as GOTO and JUMP. See also GOTO statement, jump instruction.

Stream 1 *n.* Any data transmission, such as the movement of a file between disk and memory, that occurs in a continuous flow. Manipulating a data stream is a programming task. Consumers, however, are likely to encounter references to streams and streaming in connection to the Internet, which has increased reliance on stream techniques to enable users (even those with slower equipment) to access large multimedia files—especially those containing audio and video components—and to display or play them before all the data has been transferred.

Stream 2 *vb.* To transfer data continuously, beginning to end, in a steady flow. Many aspects of computing rely on the ability to stream data: file input and output, for example, and communications. If necessary, an application receiving a stream must be able to save the information to a buffer in order to prevent loss of data. On the Internet, streaming enables users to begin accessing and using a file before it has been transmitted in its entirety.

Stream cipher *n.* A method for encrypting a data sequence of unlimited length using a key of fixed length. See also key (definition 3).

Streaming *n.* 1. On the Internet, the process of delivering information, especially multimedia sound or video, in a steady flow that the recipient can access as the file is being transmitted. 2. In magnetic tape storage devices, a low-cost technique to control the motion of the tape by removing tape buffers. Although streaming tape compromises start/stop performance, it achieves highly reliable storage and retrieval of data, and is useful when a steady supply of data is required by a particular application or computer.

Streaming buffer *n.* A small sound buffer that can play lengthy sounds because the application dynamically loads audio data into the buffer as it plays. For example, an application could use a buffer that can hold 3 seconds of audio data to play a 2-minute sound. A streaming buffer requires much less memory than a static buffer. See also static buffer.

Streaming Server *n.* A server technology designed by Apple Computer to send streaming QuickTime media files over the Internet. Built on RTP and RTSP standard Internet protocols, Streaming Server can set up a QuickTime streaming media Web broadcasting station capable of streaming digital videos and music files to more than 3000 users via the Internet. Streaming Server may be used with Mac OS X and other UNIX-based operating systems. Also called: Darwin Streaming Server, QuickTime Streaming Server.

Streaming tape *n.* See tape (definition 1).

Stream interface device driver *n.* A user-level DLL that controls devices connected to a Windows CE–based platform. A stream interface device driver presents the services of a hardware device to applications by exposing Win32 stream interface functions. Stream interface drivers also can control devices built into a Windows CE–based platform, depending on the software architecture for the drivers. Also called: installable device driver.

Stream-oriented file *n.* A file used to store a fairly continuous series of bits, bytes, or other small, structurally uniform units.

Street price *n.* The actual retail or mail-order price of a consumer hardware or software product. In most cases, the street price is somewhat lower than the "suggested retail price."

Stress test *n.* A test of a software or hardware system's functional limits, performed by subjecting the system to extreme conditions, such as peak volumes of data or extremes in temperature.

Strikethrough *n.* One or more lines drawn through a selected range of text, usually to show deletion or the intent to delete.

String *n.* A data structure composed of a sequence of characters usually representing human-readable text.

String variable *n.* An arbitrary name assigned by the programmer to a string of alphanumeric characters and used to reference that entire string. See also string.

Stripe *vb.* See disk striping.

Stripe pitch *n.* The distance, measured horizontally, between bands of phosphor that are the same colour on a cathode ray tube (CRT) display based on aperture grill technology. Although the measurements are based on different methods of applying phosphor to the screen surface, stripe pitch is comparable to dot pitch, the measurement used with CRTs based on shadow mask technology. See also aperture grill, CRT, mask (definition 2).

Striping *n.* A means of protecting data on a network by spreading it across multiple disks. In the most commonly used approach, striping is combined with parity (error-correcting information) to ensure that if some portion of the data is lost, it can be reconstructed. Striping is implemented in RAID security. See also RAID.

Strobe *n.* A timing signal that initiates and coordinates the passage of data, typically through an input/output (I/O) device interface, such as a keyboard or printer.

Stroke *n.* 1. In data entry, a keystroke—a signal to the computer that a key has been pressed. 2. In typography, a line representing part of a letter. 3. In paint programmes, a "swipe" of the brush made with the mouse or keyboard in creating a graphic. 4. In display technology, a line created as a vector (a path between two coordinates) on a vector graphics display (as opposed to a line of pixels drawn dot by dot on a raster graphics display).

Stroke font *n.* A font printed by drawing a combination of lines rather than by filling a shape, as with an outline font.

Stroke weight *n.* The width, or thickness, of the lines (strokes) that make up a character. See also font.

Stroke writer *n.* In video, a display unit that draws characters and graphic images as sets of strokes—lines or curves connecting points—rather than as sets of dots, as on a typical raster-scan monitor. See also vector graphics.

StrongARM *n.* The architecture underlying Intel's low-power, high-performance SA microprocessors. StrongARM is based on the 32-bit RISC architecture licensed by ARM Limited. StrongARM-based SA microprocessors support a number of platforms, including Windows CE and Java, and are designed for use in four primary areas: smart portable devices, such as cellular phones and handheld computers; Internet access devices, such as set-top boxes; networking devices, such as switches and routers; and embedded controls, such as entertainment devices and automation equipment. See also ARM.

Strong name *n.* A name that consists of an assembly's identity: its simple text name, version number, and often the culture information strengthened by a public key and a digital signature generated over the assembly. Assemblies with the same strong name are expected to be identical.

Strong typing *n.* A characteristic of a programming language that does not allow the programme to change the data type of a variable during programme execution. See also data type, variable.

Structure *n.* 1. The design and composition of a programme, including programme flow, hierarchy, and modularity. 2. A collection of data elements. See also data structure.

Structured graphics *n.* See object-oriented graphics.

Structured programming *n.* Programming that produces programmes with clean flow, clear design, and a degree of modularity or hierarchical structure. See also modular programming, object-oriented programming.

Structured query language *n.* A database sublanguage used in querying, updating, and managing relational databases—the de facto standard for database products. Acronym: SQL.

Structured walkthrough *n.* 1. A meeting of programmers working on different aspects of a software development project, in which the programmers attempt to coordinate the various segments of the overall project. The goals, requirements, and components of the project are systematically reviewed in order to minimise the error rate of the software under development. 2. A method for examining a computer system, including its design and implementation, in a systematic fashion.

STT *n.* See Secure Transaction Technology.

Stub *n.* A routine that contains no executable code and that generally consists of comments describing what will eventually be there; it is used as a placeholder for a routine to be written later. Also called: dummy routine. See also top-down programming.

StuffIt *n.* A file compression programme originally written for the Apple Macintosh, used for storing a file on one or more disks. Originally shareware, StuffIt is now a commercial product for Macs and PCs that supports multiple compression techniques and allows file viewing. StuffIt files can be uncompressed using a freeware programme, StuffIt Expander.

Style sheet *n.* 1. A file of instructions used to apply character, paragraph, and page layout formats in word processing and desktop publishing. 2. A text file containing code to apply semantics such as page layout specifications to an HTML document. See also HTML document, semantics (definition 1).

Stylus *n.* A pointing device, similar to a pen, used to make selections, usually by tapping, and to enter information on the touch-sensitive surface.

Subclass *n.* A class in object-oriented programming that is derived from, and inherits its attributes and methods from, another class known as a superclass.

Subcommand *n.* A command in a submenu (a menu that appears when a user selects an option in a higher-level menu).

Subdirectory *n.* A directory (logical grouping of related files) within another directory.

Subdomain *n.* A domain, often representing an administrative or other organisational subgroup within a second-level domain. See also domain.

Subform *n.* A form contained within another form or a report.

Subject drift *n.* See topic drift.

Subject tree *n.* A type of World Wide Web index that is organised by subject categories, many of which are broken down into subcategories, or "branches." An example of a World Wide Web subject tree is Yahoo! See also Yahoo!.

Submarining *n.* A phenomenon that occurs when some part of a screen display moves more quickly than the screen can show. The object (such as the mouse pointer) disappears from the screen and reappears where it comes to rest, just as a submarine resurfaces after a dive. Submarining is especially a problem with the slowly responding passive-matrix LCD displays on many laptop computers.

Submenu *n.* A menu that appears as the result of the selection of an item on another, higher-level menu.

Subnet *n.* 1. In general, a network that forms part of a larger network. 2. In terms of the ISO/OSI reference model, the subnet comprises the layers below the transport layer—that is, the network, data link, and physical layers.

Subnet mask *n.* See address mask.

Subnetting *n.* The division of a network into subnets to improve network security and performance. See also subnet (definition 1).

Subnetwork *n.* A network that is part of another, larger network.

Subnotebook *n.* A class of portable computer that is smaller in size and lighter in weight than a full-sized laptop. Subnotebooks feature a reduced-sized keyboard and screen and often use an external floppy drive to save space and weight. Despite their size, subnotebooks retain all the functions of a full-sized portable computer.

Subportable *n.* See subnotebook.

Subprogram *n.* A term used in some languages for routine (procedure or function) because the structure and syntax of a subprogram closely model those of a programme. See also programme, routine.

Subreport *n.* A report contained within another report.

Subroutine *n.* A common term for routine, likely to be used in reference to shorter, general, frequently called routines. See also procedure, routine.

Subschema *n.* The definition of a user view of the database (in CODASYL/DBTG systems only), roughly equivalent to the external schema of an ANSI/X3/SPARC database management system or to a view in a relational database management system. See also schema.

Subscribe *vb.* 1. To add a newsgroup to the list of such groups from which a user receives all new articles. 2. To add a name to a LISTSERV distribution list. See also LISTSERV.

Subscriber Identity Module card *n.* See SIM card.

Subscript *n.* 1. One or more characters printed slightly below the baseline of surrounding text. See also baseline. 2. In programming, one or more numbers or variables that identify the location of an element in an array. See also array, index (definition 2).

Subscription site *n.* E-commerce Web site that provides information or services to customers who pay a subscription fee.

Substrate *n.* The inactive supporting material used in a manufacturing process. In circuit boards, it is the base to which the traces (foil areas) are attached. In tapes and disks, it is the material on which the magnetic particles are fused.

Substring *n.* A sequential section of a string. See also string.

Subtransaction *n.* See nested transaction.

Subtree *n.* Any node within a tree, along with any selection of connected descendant nodes. See also node (definition 3), tree.

Subweb *n.* A named subdirectory of the root Web site that is a complete FrontPage-based Web site. Each subweb can have independent administration, authoring, and browsing permissions from the root Web site and other subwebs.

Suitcase *n.* A file on Macintosh computers that contains one or more fonts or desk accessories. In early versions of the operating system, such files are indicated with the icon of a suitcase. See also font suitcase.

Suite *n.* 1. A set of application programmes sold as a package, usually at a lower price than that of the individual applications sold separately. A suite for office work, for example, might contain a word processing programme, a spreadsheet, a database management programme, and a communications programme. 2. See protocol suite.

Summarise *vb.* To post the results of a survey or vote in short form to a newsgroup or mailing list after collecting the results by e-mail.

SunOS *n.* Short for Sun Operating System. A variety of the UNIX operating system used on workstations from Sun Microsystems, Inc.

Superclass *n.* A class in object-oriented programming from which another class—a subclass—is derived. The subclass inherits its attributes and methods from the superclass.

Supercomputer *n.* A large, extremely fast, and expensive computer used for complex or sophisticated calculations. See also computer.

Superconductor *n.* A substance that has no resistance to the flow of electricity.

SuperDrive *n.* An Apple 3.5-inch disk drive that can read and write in both Apple Macintosh (400K and 800K) and MS-DOS/Windows (720K and 1.44-MB) formats.

Super-large-scale integration *n.* A reference to the density with which components (transistors and other elements) are packed onto an integrated circuit and to the fineness of the connections between them. The actual number of components is nonspecific, but generally considered to be in of 50,000 to 100,000 range. Acronym: SLSI. See also integrated circuit.

Superminicomputer *n.* See computer.

Supernetting *n.* The aggregation of multiple network addresses of the same class into a single block. See also classless interdomain routing, IP address classes.

Superpipelining *n.* A method of preprocessing used by some microprocessors in which two or more of a microprocessor's execution stages (fetch, decode, execute, and write-back) are divided into two or more pipelined stages, resulting in higher performance. See also DECchip 21064, pipelining (definition 1).

Superscalar *adj.* Of, pertaining to, or being a microprocessor architecture that enables the microprocessor to execute multiple instructions per clock cycle. See also CISC, RISC.

Superscript *n.* A character printed slightly above the surrounding text, usually in smaller type.

Superserver *n.* A network server with especially high capabilities for speed and data storage. See also server (definition 1).

Superstitial *n.* An Internet ad format that downloads in the background while a user is viewing a Web page and then plays in a pop-up window when triggered by a mouse click or a break in surfing. Because the superstitial doesn't appear until it has completely downloaded and temporarily cached itself on the user's system, attention-getting effects like animation, sound, and large graphics can be used without slowing down the ad. Unicast developed the "polite cache and play" technology used with the superstitial ad format.

Supertwist display *n.* A form of passive-matrix liquid crystal displays (LCDs) that rotates polarised light as it passes through liquid crystal molecules in which the top and bottom orientations of the molecules causes them to twist 180 to 270 degrees. This technology is used to improve contrast and widen the screen's viewing angle. Supertwist displays, also known as supertwist nematic displays, are widely used and are less expensive than active-matrix displays. Different forms of supertwist displays include DSTN (double supertwist nematic), which is based on two supertwist layers with opposite twist directions, and CSTN (colour supertwist nematic), which produces wide-angle, high-quality colour. Nematic refers to microscopic threadlike bodies characteristic of the liquid crystals used in these displays. Supertwist displays are widely used in cellular telephones and other devices that may be used in low-light environments. Also called: colour supertwist nematic display, CSTN, double supertwist nematic, DSTN, twisted nematic display

Superuser *n.* A UNIX user account with root (i.e., unrestricted) access privileges, usually that of a system administrator. See also root account, system administrator, user account.

Super VAR *n.* Short for super value-added reseller. A large value-added reseller. See also value-added reseller.

Super VGA *n.* See SVGA.

Supervisor *n.* 1. See operating system. 2. A metaoperating system under which several operating systems are active. See also metaoperating system.

Supervisor state *n.* The most privileged of the modes in which a Motorola 680x0 microprocessor can operate. Every operation of which the microprocessor is capable can be executed in the supervisor state. See also privileged mode.

Support1 *n.* Assistance, such as technical advice provided to customers.

Support2 *vb.* To work with another programme or product; for example, an application might support file transfers from another programme.

Surf *vb.* To browse among collections of information on the Internet, in newsgroups, in Gopherspace, and especially on the World Wide Web. As in channel surfing while watching television, users ride the wave of what interests them, jumping from topic to topic or from one Internet site to another. Also called: cruise.

Surface modeling *n.* A display method used by some CAD programmes that gives onscreen constructions the appearance of solidity. See also CAD.

Surface-mount technology *n.* A method of manufacturing printed circuit boards in which chips are fixed directly to the surface of the board instead of being soldered into holes predrilled to hold them. Its advantages are compactness, resistance to vibration, and the capacity for dense interconnections on both sides of the board. Acronym: SMT.

Surge *n.* A sudden—and possibly damaging—increase in line voltage. See also surge protector, voltage regulator.

Surge protector *n.* A device that prevents surges from reaching a computer or other kinds of electronic equipment. Also called: surge suppressor. See also surge, transient suppressor.

Surge suppressor *n.* See surge protector.

Suspend *vb.* To halt a process temporarily. See also sleep.

Suspend command *n.* A power management feature of Windows 9x and Windows NT 4 and later for portable computers. Clicking on the Suspend command in the Start menu allows the user to temporarily suspend operations of the machine (enter "Suspend mode") without turning the power off, saving battery power without having to restart applications or reload data.

Suspend mode *n.* See sleep mode.

Sustained transfer rate *n.* A measure of the speed at which data can be transferred to a storage device such as a disk or a tape. The sustained transfer rate is the data transfer speed that can be kept up by the device for an extended period of time.

SVC *n.* Acronym for switched virtual circuit. A logical connection between two nodes on a packet-switching network that is established only when data is to be transmitted. See also node (definition 1), packet switching.

SVG *n.* Acronym for Scalable Vector Graphics. An XML-based language for device-independent description of two-dimensional graphics. SVG images maintain their appearance when printed or when viewed with different screen sizes and resolutions. SVG is a recommendation of the World Wide Web Consortium (W3C).

SVGA *n.* Acronym for Super Video Graphics Array. A video standard established by the Video Electronics Standards Association (VESA) in 1989 to provide high-resolution colour display on IBM-compatible computers. Although SVGA is a standard, compatibility problems can occur with the video BIOS. See also BIOS, video adapter.

S-video connector *n.* A hardware interface for video devices that handles chrominance (colour) and luminance (black and white) separately. An S-video connector is capable of providing a sharper image than those achieved with systems using RCA-type, or composite, connectors.

S/WAN *n.* See secure wide area network.

Swap *vb.* 1. To exchange one item for another, as in swapping floppy disks in and out of a single drive. 2. To move segments of programmes or data between memory and disk storage. See also virtual memory.

Swap file *n.* A hidden file on the hard drive that Windows uses to hold parts of programmes and data files that do not fit in memory. The operating system moves data from the swap file to memory as needed and moves data out of memory to the swap file to make room for new data. The swap file is a form of virtual memory. See also memory, virtual memory.

Swap-on-the-fly *n.* In Linux, a process which allows swap space to be added as needed. Swap-on-the-fly allows a swap file to be created at any time on any available disk, and active only until the system is shut down.

Swapping *n.* 1. A technique for enabling an operating system, and therefore a computer, to address—roughly, have available—more memory than is physically present in the system. Swapping in this sense (as opposed to swapping disks in and out of a drive, for example) involves moving blocks of information in units known as pages between memory and disk as they are needed during the execution of the application Swapping is supported by operating systems such as Windows NT and later, Windows 9x and later, OS/2, and Linux. 2. A technique for moving entire processes in and out of main memory. 3. In programming, the process of exchanging two values—for example, exchanging values between two variables. See also page (definition 2), swap, swap file, virtua memory.

Swap space *n.* See swap file.

Swarm intelligence *n.* An emerging subfield of artificia intelligence that relies on the collective knowledge of relativel simple particles or agents. Based loosely on the principles c social insect colonies, it seeks to apply the collectiv intelligence of fragmented agents or groups. It emphasize distributedness, direct or indirect interactions, flexibility, an robustness. Successful applications of its principles have bee evidenced in communications networks, and robotics. See als artificial intelligence, robotics.

Swatch *n.* Short for Simple Watcher. A UNIX log monitoring an alarm programme. Swatch filters system log data as specifie by the user, forwarding only important data. Swatch also lool for patterns of changes made in the log file and alerts the us to system problems as they occur.

Swim *n.* A condition in which images slowly move about tl positions they are supposed to occupy on screen.

SWING set *n.* A library of Java GUIs that run uniformly on ar native platform that supports the Java Virtual Machine (JVM

Swing Set components have largely supplanted Sun Microsystems's Abstract Window Toolkit. See also Abstract Window Toolkit, graphical user interface, Java Virtual Machine.

Switch *n.* 1. A circuit element that has two states: on and off. 2. A control device that allows the user to choose one of two or more possible states. 3. In communications, a computer or electromechanical device that controls routing and operation of a signal path. 4. In networking, a device capable of forwarding packets directly to the ports associated with particular network addresses. See also bridge, multilayer, router. 5. In operating systems such as MS-DOS, an argument used to control the execution of a command or an application, typically starting with a slash character (/).

Switch box *n.* An enclosure that contains a selector switch. When a user selects a switch setting, the signal passing through the box may be directed either from a single input to one of multiple outputs, or from the selected input to a single output. Switch boxes are often used to connect multiple peripherals, such as printers, to a single port.

Switched configuration *n.* A communications link in which a signal moves from the origin to a switch that routes the signal to one of several possible destinations.

Switched Ethernet *n.* An Ethernet network run through a high-speed switch instead of an Ethernet hub. A switched Ethernet involves dedicated bandwidth of 10 Mbps between stations rather than a shared medium. See also Ethernet (definition 1), switch (definition 3).

Switched line *n.* A standard dial-up telephone connection; the type of line established when a call is routed through a switching station.

Switched Multimegabit Data Services *n.* See SMDS.

Switched network *n.* A communications network that uses switching to establish a connection between parties, such as the dial-up telephone system.

Switched T1 *n.* A circuit-switched form of T1 communications. See also T1.

Switched virtual circuit *n.* See SVC.

Switcher *n.* A special Macintosh utility that allowed more than one programme to be resident in memory at one time. Switcher was made obsolete by MultiFinder. See also MultiFinder.

Switching *n.* A communications method that uses temporary rather than permanent connections to establish a link or to route information between two parties. In the dial-up telephone network, for example, a caller's line goes to a switching center, where the actual connection is made to the called party. In computer networks, message switching and packet switching allow any two parties to exchange information. In both instances, messages are routed (switched) through intermediary stations that together serve to connect the sender and the receiver.

Switching hub *n.* A central device (switch) that connects separate communication lines in a network and routes messages and packets among the computers on the network. The switch functions as a hub, or PBX, for the network. See also hub, packet (definition 1), PBX, switch (definition 3), switched Ethernet, switched network.

Switching speed *n.* In a packet-switching telecommunications technology, such as ATM, the speed at which data packets are sent through the network. Switching speed is generally measured in kilobits or megabits per second. See also ATM (definition 1), packet switching.

SYLK file *n.* Short for symbolic linkfile. A file constructed with a proprietary Microsoft format, used primarily for exchanging spreadsheet data in such a way that formatting information and intercellular data value relationships are preserved.

Symbol *n.* In programming, a name that represents a register, an absolute value, or a memory address (relative or absolute). See also identifier, operator (definition 1).

Symbol font *n.* A special font or typeface that replaces the characters normally accessible from the keyboard with alternative characters used as symbols, such as scientific, linguistic, or foreign-alphabet characters.

Symbolic address *n.* A memory address that can be referred to in a programme by name rather than by number.

Symbolic coding *n.* The expression of an algorithm in words, decimal numbers, and symbols rather than in binary numbers, so that a person can read and understand it. Symbolic coding is used in high-level programming languages. See also algorithm, high-level language.

Symbolic language *n.* A computer language that uses symbols such as keywords, variables, and operators to form instructions. All computer languages except machine language are symbolic.

Symbolic link *n.* A disk directory entry that takes the place of a directory entry for a file but is actually a reference to a file in a different directory. Also called: alias, shortcut, soft link, symlink.

Symbolic logic *n.* A representation of the laws of reasoning, so named because symbols rather than natural-language expressions are used to state propositions and relationships. See also logic.

Symbol set *n.* Any collection of symbols legitimised by a data-coding system, such as extended ASCII, or a programming language.

Symbol table *n.* A list of all identifiers encountered when a programme is compiled (or assembled), their locations in the programme, and their attributes, such as variable, routine, and so on. See also compile, identifier, linker, module (definition 1), object code.

SYN *n.* Short for synchronous idle character. A character used in synchronous (timed) communications that enables the sending and receiving devices to maintain the same timing. Also called: sync character.

Sync character *n.* See SYN.

SyncDRAM *n.* See SDRAM.

Synchronisation *n.* 1. In networking, a communications transmission in which multibyte packets of data are sent and received at a fixed rate. See also packet (definition 1). 2. In networking, the matching of timing between computers on the network. All of the computers are generally assigned identical times to facilitate and coordinate communications. 3. In a computer, the matching of timing between components of the computer so that all are coordinated. For instance, operations performed by the operating system are generally synchronised with the signals of the machine's internal clock. See also clock (definition 1), operating system. 4. In application or database files, version comparisons of copies of the files to ensure they contain the same data. 5. In multimedia, precise real-time processing. Audio and video are transmitted over a network in synchronisation so that they can be played back together without delayed responses. See also real-time.

Synchronisation signal *n.* See sync signal.

Synchronise *vb.* To cause to occur at the same time.

Synchronised Multimedia Integration Language *n.* See SMIL.

Synchronous *adj.* Occurring at the same time. In computer transmissions, a reference to activity governed by a clock or by synchronised timing.

Synchronous burst static RAM *n.* A type of static RAM that is synchronised with the system clock. Synchronous burst static RAM is used in a computer's L2 cache, where frequently accessed information is stored for fast retrieval by the CPU. Synchronous burst static RAM is faster than asynchronous static RAM but is limited to a maximum bus speed of 66 MHz. Computers running at faster speeds can use another form of cache memory known as pipeline burst static RAM. Also called: sync SRAM. See also L2 cache, static RAM.

Synchronous communications *n.* Computer-to-computer communications in which transmissions are synchronised by timing between the sending and receiving machines.

Synchronous Data Link Control *n.* See SDLC.

Synchronous Digital Hierarchy *n.* An ITU recommendation implemented in Europe and similar in most respects to the SONET standard used in North America and Japan. See also SONET.

Synchronous DRAM *n.* See SDRAM.

Synchronous graphics RAM *n.* A form of dynamic RAM optimised for the high-speed, high-volume data transfers required by 3D graphics, video, and other memory-intensive applications. Used primarily on video accelerator cards, synchronous graphics RAM makes use of burst operations and includes features such as block writes that increase efficiency in retrieving and writing graphics data to the screen. Acronym: SGRAM. See also block, mask.

Synchronous idle character *n.* See SYN.

Synchronous operation *n.* 1. Any procedure under the control of a clock or timing mechanism. 2. In communications and bus operation, data transfer accompanied by clock pulses either embedded in the data stream or provided simultaneously on a separate line.

Synchronous operation *n.* 1. Two or more processes that depend on the occurrences of specific events such as common timing signals. 2. A data transmission method in which there is constant time between successive bits, characters, or events. The timing is achieved by the sharing of a single clock. Each end of the transmission synchronises itself with the use of clocks and information sent along with the transmitted data. Characters are spaced by time and not by start and stop bits. 3. A function call that blocks execution of a process until it returns. See also asynchronous operation.

Synchronous Optical Network *n.* See SONET.

Synchronous protocol *n.* A set of guidelines developed to standardise synchronous communications between computers, usually based on either bit stream transmission or recognised character codes. Examples include the character-oriented binary synchronous (BISYNC) protocol and the bit-oriented High-level Data Link Control (HDLC) and Synchronous Data Link Control (SDLC) protocols. See also BISYNC, HDLC, SDLC.

Synchronous transmission *n.* Data transfer in which information is transmitted in blocks (frames) of bits separated by equal time intervals.

Synchronous UART *n.* A universal asynchronous receiver/transmitter (UART) that supports synchronous serial transmission, where the sender and receiver share a timing signal. See also UART.

Sync signal *n.* Short for synchronisation signal. The part of a raster-display video signal that denotes the end of each scan line (the horizontal sync signal) and the end of the last scan line (the vertical sync signal).

Sync SRAM *n.* See synchronous burst static RAM.

SYN flood *n.* A method of overwhelming a host computer on a network, especially the Internet, by sending the host a high volume of SYN (synchronisation) packets requesting a connection, but never responding to the acknowledgement packets returned by the host. A SYN flood is a form of denial of service attack. See also denial of service attack.

Synonym *n.* 1. A word that is an equivalent of another word. When used in reference to data input, for example, the verbs type and keyboard are synonyms. 2. In hashing, one of two distinct keys that produce the same hash address. See also hash2.

Syntax *n.* The grammar of a language; the rules governing the structure and content of statements. See also logic, programming language, syntax error.

Syntax checker *n.* A programme for identifying errors in syntax for a programming language. See also syntax, syntax error.

Syntax error *n.* An error resulting from a statement that violates one or more of the grammatical rules of a language and is thus not "legal." See also logic, semantics (definition 1), syntax.

Synthesis *n.* The combining of separate elements to form a coherent whole, or the result of such a combining (for example, combining digital pulses to replicate a sound, or combining digitised words to synthesize human speech). See also speech synthesis.

Synthesizer *n.* A computer peripheral, chip, or stand-alone system that generates sound from digital instructions rather than through manipulation of physical equipment or recorded sound. See also MIDI.

.sys *n.* A file extension for system configuration files.

Sysadmin *n.* The usual logon name or e-mail address for the system administrator of a UNIX-based system. See also system administrator.

Sysgen *n.* See system generation.

Sysop *n.* Short for system operator. The overseer of a bulletin board system (BBS) or a small multiuser computer system.

Sys Req key *n.* Short for System Request key. A key on some IBM and compatible keyboards that is intended to provide the same function as the Sys Req key on an IBM mainframe computer terminal: to reset the keyboard or to change from one session to another.

System *n.* Any collection of component elements that work together to perform a task. Examples are a hardware system consisting of a microprocessor, its allied chips and circuitry, input and output devices, and peripheral devices; an operating system consisting of a set of programmes and data files; or a database management system used to process specific kinds of information.

System administrator *n.* The person responsible for administering use of a multiuser computer system, communications system, or both. A system administrator performs such duties as assigning user accounts and passwords, establishing security access levels, allocating storage space, and watching for unauthorised access to prevent virus or Trojan horse programmes from entering the system. Also called: sysadmin. See also superuser, Trojan horse, virus.

System area network *n.* See storage area network.

System board *n.* See motherboard.

System clock *n.* See clock (definition 1).

System console *n.* The control center of a computer system, primarily with reference to mainframe and minicomputers. In networked or distributed systems, one workstation is designated as the system administrator's; this workstation is analogous to the LAN system console. See also console, LAN.

System conversion *n.* Changing from one operating system to another—for example, from Windows 98 to Windows 2000, UNIX, or OS/2.

System development *n.* The process of defining, designing, testing, and implementing a new system.

System disk *n.* A disk that contains an operating system and can be used to boot a computer. Also called: startup disk. See also boot2, operating system.

System error *n.* A software condition that renders the operating system incapable of continuing to function normally. This type of error usually requires rebooting the system.

System failure *n.* The inability of a computer to continue functioning, usually caused by software rather than hardware.

System file *n.* A resource file on the Macintosh that contains the resources needed by the operating system, such as fonts, icons, and default dialog boxes.

System folder *n.* The Macintosh file folder (directory) that contains the System file and other vital files, such as Finder, device drivers, INIT files, and control panel files. See also control panel, Finder, INIT, System file.

System font *n.* On the Macintosh and in some PC applications, the font used by the computer for onscreen text, such as menu titles and items (but not onscreen text within a word processor or other application). See also font.

System generation *n.* The process of configuring and installing system software for a particular set of hardware components. Complex operating systems such as UNIX are shipped with device drivers and utilities that are often not relevant to a particular hardware configuration; putting together only the necessary components, as well as specifying important system characteristics, is part of the system generation process. Also called: sysgen.

System heap *n.* See heap (definition 1).

System.ini *n.* In Windows 3.x, the initialisation file used to store the hardware configuration information necessary to run the Windows operating environment. The system.ini file was replaced by the registry database in Windows 9x and in Windows NT. See also ini file.

System life cycle *n.* An information system's useful life. At the end of a system's life cycle it is not feasible to repair or expand it, so it must be replaced.

System memory *n.* See memory.

System prompt *n.* See prompt (definition 1).

System recovery *n.* Processing that takes place after a system failure in order to restore a system to normal operation. System recovery takes place after the operating system is initiated. It sometimes requires that tasks in process during the failure be backed out of and that structures in memory during the failure be reconstructed.

System Registry *n.* See registry.

System replacement *n.* See replacement strategy.

System Request key *n.* See Sys Req key.

System resource *n.* On the Macintosh, any of numerous routines, definitions, and data fragments that are stored in the Macintosh System file, such as floating-point arithmetic routines, font definitions, and peripheral drivers. See also resource (definition 2).

Systems analysis *n.* The examination of a system or problem with the goal of either improving an existing system or designing and implementing a new one. As a science, systems analysis is related to cybernetics, a branch of engineering that studies the behaviour of systems.

Systems analyst *n.* A person who works on designing and developing systems. Systems analysts generally combine technical, managerial, and human-relations activities in order to complete their analyses.

Systems Application Architecture *n.* See SAA.

Systems integration *n.* The development of a computer system for a particular customer by combining products from different original equipment manufacturers (OEMs).

Systems Management Server *n.* A Microsoft Back-Office component that provides services for centralised network management. Acronym: SMS.

Systems Network Architecture *n.* See SNA.

System software *n.* The collection of programmes and data that make up and relate to the operating system.

Systems programming *n.* The development or maintenance of programmes designed to execute as part of an operating system, such as I/O routines, user interfaces, command-line interpreters, and task-scheduling and memory management routines.

System support *n.* The provision of services and material resources for the use, maintenance, and improvement of an implemented system.

System timer *n.* See clock (definition 1).

System unit *n.* See console.

System V *n.* A version of the UNIX system provided by AT&T and others. It is both a standard (principally controlled by AT&T) and a set of commercial products.

T

T prefix See tera-.

T1 or T-1 *n.* A high-speed communications line that can handle digital communications and Internet access at the rate 1.544 Mbps (megabits per second). Although originally designed by AT&T to carry multiple voice calls over standard twisted-pair telephone wiring, this high-bandwidth telephone line can also transmit text and images. T1 speed is attained through multiplexing 24 separate 64 Kbps channels into a single data stream. T1 lines are commonly used by larger organisations for Internet connectivity. Also called: T-1 carrier. See also T-carrier.

T.120 standard *n.* A family of International Telecommunications Union (ITU) specifications for multipoint data communications services within computer applications, such as conferencing and multipoint file transfer.

T2 or T-2 *n.* A T-carrier that can handle 6.312 Mbps (megabits per second) or 96 voice channels. See also T-carrier.

T3 or T-3 *n.* A T-carrier that can handle 44.736 Mbps (megabits per second) or 672 voice channels. See also T-carrier.

T4 or T-4 *n.* A T-carrier that can handle 274.176 Mbps (megabits per second) or 4032 voice channels. See also T-carrier.

TA *n.* See terminal adapter.

Tab character *n.* A character used to align lines and columns on screen and in print. Although a tab is visually indistinguishable from a series of blank spaces in most programmes, the tab character and the space character are different to a computer. A tab is a single character and therefore can be added, deleted, or overtyped with a single keystroke. The ASCII coding scheme includes two codes for tab characters: a horizontal tab for spacing across the screen or page and a vertical tab for spacing down the screen or page. See also Tab key.

Tab key *n.* A key, often labeled with both a left-pointing and a right-pointing arrow, that traditionally (as in word processing) is used to insert tab characters into a document. In other applications, such as menu-driven programmes, the Tab key is often used to move the onscreen highlight from place to place. Many database and spreadsheet programmes allow the user to press the Tab key to move around within a record or between cells. The word tab is short for "tabulator," which was the name given to this key on typewriters, where it was used in creating tables. See also tab character.

Table *n.* 1. In programming, a data structure usually consisting of a list of entries, each entry being identified by a unique key and containing a set of related values. A table is often implemented as an array of records, a linked list, or (in more primitive languages) several arrays of different data types, all using a common indexing scheme. See also array, list, record. 2. In relational databases, a data structure characterised by rows and columns, with data occupying or potentially occupying each cell formed by a row-column intersection. The table is the underlying structure of a relation. See also relational database. 3. In word processing, desktop publishing, and in HTML documents, a block of text formatted in aligned rows and columns.

Table lookup *n.* The process of using a known value to search for data in a previously constructed table of values—for example, using a purchase price to search a tax table for the appropriate sales tax. See also lookup.

Tablet *n.* See graphics tablet.

Tablet PC *n.* A touch-sensitive computer screen tablet designed by Microsoft for the entry of handwritten text using a stylus or digital pen. The Tablet PC runs Windows applications and can function as a primary personal computer as well as a note-taking device.

Tabulate *vb.* 1. To total a row or column of numbers. 2. To arrange information in table form.

TACACS *n.* Acronym for Terminal Access Controller Access Control System. A network access technique in which users log into a single centralised server that contains a database of authorised accounts. After the access server authenticates the user, it forwards the login information to the data server requested by the user. See also authentication, server (definition 2).

Tag *n.* 1. In programming, one or more characters containing information about a file, record type, or other structure. 2. In certain types of data files, a key or an address that identifies a record and its storage location in another file. See also tag sort. 3. In markup languages such as SGML and HTML, a code that identifies an element in a document, such as a heading or a paragraph, for the purposes of formatting, indexing, and linking information in the document. In both SGML and HTML, a tag is generally a pair of angle brackets that contain one or more letters and numbers. Usually one pair of angle brackets is placed before an element, and another pair is placed after, to indicate where the element begins and ends. For example, in HTML, <I>hello world</I> indicates that the phrase "hello world" should be italicised. See also <>, element, emotag, HTML, SGML. 4. An early-generation raster graphics format used for Macintosh Ready, Set, Go programmes and Letraset's ImageStudio. See also raster graphics.

Tagged Image File Format *n.* See TIFF.

Tag sort *n.* A sort performed on one or several key fields for the purpose of establishing the order of their associated records. Also called: key sort.

Tag switching *n.* A multilayer Internet switching technology developed by Cisco Systems that integrates routing and switching.

Talk 1 *n.* The UNIX command that, when followed by another user's name and address, is used to generate a request for a synchronous chat session on the Internet. See also chat1 (definition 1).

Talk 2 *vb.* See chat2.

Talker *n.* An Internet-based synchronous communication mechanism most commonly used to support multiuser chat functions. Such systems typically provide specific commands for movement through separate rooms, or chat areas, and allow users to communicate with other users in real time through text messages, indicate simple gestures, use a bulletin board system (BBS) for posting comments, and send internal e-mail. See also BBS (definition 1), chat (definition 1).

Talk. newsgroups *n.* Usenet newsgroups that are part of the talk. hierarchy and have the prefix talk. as part of their names. These newsgroups are devoted to debate and discussion of controversial topics. Talk. newsgroups are one of the seven original Usenet newsgroup hierarchies. The other six are comp., misc., news., rec., sci., and soc. See also newsgroup, traditional newsgroup hierarchy, Usenet.

Tandem processors *n.* Multiple processors wired so that the failure of one processor transfers central processing unit (CPU) operation to another processor. Using tandem processors is part of the strategy for implementing fault-tolerant computer systems. See also central processing unit.

TANSTAAFL *n.* Acronym for There ain't no such thing as a free lunch. An expression used on the Internet in e-mail, chat sessions, mailing lists, newsgroups, and other online forums; derived from The Moon Is a Harsh Mistress, a science-fiction classic by Robert A. Heinlein. See also chat1 (definition 1), e-mail1 (definition 1), mailing list, newsgroup.

Tap 1 *n.* A device that can be attached to an Ethernet bus to enable a computer to be connected.

Tap 2 *vb.* To use a stylus to quickly touch a device screen to perform an activity. Tapping is analogous to clicking with a mouse.

Tap and hold *vb.* To hold a stylus on a device screen to open a pop-up or shortcut menu. Analogous to right-clicking with a mouse.

Tape *n.* 1. A thin strip of polyester film coated with magnetic material that permits the recording of data. Because tape is a continuous length of data storage material and because the read/write head cannot "jump" to a desired point on the tape without the tape first being advanced to that point, tape must be read or written sequentially, not randomly (as can be done on a floppy disk or a hard disk). 2. A storage medium consisting of a thin strip of paper used to store information in the form of sequences of punched holes, chemical impregnation, or magnetic ink imprinting.

Tape cartridge *n.* A module that resembles an audio cassette and contains magnetic tape that can be written on and read from by a tape drive. Tape cartridges are primarily used to back up hard disks. See also tape (definition 1).

Tape drive *n.* A device for reading and writing tapes. See also tape (definition 1).

Tape dump *n.* The process of simply printing the data contained on a tape cartridge without performing any report formatting. See also tape cartridge.

Tape tree *n.* A means of audiotape distribution, used in Usenet music newsgroups and mailing lists, in which a recording is copied and sent to a number of branch participants, who in turn send copies to their children, or leaves. See also branch (definition 1), child (definition 2), leaf, tree structure.

TAPI *n.* Acronym for Telephony Application Programming Interface. In the Windows Open Systems Architecture (WOSA), a programming interface that gives Windows client applications access to a server's voice services. TAPI facilitates interoperability between personal computers and telephone equipment. Also called: Telephony API. See also application programming interface, WOSA.

.tar *n.* The file extension that identifies uncompressed UNIX archives in the format produced by the tar programme.

Tar 1 *n.* Acronym for tape archive. A UNIX utility for making a single file out of a set of files that a user wishes to store together. The resulting file has the extension .tar. Unlike PKZIP, tar does not compress files, so compress or gzip is usually run on the .tar file to produce a file with extensions .tar.gz or .tar.Z. See also compress1, gzip, PKZIP.

Tar 2 *vb.* To make a single file out of a set of files using the tar utility. See also compress1, PKZIP.

Target *n.* Loosely, the objective of a computer command or operation. Examples are a computer that is to run a programme translated for its use, a "foreign" language (for another computer) into which a programme is to be translated, or a group of people for whom a particular product is designed. In MS-DOS usage, the target is often the disk referred to by prompts in a copy operation (for example, "insert target diskette"). In terms of the SCSI (small computer system interface) connection, the target is the device that receives commands. See also SCSI, target computer, target disk, target language.

Target computer *n.* The computer that receives data from a communications device, a hardware add-in, or a software package.

Target disk *n.* The disk to which data is to be written, as in a copy operation. See also target.

Target language *n.* The language into which source code is compiled or assembled. See also assembler, compiler (definition 2), cross-compiler.

Task *n.* A stand-alone application or a subprogram that is run as an independent entity.

Taskbar *n.* A graphic toolbar used in Windows 9x, Windows CE Windows NT, and Windows 2000 to select, via the mouse one of a number of active applications. See also task button toolbar.

Task button *n.* In Windows 9x, Windows CE, Windows NT, and Windows 2000, a button that appears on the taskbar on the screen when an application is run. By clicking on the button the user can switch from another application to the application corresponding to the button. See also taskbar.

Task management *n.* The operating-system process of tracking the progress of and providing necessary resources for separate tasks that are running on a computer, especially in a multitasking environment.

Task swapping *n.* The process of switching from one application to another by saving the data for the application presently running in the foreground to a storage device and loading the other application. See also foreground(definition 2), task, task switching.

Task switching *n.* The act of moving from one programme to another without shutting down the first programme. Task switching is a single act, as compared to multitasking, in which the central processing unit rapidly switches back and forth between two or more programmes. See also task, task swapping.

TB *n.* See terabyte.

T-carrier *n.* A long-distance, digital communications line provided by a common carrier. Multiplexers at either end merge several voice channels and digital data streams for transmission and separate them when received. T-carrier service, introduced by AT&T in 1993, is defined at several capacity levels: T1, T2, T3, and T4. In addition to voice communication, T-carriers are used for Internet connectivity. See also T1, T2, T3, T4.

TCB *n.* Acronym for Trusted Computing Base. The complete set of security mechanisms that create security on a network. The TCB includes all the hardware, software, and firmware components that are responsible for system security.

Tcl/Tk *n.* Acronym for Tool Command Language/Tool Kit. A programming system that includes a scripting language (Tcl) and a graphical user interface toolkit (Tk). The Tcl language issues commands to interactive programmes, such as text editors, debuggers, and shells, which tie together complex data structures into scripts. See also graphical user interface, script, scripting language.

TCM *n.* See trellis-coded modulation.

TCO *n.* See total cost of ownership.

TCP *n.* Acronym for Transmission Control Protocol. The protocol within TCP/IP that governs the breakup of data messages into packets to be sent via IP (Internet Protocol), and the reassembly and verification of the complete messages from packets received by IP. A connection-oriented, reliable protocol (reliable in the sense of ensuring error-free delivery), TCP corresponds to the transport layer in the ISO/OSI reference model. See also ISO/OSI reference model, packet, TCP/IP.

TCP/IP *n.* Acronym for Transmission Control Protocol/Internet Protocol. A protocol suite (or set of protocols) developed by the U.S. Department of Defense for communications over interconnected, sometimes dissimilar, networks. It is built into the UNIX system and has become the de facto standard for data transmission over networks, including the Internet.

TCP/IP reference model *n.* A networking model designed around the concept of internetworking—the exchange of information among different networks, often built on different architectures. The TCP/IP reference model, often called the Internet reference model, consists of four layers, the most distinctive of which is the internetwork that deals with routing messages and that has no equivalent in the ISO/OSI reference model or the SNA model.

TCP/IP stack *n.* The set of TCP/IP protocols. See also protocol stack, TCP/IP.

TDM *n.* See time-division multiplexing.

TDMA *n.* Short for Time Division Multiple Access. A multiplexing technology used to divide a single cellular phone channel into multiple subchannels. TDMA works by allocating separate time slots to each user. It is implemented in D-AMPS (Digital Advanced Mobile Phone Service), which relies on TDMA to divide each of the 30 analog AMPS channels into 3 separate subchannels, and GSM (Global System for Mobile Communications). See also D-AMPS, Global System for Mobile Communications.

Team Web site *n.* See SharePoint team Web site.

Teardrop attack *n.* An Internet-based attack that breaks a message into a series of IP fragments with overlapping offset fields. When these fragments are reassembled at their destination, the fields don't match, causing the system to hang, reboot, or crash.

Tearing *n.* A visual artifact produced when the screen refresh rate is out of sync with an application's frame rate. The top portion of one frame is displayed at the same time as the bottom portion of another frame, with a discernible tear between the two partial images.

Tear-off *adj.* Capable of being dragged from an original position in a graphical user interface and placed where the user desires. For example, many graphics applications feature tear-off menus of tool palettes that can be dragged to locations other than the menu bar.

Techie *n.* A technically oriented person. Typically, a techie is the person on whom a user calls when something breaks or the user cannot understand a technical problem. A techie may be an engineer or a technician, but not all engineers are techies. See also guru.

Technical author *n.* See tech writer.

Technobabble *n.* Language that includes incomprehensible technical terms and jargon. In ordinary conversation, many of the words in this dictionary might be considered technobabble.

Technology *n.* The application of science and engineering to the development of machines and procedures in order to enhance or improve human conditions, or at least to improve human efficiency in some respect. See also high tech.

Technophile *n.* Someone who is enthusiastic about emerging technology.

Technophobe *n.* A person who is afraid of or dislikes technological advances, especially computers. See also Luddite.

Tech writer *n.* Short for technical writer. One who writes the documentation material for a hardware or software product. Also called: technical author. See also documentation.

Telco *n.* Short for telephone company. A term generally used in reference to a telephone company's provision of Internet services.

Telecom closet *n.* See wiring closet.

Telecommunications *n.* The transmission and reception of information of any type, including data, television pictures, sound, and facsimiles, using electrical or optical signals sent over wires or fibers or through the air.

Telecommunications closet *n.* See wiring closet.

Telecommute *vb.* To work in one location (often at home) and communicate with a main office at a different location through a personal computer equipped with a modem and communications software.

Telecommuter *n.* A member of the workforce who conducts business outside the traditional office setting, collaborating with business associates and colleagues through communications and computer technologies. Some workers telecommute full-time; others part-time. The telecommuting ranks include self-employed home workers, small-business entrepreneurs, and employees of large corporations or organisations. See also distributed workplace, SOHO.

Teleconferencing *n.* The use of audio, video, or computer equipment linked through a communications system to enable geographically separated individuals to participate in a meeting or discussion. See also video conferencing.

Telecopy *vb.* See fax.

Telematics *n.* In communications technology, the linking of computers and telecommunications. Telematics technology is becoming standard in the automotive industry, with dashboard navigation systems, roadside assistance, entertainment, Internet, and cellular services available in vehicles.

Telephony *n.* Telephone technology—voice, fax, or modem transmissions based on either the conversion of sound into electrical signals or wireless communication via radio waves.

Telephony API *n.* See TAPI.

Telephony device *n.* A mechanism designed to translate sound into electrical signals, transmit them, and then convert them back to sound.

Telephony Service Provider *n.* A modem driver that enables access to vendor-specific equipment through a standard device driver interface. Acronym: TSP. See also Telephony Service Provider Interface.

Telephony Service Provider Interface *n.* The external interface of a service provider to be implemented by vendors of telephony equipment. A telephony service provider accesses vendor-specific equipment through a standard device driver interface. Installing a service provider allows Windows CE–based applications that use elements of telephony to access the corresponding telephony equipment. Acronym: TSPI. See also Telephony Service Provider.

Teleprocess *vb.* To use a terminal or computer and communications equipment to access computers and computer files located elsewhere. Teleprocess is a term originated by IBM. See also distributed processing, remote access.

Teleprocessing monitor *n.* See TP monitor.

Telescript *n.* A communications-oriented programming language, released in 1994 by General Magic, that was designed to address the need for cross-platform, network-independent messaging and abstraction of complex network protocols. See also communications protocol.

Teletext *n.* All-text information broadcast by a television station to a subscriber's television set.

Teletype *n.* The Teletype Corporation, developer of the teletypewriter (TTY) and various other printers used with computers and communications systems. See also TTY.

Teletype mode *n.* A mode of operation in which a computer or an application limits its actions to those characteristic of a teletypewriter (TTY). On the display, for example, teletype mode means that only alphanumeric characters can be shown, and they are simply "typed" on the screen, one letter after the other, and cannot be placed in any desired position. See also Teletype, TTY.

Teletypewriter *n.* See TTY.

Teleworker *n.* A businessperson who substitutes information technologies for work-related travel. Teleworkers include home-based and small business workers who use computer and communications technologies to interact with customers and/or colleagues. See also distributed workplace, SOHO.

Telnet 1 *n.* 1. A client programme that implements the Telnet protocol. 2. A protocol in the TCP/IP suite that enables individuals to log on to and use a remote computer as if they were sitting at a terminal directly connected to the machine.

Telnet 2 *vb.* To access a remote computer over the Internet using the Telnet protocol. See also telnet1.

Telnet *n.* A protocol that enables an Internet user to log on to and enter commands on a remote computer linked to the Internet, as if the user were using a text-based terminal directly attached to that computer. Telnet is part of the TCP/IP suite of protocols.

Template *n.* 1. In an application package, an overlay for the keyboard that identifies special keys and key combinations. 2. In image processing, a pattern that can be used to identify or match a scanned image. 3. In spreadsheet programmes, a predesigned spreadsheet that contains formulas, labels, and other elements. 4. In MS-DOS, a small portion of memory that holds the most recently typed MS-DOS command. 5. In word processing and desktop publishing programmes, a predesigned document that contains formatting and, in many cases, generic text.

Temporary file *n.* A file created either in memory or on disk, by the operating system or some other programme, to be used during a session and then discarded. Also called: temp file. See also scratch1.

Temporary storage *n.* A region in memory or on a storage device that is temporarily allocated for use in storing intermediate data in a computational, sorting, or transfer operation.

Ten's complement *n.* A number in the base-10 system that is the true complement of another number and is derived either by subtracting each digit from 1 less than the base and adding 1 to the result or by subtracting each number from the next higher power of the base. For example, the ten's complement of 25 is 75, and it can be derived either by subtracting each digit from 9, which is 1 less than the base (9 – 2 = 7, 9 – 5 = 4) and then adding 1 (74 + 1 = 75) or by subtracting 25 from the next higher power of 10, which is 100 (100 – 25 = 75). See also complement.

tera- prefix A prefix meaning 1012: 1 trillion in the American numbering system, 1 million million in British numbering. Abbreviation: T. See also terabyte.

Terabyte *n.* A measurement used for high-capacity data storage. One terabyte equals 240, or 1,099,511,627,776, bytes, although it is commonly interpreted as simply one trillion bytes. Abbreviation: TB.

Teraflops *n.* One trillion floating-point operations (FLOPS) per second. Teraflops serves as a benchmark for larger computers that measures the number of floating-point operations they can perform in a set amount of time. Also called: TFLOPS. See also FLOPS.

Terminal *n.* 1. In networking, a device consisting of a video adapter, a monitor, and a keyboard. The adapter and monitor and, sometimes, the keyboard are typically combined in a single unit. A terminal does little or no computer processing on its own; instead, it is connected to a computer with a communications link over a cable. Terminals are used primarily in multiuser systems and today are not often found on single-user personal computers. See also dumb terminal, smart terminal, terminal emulation. 2. In electronics, a point that can be physically linked to something else, usually by a wire, to form an electrical connection.

Terminal *n.* An application that provides command-line access to the Mac OS X UNIX core. The Terminal command-line environment allows UNIX functions from within Mac OS X.

Terminal Access Controller Access Control System *n.* See TACACS.

Terminal adapter *n.* The correct name for an ISDN modem, which connects a PC to an ISDN line but does not modulate or demodulate signals as a typical modem does.

Terminal emulation *n.* The imitation of a terminal by using software that conforms to a standard, such as the ANSI standard for terminal emulation. Terminal-emulation software is used to make a microcomputer act as if it were a particular type of terminal while it is communicating with another computer, such as a mainframe. See also VT-52, VT-100, VT-200.

Terminal server *n.* In a LAN (local area network), a computer or a controller that allows terminals, microcomputers, and other devices to connect to a network or host computer, or to devices attached to that particular computer. See the illustration. See also controller, LAN, microcomputer, terminal.

Terminal session *n.* The period of time spent actively using a terminal. See also session.

Terminal strip *n.* A usually long and narrow assembly containing one or more electrical connectors. Commonly, terminal strips consist of screws on which bare wires are wrapped before the screws are tightened; for example, some consumer-grade stereo receiver/amplifiers incorporate a set of terminal strips on the rear panel for attaching speaker wires to the unit.

Terminate *vb.* 1. With reference to software, to end a process or programme. Abnormal termination occurs in response to user intervention or because of a hardware or software error. 2. With reference to hardware, to install a plug, jack, or other connector at the end of a wire or cable.

Terminator *n.* 1. A character that indicates the end of a string, such as the null character in an ASCIIZ string. See also ASCII, ASCIIZ string. 2. An item of hardware that must be installed in the last device in a daisy chain or bus network, such as Ethernet or SCSI. The terminator caps the end of a cable in a bus network in order to keep signals from bouncing back along the line. See also terminator cap.

Terminator cap *n.* A special connector that must be attached to each end of an Ethernet bus. If one or both terminator caps are missing, the Ethernet network will not work.

Ternary *adj.* In programming, of, pertaining to, or characteristic of an element with three possible values, a condition that has three possible states, or a base-3 number system.

Tessellate *vb.* To break an image into small, square regions for processing or output.

Test *vb.* To check programme correctness by trying out various sequences and input values. See also debug, test data.

Test automation software *n.* A programme that automatically enters a predetermined set of characters or user commands in order to test new or modified versions of software applications.

Test data *n.* A set of values used to test proper functioning of a programme. Reasons for choosing particular test data include verifying known output (anticipated output) and pushing boundary conditions that might cause the programme to fail.

Test post *n.* A newsgroup article that contains no actual message but is used simply as a means of checking the connection. See also article, newsgroup.

TeX or TEX *n.* A text-formatting software system created by mathematician and computer scientist Donald Knuth for producing typeset-quality scientific, mathematical, or other complex technical documents from plain ASCII text input. Implementations of TeX for UNIX systems, MS-DOS and Windows, and the Apple Macintosh are available free over the Internet (ftp://ftp.tex.ac.uk/tex-archive/) or in commercial distributions (which often include enhancements). Commands in the input file produce format elements and special symbols; for example, ${\pi}r^2$ produces the expression pr 2. TeX is extensible through macros, and macro files are available for a wide variety of applications. See also LaTeX.

Texas Instruments Graphics Architecture *n.* See TIGA.

Texel *n.* A single element in a texture. When a texture has been applied to an object, the texels rarely correspond to pixels on the screen. Applications can use texture filtering to control how texels are sampled and interpolated to pixels.

Text *n.* 1. Data that consists of characters representing the words and symbols of human speech; usually, characters coded according to the ASCII standard, which assigns numeric values to numbers, letters, and certain symbols. 2. In word processing and desktop publishing, the main portion of a document, as opposed to headlines, tables, figures, footnotes, and other elements.

Text box *n.* In a dialog box or HTML form, a box in which the user may enter text.

TextEdit *n.* A standard set of routines in the Macintosh operating system that are available to programmes for controlling the way text is displayed. See also Toolbox.

Text editor *n.* See editor.

Text entry *n.* The inputting of text characters by means of a keyboard.

Text file *n.* A file composed of text characters. A text file can be a word-processing file or a "plain" ASCII file encoded in a format practically all computers can use. See also ASCII file, text (definition 1).

Text mode *n.* A display mode in which the monitor can display letters, numbers, and other text characters but no graphical images or WYSIWYG ("what-you-see-is-what-you-get") character formatting (italics, superscript, and so on). Also called: alphanumeric mode, character mode.

Text-to-speech *n.* The conversion of text-based data into voice output by speech synthesis devices to allow users to gain access to information by telephone or to allow blind or illiterate people to use computers.

Text-to-Speech *n.* See TTS (definition 1).

Texture *n.* In computer graphics, shading or other attributes added to the "surface" of a graphical image to give it the illusion of a physical substance. For example, a surface could be made to appear reflective to simulate metal or glass, or a scanned image of wood grain could be applied to a shape intended to simulate an object made of wood.

Texture mapping *n.* In 3-D graphics, the process of adding detail to an object by creating a picture or a pattern that can be "wrapped" around the object. For example, a texture map of stones might be wrapped around a pyramid shape to create a realistic image. Texture mapping can also account for changes in perspective as the picture is wrapped around the shape. The technique is valued in 3-D graphics because it enables creation of detailed images without the performance degradation that can result from the computation required to manipulate images created with large numbers of polygons.

TFLOPS *n.* See teraflops.

TFT *n.* Acronym for thin film transistor. A transistor created using thin film methodology. See also active matrix display, thin film, transistor.

TFT display *n.* See active matrix display.

TFT LCD *n.* Acronym for thin film transistor liquid crystal display. See active matrix display.

TFTP *n.* See Trivial File Transfer Protocol.

TGA *n.* 1. Short for Targa. A raster graphics file format from Truevision, Inc., that handles 16-, 24-, and 32-bit colour. See also 16-bit colour, 24-bit colour, 32-bit colour, raster graphics, video graphics board. 2. The brand name of a series of high-resolution video graphics boards.

Theme *n.* 1. A set of visual elements that provide a unified look for your computer desktop. A theme determines the look of the various graphic elements of your desktop, such as the windows, icons, fonts, colours, and the background and screen saver pictures. It can also define sounds associated with events, such as opening or closing a programme. 2. A set of coordinated graphic elements applied to a document or Web page, or across all pages in a Web site. Themes can consist of designs and colour schemes for fonts, link bars, and other page elements.

Thermal printer *n.* A nonimpact printer that uses heat to generate an image on specially treated paper. The printer uses pins to produce an image, but rather than striking the pins against a ribbon to mark the paper as does a wire-pin dot-matrix printer, it heats the pins and brings them into gentle contact with the paper. The special coating on the paper discolours when it is heated.

Thermal wax-transfer printer *n.* A special type of nonimpact printer that uses heat to melt coloured wax onto paper to create an image. Like a standard thermal printer, it uses pins to apply the heat. Rather than making contact with coated paper, however, the pins touch a wide ribbon saturated with different coloured waxes. The wax melts under the pins and adheres to the paper.

Thesaurus *n.* 1. A book of words and their synonyms. 2. In microcomputer applications, both a file of synonyms stored on disk and the programme used to search the file.

The World—Public Access UNIX *n.* One of the oldest public access Internet service providers, based in Boston. In 1990, The World began offering full dial-up Internet access to the public. Other services include World Wide Web access, Usenet, SLIP/PPP support, telnet, FTP, IRC, Gopher, and e-mail. In 1995, The World began supporting local dial-up access via UUNET. See also ISP.

Thick Ethernet *n.* See 10Base5.

Thick film *adj.* A term describing a method used in the manufacture of integrated circuits. Thick film technology uses a stencil-like technique called photosilkscreening to deposit multiple layers of special inks or pastes on a ceramic substrate. The inks or pastes can be conducting, insulating, or resistive. The passive components (wires, resistors, and capacitors) of the integrated circuits are formed by depositing a series of films of different characteristics and patterns.

ThickNet *n.* See 10Base5.

ThickWire *n.* See 10Base5.

Thimble *n.* A type element, similar to a daisy wheel, that bears a full character set, with each character on a separate type bar. As with a daisy wheel, the spokes, or type bars, radiate out from a central hub. On a thimble print element, however, each type bar is bent 90 degrees at its halfway point, so the type bars stick straight up with the type facing away from the hub. See also thimble printer.

Thimble printer *n.* A printer that uses a thimble print element, best known in a line of printers from NEC. Because these printers use fully formed characters like those on a typewriter, they generate letter-quality output that is indistinguishable from that of a typewriter. This includes the slight impression created by the type hitting the paper hard through the ribbon, which distinguishes this type of printout from that of laser printers. See also thimble.

Thin client *n.* A software layer of a small client for a centrally managed, network terminal. The thin client allows the user access to server-hosted applications and data.

Thin Ethernet *n.* See 10Base2.

Thin film *adj.* A method used in the fabrication of integrated circuits. Thin film technology operates on the same basic principles as thick film technology. Rather than using inks or pastes, however, thin film technology uses metals and metal oxides that are "evaporated" and then deposited on the substrate in the desired pattern to form the integrated circuit's passive components (wires, resistors, and capacitors). See also molecular beam epitaxy.

Thin film transistor *n.* See TFT.

ThinNet *n.* See 10Base2.

Thin server *n.* A client/server architecture in which most of an application is run on the client machine, which is called a fat client, with occasional data operations on a remote server. Such a configuration yields good client performance, but complicates administrative tasks, such as software upgrades. See also client/server architecture, fat client, thin client.

Thin space *n.* An amount of horizontal space in a font, equal to one-quarter the point size of the font. For example, a thin space in a 12-point font is 3 points wide. See also point1 (definition 1).

Third-generation computer *n.* Any of the computers produced from the mid-1960s to the 1970s that were based on integrated circuits rather than on separately wired transistors. See also computer.

Third-generation language *n.* See 3GL.

Third normal form *n.* See normal form (definition 1).

Third-party1 *adj.* In computer console games, a game made for a specific console by a company other than the console manufacturer.

Third party2 *n.* A company that manufactures and sells accessories or peripherals for use with a major manufacturer's computer or peripheral, usually without any involvement from the major manufacturer.

Thrashing *n.* The state of a virtual memory system that is spending almost all its time swapping pages in and out of memory rather than executing applications. See also swap (definition 2), virtual memory.

Thread *n.* 1. In programming, a process that is part of a larger process or programme. 2. In a tree data structure, a pointer that identifies the parent node and is used to facilitate traversal of the tree. 3. In electronic mail and Internet newsgroups, a series of messages and replies related to a specific topic.

Threaded discussion *n.* In a newsgroup or other online forum, a series of messages or articles in which replies to an article are nested directly under it, instead of the articles being arranged in chronological or alphabetical order. See also newsgroup, thread (definition 3).

Threaded newsreader *n.* A newsreader that displays posts in newsgroups as threads. Replies to a post appear directly after the original post, rather than in chronological or any other order. See also newsreader, post, thread (definition 3).

Threaded tree *n.* A tree in which the leaf (end) nodes contain pointers to some of the nodes from which they arise. The pointers facilitate searching the tree for information. See also thread (definition 2).

Threading *n.* A technique used by certain interpretive languages, such as many Forth implementations, to speed execution. The references to other support routines in each threaded support routine, such as a predefined word in Forth, are replaced by pointers to those routines. See also Forth, thread (definition 1).

Three-dimensional array *n.* An ordered arrangement of information in which three numbers (integers) are used to locate a particular item. A three-dimensional array treats data as if it were laid out in rows, columns, and layers. See also 3-D array, array, two-dimensional array.

Three-dimensional model *n.* A computer simulation of a physical object in which length, width, and depth are real attributes—a model, with x-, y-, and z-axes, that can be rotated for viewing from different angles.

Three-finger salute *n.* Slang term for a warm, or soft, boot, in which the Ctrl, Alt, and Delete keys are pressed simultaneously to restart a computer without first turning off the power. Also called: Vulcan death grip. See also warm boot.

Three-nines availability *n.* The availability of a system 99.9% of the time. Three-nines availability equates to approximately 526 minutes of downtime in a standard 365-day year. See also high availability.

Three-point editing *n.* In digital video editing, a feature that simplifies the process of placing new video within a sequence by assisting in calculating edit points. To make an edit, in and out points must be defined in the video clip to be added and in the sequence into which the clip is to be inserted. The user provides any three of these edit points and the editing software determines the fourth.

Three-tier client/server *n.* A client/server architecture in which software systems are structured into three tiers or layers: the user interface layer, the business logic layer, and the database layer. Layers may have one or more components. For example, there can be one or more user interfaces in the top tier, each user interface may communicate with more than one application in the middle tier at the same time, and the applications in the middle tier may use more than one database at a time. Components in a tier may run on a computer that is separate from the other tiers, communicating with the other components over a network. See also client/server architecture.

Throbber *n.* An animated icon that moves while an application is completing a task, such as a browser loading a Web page. Throbbers serve to reassure the user that the application is still working on the task and has not frozen. Web browsers and some other applications come with a throbber icon. In some cases, the user can replace the original throbber with a customised icon of the user's choice.

Throttle control *n.* A device that enables the user of a flight simulator or game to control simulated engine power. The throttle control is used along with a joystick (which controls the simulated ailerons and elevators) and possibly a rudder control.

Throughput *n.* 1. The data transfer rate of a network, measured as the number of bits per second transmitted. 2. A measure of the data processing rate in a computer system.

Throughput test *n.* See bandwidth test.

Thumb *n.* See elevator.

Thumbnail *n.* A miniature version of an image or electronic version of a page that is generally used to allow quick browsing through multiple images or pages. For example Web pages often contain thumbnails of images (which can be loaded much more quickly by the Web browser than the full size image). Many of these thumbnails can be clicked on to load the complete version of the image.

Thumbwheel *n.* A wheel embedded in a case so that only portion of the outside rim is revealed. When rolled with the thumb, the wheel can control an onscreen element such as pointer or a cursor. Thumbwheels are used with three-dimensional joysticks and trackballs to control the depth aspect of the pointer or cursor. See also joystick, relative pointing device, trackball.

Thunk1 *n.* Code that enables 16-bit code to call 32-bit code, and vice versa. There are three different types of thunk: a flat thunk relies on a thunk compiler to allow 32-bit code to call a 16-bit DLL and 16-bit code to call a 32-bit DLL; a generic thunk enables a 16-bit application to load and call a 32-bit DLL; and a universal thunk allows 32-bit code to load and call a 16-bit DLL. All thunks are Windows-based, but the type of thunk used depends on the Windows version.

Thunk2 *vb.* To call 32-bit code from 16-bit code, or vice versa. Thunking involves, in large part, the translation to and from 16-bit segment offset memory addressing and 32-bit flat, or linear, memory addressing. See also address space, flat address space, segmented address space.

TIA *n.* Acronym for thanks in advance. On the Internet, a popular sign-off to a request of some sort. Also called: aTdHvAaNnKcSe.

Tick *n.* 1. A regular, rapidly recurring signal emitted by a clocking circuit; also, the interrupt generated by this signal. 2. In some microcomputer systems, notably Macintosh, one sixtieth of a second, the basic time unit used by the internal clock that is accessible by programmes.

Tiebreaker *n.* A circuit that arbitrates competing circuits and resolves bottlenecks by giving priority to one circuit at a time.

Tie line *n.* A private line leased from a communications carrier and often used to link two or more points in an organisation.

Tier 1 *n.* An Internet Network Access Point that provides access to and interconnection among major national and international network backbone providers, such as MCI WorldCom, Sprint, BBN, and IBM. See also Network Access Point.

Tier 2 *n.* A regional Internet Network interchange location where local ISPs exchange data. By using a Tier 2 exchange point, ISPs in the same area can move data between their users without the need to transport that data over long distances. For example, if a user in Singapore connects to a Web site in the same city through a local Tier 2 exchange point, it is not necessary to move the data through a major Network Access Point, or NAP, in Japan or North America. Tier 2 locations generally have much smaller capacities than the national and international Tier 1 NAPs. See also Network Access Point.

.tif or .tiff *n.* The file extension that identifies bitmap images in Tagged Image File Format (TIFF). See also TIFF.

TIFF or TIF *n.* Acronym for Tagged Image File Format or Tag Image File Format. A standard file format commonly used for scanning, storage, and interchange of gray-scale graphic images. TIFF may be the only format available for older programmes (such as older versions of MacPaint), but most modern programmes are able to save images in a variety of other formats, such as GIF or JPEG. See also gray scale.

TIFF JPEG *n.* Acronym for Tagged Image File Format JPEG. A means of saving photographic images compressed according to the JPEG (Joint Photographic Experts Group) standard. TIFF JPEG saves more information about an image than does the lower-end JFIF (JPEG File Interchange Format), but TIFF JPEG files are limited in portability because of differences in implementation among applications. See also JFIF, JPEG.

TIGA *n.* Acronym for Texas Instruments Graphics Architecture. A video adapter architecture based on the Texas Instruments 340x0 graphics processor.

Tiger team *n.* A group of users, programmers, or hackers who are charged with finding flaws in networks, applications, or security procedures. Tiger teams may be hired or may be composed of volunteers, and may have a single, short-term goal or may be used for a number of investigative purposes over a longer period of time. The term "tiger team" was originally used by the military to describe infiltration groups, and was first used in the computer industry to refer to hackers hired to expose flaws in network security.

Tightly coupled *adj.* 1. Refers to two computing processes whose successful completion and individual performance rates are highly interdependent. 2. Of, pertaining to, or characteristic of a relationship of interdependency between computers, as in multiprocessing.

Tile *vb.* 1. In computer-graphics programming, to fill adjacent blocks of pixels on the screen with a design or pattern without allowing any blocks to overlap. 2. To fill the space on a monitor or within a smaller area with multiple copies of the same graphic image. 3. In an environment with multiple windows, to rearrange and resize all open windows so that they appear fully on the screen without any overlap.

Time and date *n.* In computing, the timekeeping and datekeeping functions maintained by the computer's operating system, used most visibly as a means of "stamping" files with the date and time of creation or last revision.

Time and date stamp *n.* See time stamp.

Time bomb *n.* 1. A feature often built into evaluation or beta versions of software that renders the software unusable after a certain period of time. With some evaluation versions of software containing time bombs, users are given codes or registration numbers after purchasing the software that will deactivate the time bomb. 2. See logic bomb. 3. See Year 2000 problem.

Time Division Multiple Access *n.* See TDMA.

Time-division multiplexing *n.* A form of multiplexing in which transmission time is broken into segments, each of which carries one element of one signal. Acronym: TDM. See also statistical multiplexer.

Time horizon to failure *n.* See event horizon.

Time out or timeout or time-out *n.* An event that indicates that a predetermined amount of time has elapsed without some other expected event taking place. The time-out event is used to interrupt the process that had been waiting for the other expected event. For example, a dial-up remote system might allow the user 60 seconds to log in after making a connection. If the user fails to enter a valid login name and password within this time, the computer breaks the connection, thus protecting itself against crackers as well as freeing a phone line that may have gone dead.

Timer *n.* A register (high-speed memory circuit) or a special circuit, chip, or software routine used to measure time intervals. A timer is not the same as the system clock, although its pulses can be derived from the system clock frequency. See also time and date.

Time server *n.* A computer that periodically synchronises the time on all computers within a network. This ensures that the time used by network services and local functions remains accurate.

Time-sharing or timesharing *n.* 1. The use of a computer system by more than one individual at the same time. Time-sharing runs separate programmes concurrently by interleaving portions of processing time allotted to each programme (user). See also quantum (definition 2), time slice. 2. A method, used primarily in the 1960s and 1970s, for sharing the capabilities (and cost) of a computer, such as a mainframe. Time-sharing allowed different clients to "rent" time on a large computer and pay for only the portion of time they used.

Time shifting *n.* A method of dealing with programmes with Year 2000 problems that entails modifying the date either in data with which a programme works (programme encapsulation) or in the input/output logic of the programme (data encapsulation). In both cases, the date is moved back in time to process the input, and forward in time to the correct date to produce output. See also encapsulation.

Time slice *n.* A brief period of time during which a particular task is given control of the microprocessor in a time-sharing multitasking environment. See also multitasking, preemptive multitasking.

Time-slice multitasking *n.* See preemptive multitasking.

Timestamp *n.* A certification by a trusted third party specifying that a particular message existed at a specific time and date. In a digital context, trusted third parties generate a trusted timestamp for a particular message by having a timestamping service append a time value to a message and then digitally signing the result. See also digital signature, service.

Time stamp *n.* A time signature that is added by a programme or system to files, e-mail messages, or Web pages. A time stamp indicates the time and usually the date when a file or Web page was created or last modified or when an e-mail message was sent or received. Most time stamps are created by programmes and are based on the time kept by the system clock of a computer on which the programme resides. Commercial time stamp services are available on the Web or by e-mail, and offer proof of posting certificates to corroborate the time and date a message was sent. Also called: date and time stamp, date stamp, time and date stamp.

Time-synchronisation service *n.* A programme used to ensure that all systems on a network use a common time. Time-synchronisation services on the Internet typically update real-time clocks to Universal Time Coordinate (UTC) using Network Time Protocol (NTP). Windows Time Synchronisation Service (Win32Time) is a time-synchronisation service. See also clock (definition 2), Network Time Protocol, Universal Time Coordinate.

Time to Live *n.* A header field for a packet sent over the Internet indicating how long the packet should be held. Acronym: TTL. See also header (definition 2), packet (definition 1).

Timing attack *n.* An attack on a cryptographic system that exploits the fact that different cryptographic operations take slightly different amounts of time to process. The attacker exploits these slight time differences by carefully measuring the amount of time required to perform private key operations. Taking these measurements from a vulnerable system can reveal the entire secret key. Cryptographic tokens, network-based cryptosystems, and other applications where attackers can make reasonably accurate timing measurements are potentially at risk from this form of attack.

Timing signals *n.* 1. Any of several types of signals used to coordinate activities within a computer system. 2. A signal used to coordinate data transfer operations.

Tinkerbell programme *n.* A programme used to monitor network traffic and alert security administrators when connections are made from a predetermined list of sites and individuals. A Tinkerbell programme acts as a low-level security reporting feature.

Tiny model *n.* A memory model in the Intel 80x86 processor family. The tiny model allows a combined total of only 64 kilobytes (KB) for code and for data. See also 8086, memory model.

Title bar *n.* In a graphical user interface, a horizontal space at the top of a window that contains the name of the window. Most title bars also contain boxes or buttons for closing and resizing the window. Clicking on the title bar allows the user to move the entire window.

TLA *n.* Acronym for three-letter acronym. An ironic term, usually used in jest on the Internet in e-mail, newsgroups, and other online forums, referring to the large number of acronyms in computer terminology, particularly those consisting of three letters.

TLD *n.* See top-level domain.

TLS *n.* Acronym for Transport Layer Security. A standard protocol that is used to provide secure Web communications on the Internet or intranets. It enables clients to authenticate servers or, optionally, servers to authenticate clients. It also provides a secure channel by encrypting communications. TLS is the latest and a more secure version of the SSL protocol. See also authentication, communications protocol, SSL.

TMS34010 *n.* See 34010, 34020.

TN display *n.* See twisted nematic display.

TOF *n.* See top-of-file.

Toggle1 *n.* An electronic device with two states or a programme option that can be turned on or off using the same action, such as a mouse click.

Toggle2 *vb.* To switch back and forth between two states. For example, the Num Lock key on an IBM-style keyboard toggles the numeric keypad between numbers and cursor movement.

ToggleKeys *n.* A feature of Windows 9x and Windows NT 4 that sounds high and low beeps when one of the toggle keys (Caps Lock, Num Lock, or Scroll Lock) is turned on or off. See also typematic.

Token *n.* 1. A unique structured data object or message that circulates continuously among the nodes of a token ring and describes the current state of the network. Before any node can send a message, it must first wait to control the token. See also token bus network, token passing, token ring network. 2. Any nonreducible textual element in data that is being parsed—for example, the use in a programme of a variable name, a reserved word, or an operator. Storing tokens as short codes shortens programme files and speeds execution. See also Basic, parse.

Token bus *n.* The IEEE 802.4 specification for token-passing networks based on a bus or tree topology. Token bus networks were designed primarily for manufacturing but the specification also corresponds to the ARCnet architecture used for LANs.

Token bus network *n.* A LAN (local area network) formed in a bus topology (stations connected to a single, shared data highway) that uses token passing as a means of regulating traffic on the line. On a token bus network, a token governing the right to transmit is passed from one station to another, and each station holds the token for a brief time, during which it alone can transmit information. The token is transferred in order of priority from an "upstream" station to the next "downstream" station, which might or might not be the next station on the bus. In essence, the token "circles" through the network in a logical ring rather than a physical one. Token bus networks are defined in the IEEE 802.4 standards. See also bus network, IEEE 802 standards, token passing.

Token passing *n.* A method of controlling network access through the use of a special signal, called a token, that determines which station is allowed to transmit. The token, which is actually a short message or a small packet, is passed from station to station around the network. Only the station with the token can transmit information. See also token bus network, token ring network.

Token ring *n.* Spelled with lowercase t and r, the IEEE specification 802.5 for token ring networks. See also token ring network.

Token Ring *n.* See Token Ring network.

Token ring network *n.* A LAN (local area network) formed in a ring (closed loop) topology that uses token passing as a means of regulating traffic on the line. On a token ring network, a token governing the right to transmit is passed from one station to the next in a physical circle. If a station has information to transmit, it "seizes" the token, marks it as being in use, and inserts the information. The "busy" token, plus message, is then passed around the circle, copied when it arrives at its destination, and eventually returned to the sender. The sender removes the attached message and then passes the freed token to the next station in line. Token ring networks are defined in the IEEE 802.5 standards. See also IEEE 802 standards, ring network, token passing.

Token Ring network *n.* A token-passing, ring-shaped local area network (LAN) developed by IBM that operates at 4 megabits (4 million bits) per second. With standard telephone wiring, the Token Ring network can connect up to 72 devices; with shielded twisted-pair (STP) wiring, the network supports up to 260 devices. Although it is based on a ring (closed loop) topology, the Token Ring network uses star-shaped clusters of up to eight workstations connected to a wiring concentrator (Multistation Access Unit, or MSAU), which, in turn, is connected to the main ring. The Token Ring network is designed to accommodate microcomputers, minicomputers, and mainframes; it follows the IEEE 802.5 standards for token ring networks.

Tone *n.* 1. A particular tint of a colour. Also called: shade, value. See also brightness, colour model. 2. One sound or signal of a particular frequency.

Tone compression *n.* In digital graphics, the compression of the complete colour range of an image to the narrower range of the chosen output device. Allowing for tone compression in scanning and graphics editing may improve the quality of the final printed image.

Toner *n.* Powdered pigment that is used in office copiers and in laser, LED, and LCD printers. See also electrophotographic printers.

Toner cartridge *n.* A disposable container that holds toner for a laser printer or other page printer. Some types of toner cartridge contain toner only; however, the most popular printer engines pack all expendables, including toner and the photosensitive drum, in a single cartridge. Toner cartridges are interchangeable among printers that use the same engine.

Toolbar *n.* In an application in a graphical user interface, a row, column, or block of onscreen buttons or icons. When these buttons or icons are clicked on with the mouse, macros or certain functions of the application are activated. For example, word processors often feature toolbars with buttons for changing text to italic, boldface, and other styles. Toolbars often can be customised by the user and usually can be moved around on the screen according to the user's preference.

Toolbox *n.* A set of predefined (and usually precompiled) routines a programmer can use in writing a programme for a particular machine, environment, or application. Also called: toolkit. See also library (definition 1).

Toolbox *n.* A set of routines stored mostly in the read-only memory of a Macintosh that provides application programmers with the tools needed to support the graphical interface characteristic of the computer. Also called: User Interface Toolbox.

Tool Command Language/Tool Kit *n.* See Tcl/Tk.

Toolkit *n.* See toolbox.

ToolTips *n.* Brief descriptions of the names of buttons and boxes on toolbars and in the toolbox. A ToolTip is displayed when the mouse pointer rests on the button or combo box. See also ScreenTips.

Top-down design *n.* A programme design methodology that starts with defining programme functionality at the highest level (a series of tasks) and then breaks down each task into lower-level tasks, and so on. See also bottom-up programming, top-down programming.

Top-down programming *n.* An approach to programming that implements a programme in top-down fashion. Typically, this is done by writing a main body with calls to several major routines (implemented as stubs). Each routine is then coded, calling other, lower-level, routines (also done initially as stubs). See also bottom-up design, stub, top-down design.

Topic drift *n.* The tendency of an online discussion to move from its original subject to other related or unrelated subjects. For example, someone in a conference devoted to television may ask about a news programme; then somebody else may say something about a story on that programme about food poisoning, which leads somebody else to start a general discussion on the advantages of organic fruits and vegetables.

Topic group *n.* An online discussion area for participants with a common interest in a particular subject.

Top-level domain *n.* In the domain-name system of Internet addresses or DNS hierarchy, any of the broadest category of names, under which all domain names fit. Top-level domains for sites in the United States include .com, .edu, .gov, .net, and .org. See also DNS (definition 1), major geographic domain.

Top-of-file *n.* 1. The beginning of a file. 2. A symbol used by a programme to mark the beginning of a file—the first character in the file or, in an indexed (ordered) database, the first indexed record. Acronym: TOF. See also beginning-of-file.

Topology *n.* The configuration or layout of a network formed by the connections between devices on a LAN (local area network) or between two or more LANs. See also bus network, LAN, ring network, star network, token ring network, tree network.

Top posting *n.* In e-mail and newsgroup discussions, placing new material before material quoted from earlier posts rather than after. Because top-posted messages are read out of chronological order, top-posting is considered an undesirable practice.

Total bypass *n.* A communications network that uses satellite transmission to bypass both local and long-distance telephone links.

Total cost of ownership *n.* Specifically, the cost of owning, operating, and maintaining a single PC; more generally, the cost to businesses and organisations of setting up and maintaining complex and far-reaching networked computer systems. Total cost of ownership includes the up-front costs of hardware and software added to later costs of installation, personnel training, technical support, upgrades, and repairs. Industry initiatives designed to lower the total cost of ownership include centralised network management and administration, as well as hardware solutions in the form of network-based computers with or without local storage and expansion capability. Acronym: TCO.

Touch pad *n.* A variety of graphics tablet that uses pressure sensors, rather than the electromagnetics used in more expensive high-resolution tablets, to track the position of a device on its surface. See also absolute pointing device, graphics tablet.

Touch screen *n.* A computer screen designed or modified to recognise the location of a touch on its surface. By touching the screen, the user can make a selection or move a cursor. The simplest type of touch screen is made up of a grid of sensing lines, which determine the location of a touch by matching vertical and horizontal contacts. Another, more accurate type uses an electrically charged surface and sensors around the outer edges of the screen to detect the amount of electrical disruption and pinpoint exactly where contact has been made. A third type has infrared light-emitting diodes (LEDs) and sensors around the outer edges of the screen. These LEDs and sensors create an invisible infrared grid, which the user's finger interrupts, in front of the screen.

Touch-sensitive display *n.* See touch screen.

Touch-sensitive tablet *n.* See touch pad.

Touch tone dialing *n.* The signaling system used in telephones with touch-tone keypads, in which each digit is associated with two specific frequencies. During dialing, these frequencies—for example, 1336 Hz and 697 Hz for the number 2—are transmitted to the telephone company. Also called: DTMF, Dual Tone Multiple Frequency.

Tower *n.* A microcomputer system in which the cabinet for the central processing unit (CPU) is tall, narrow, and deep rather than short, wide, and deep. The motherboard is usually vertical, and the disk drives are often perpendicular to the motherboard. A tower cabinet is at least 24 inches tall. See also cabinet, microcomputer, motherboard.

TP *n.* See transaction processing.

TPC *n.* See Transaction Processing Council.

TPC-D *n.* Acronym for Transaction Processing Council Benchmark D. A benchmark standard that addresses a broad range of decision support applications working with complex data structures. See also Transaction Processing Council.

TPI *n.* See tracks per inch.

TP monitor *n.* Short for teleprocessing monitor or transaction processing monitor. A programme that controls the transfer of data between terminals (or clients) and a mainframe (or one or more servers) so as to provide a consistent environment for one or more online transaction processing (OLTP) applications. A TP monitor may also control the appearance of the screen displays and check input data for proper format. See also client (definition 3), mainframe computer, OLTP, server (definition 1).

Trace *vb.* To execute a programme in such a way that the sequence of statements being executed can be observed. See also debugger, single step.

Traceroute *n.* A utility that shows the route a packet takes through a network to arrive at a remote host. A traceroute also reports the IP addresses of all intermediate hosts or routers and the time required for the packet to reach each of them. See also IP address, packet.

Track1 *n.* One of numerous circular data storage areas on a floppy disk or a hard drive, comparable to a groove on a record but not spiral. Tracks, composed of sectors, are recorded on a disk by an operating system during a disk format operation. On other storage media, such as tape, a track runs parallel to the edge of the medium.

Track2 *vb.* 1. To follow a path. 2. In data management, to follow the flow of information through a manual or an automated system. 3. In data storage and retrieval, to follow and read from a recording channel on a disk or a magnetic tape. 4. In computer graphics, to cause a displayed symbol, such as a pointer, to match on the screen the movements of a mouse or another pointing device.

Trackball *n.* A pointing device that consists of a ball resting on two rollers at right angles to each other, which translate the ball's motion into vertical and horizontal movement on the screen. A trackball also typically has one or more buttons to initiate other actions. A trackball's housing is stationary; its ball is rolled with the hand.

Tracked change *n.* A mark that shows where a deletion, insertion, or other editing change has been made in a document.

Trackpad *n.* A pointing device consisting of a small, flat pad that is sensitive to touch. Users move the mouse cursor on screen by touching the trackpad and moving their fingers across the trackpad's surface. Such devices are most commonly installed on laptop computers. See also pointing device.

Tracks per inch *n.* The density with which concentric tracks (data storage rings) are recorded or can be recorded in an inch of radius on a disk. The greater the density (the more tracks per inch), the more information a disk can hold. Acronym: TPI.

Tractor feed *n.* A method of feeding paper through a printer using pins mounted on rotating belts. The pins engage holes near the edges of continuous-form paper and either push or pull the paper through. See also continuous-form paper.

Trademark *n.* A word, phrase, symbol, or design (or some combination thereof) used to identify a proprietary product, often accompanied by the symbol TM or ®.

Trade show *n.* A multivendor sales event or exposition that showcases companies' products. The computer industry has a number of trade shows every year, including COMDEX.

Traditional newsgroup hierarchy *n.* The seven standard newsgroup categories in Usenet: comp., misc., news., rec., sci., soc., and talk. Newsgroups can be added within the traditional hierarchy only following a formal voting process. See also comp. newsgroups, misc. newsgroups, newsgroup, news. newsgroups, rec. newsgroups, Request for Discussion, sci. newsgroups, soc. newsgroups, talk. newsgroups, Usenet.

Traffic *n.* The load carried by a communications link or channel.

Traffic management *n.* See ITM.

Traffic shaping *n.* A technique for allocating bandwidth and preventing packet loss by enforcing prioritisation policies on the transmission of data over a network. Also called: bandwidth shaping. See also bandwidth management, bandwidth reservation, token passing.

Trailer *n.* Information, typically occupying several bytes, at the tail end of a block (section) of transmitted data and often containing a checksum or other error-checking data useful for confirming the accuracy and status of the transmission. See also checksum.

Trailer label *n.* 1. A small block of information used in tape processing that marks the end of a file or the end of the tape and that can contain other information, such as the number of records in the file or files on the tape. 2. A label used in communications data frames that follows the data and might contain an end-of-message mark, a checksum, and some synchronisation bits.

Trailing edge *n.* The latter part of an electronic signal. When a digital signal switches from on to off, the transition is the trailing edge of the signal.

Train1 *n.* A sequence of items or events, such as a digital pulse train consisting of transmitted binary signals.

Train2 *vb.* To teach an end user how to use a software or hardware product.

Transaction *n.* A discrete activity within a computer system, such as an entry of a customer order or an update of an inventory item. Transactions are usually associated with database management, order entry, and other online systems.

Transactional e-mail *n.* A form of Web-based marketing in which goods and services are sold to consumers directly from an e-mail message. Unlike traditional e-mail marketing that requires the e-mail recipient to visit the seller's Web site, transactional e-mail allows an entire sales transaction to be completed from within the marketing e-mail. To take advantage of transactional e-mail buying options, the recipient must view the e-mail message in HTML format.

Transaction file *n.* A file that contains the details of transactions, such as items and prices on invoices. It is used to update a master database file. See also transaction.

Transaction log *n.* See change file.

Transaction processing *n.* A processing method in which transactions are executed immediately after they are received by the system. Acronym: TP. See also transaction.

Transaction Processing Council *n.* A group of hardware and software vendors with the goal of publishing benchmark standards. Acronym: TPC.

Transaction processing monitor *n.* See TP monitor.

Transaction Tracking System *n.* See TTS (definition 2).

Transact-SQL *n.* A query language. Transact-SQL is sophisticated SQL dialect loaded with additional features beyond what is defined in the ANSI SQL 92 Standard. Also called: T-SQL, TSQL.

Transceiver *n.* Short for transmitter/receiver. A device that can both transmit and receive signals. On LANs (local area networks), a transceiver is the device that connects a computer to the network and that converts signals to and from parallel and serial form.

Transceiver cable *n.* A cable that is used to connect a host adapter within a computer to a LAN (local area network). See also AUI cable, LAN.

Transfer1 *n.* 1. The movement of data from one location to another. 2. The passing of programme control from one portion of code to another.

Transfer2 *vb.* To move data from one place to another, especially within a single computer.

Transfer rate *n.* The rate at which a circuit or a communications channel transfers information from source to destination, as over a network or to and from a disk drive. Transfer rate is measured in units of information per unit of time—for example, bits per second or characters per second—and can be measured either as a raw rate, which is the maximum transfer speed, or as an average rate, which includes gaps between blocks of data as part of the transmission time.

Transfer statement *n.* A statement in a programming language that transfers the flow of execution to another location in the programme. See also branch instruction, CALL statement, GOTO statement, jump instruction.

Transfer time *n.* The time elapsed between the start of a data transfer operation and its completion.

Transform *vb.* 1. To change the appearance or format of data without altering its content; that is, to encode information according to predefined rules. 2. In mathematics and computer graphics, to alter the position, size, or nature of an object by moving it to another location (translation), making it larger or smaller (scaling), turning it (rotation), changing its description from one type of coordinate system to another, and so on.

Transformer *n.* A device used to change the voltage of an alternating current signal or to change the impedance of an alternating current circuit.

Transient *adj.* 1. Fleeting, temporary, or unpredictable. 2. Of or pertaining to the region of memory used for programmes, such as applications, that are read from disk storage and that reside in memory temporarily until they are replaced by other programmes. In this context, transient can also refer to the programmes themselves. 3. In electronics, of or pertaining to a short-lived, abnormal, and unpredictable increase in power supply, such as a voltage spike or surge. Transient time is the interval during which a change in current or voltage is building up or decaying.

Transient suppressor *n.* A circuit designed to reduce or eliminate unwanted electrical signals or voltages.

Transistor *n.* Short for transfer resistor. A solid-state circuit component, usually with three leads, in which a voltage or a current controls the flow of another current. The transistor can serve many functions, including those of amplifier, switch, and oscillator, and is a fundamental component of almost all modern electronics.

Transistor-transistor logic *n.* A type of bipolar circuit design that utilises transistors connected to each other either directly or through resistors. Transistor-transistor logic offers high speed and good noise immunity and is used in many digital circuits. A large number of transistor-transistor logic gates can be fabricated on a single integrated circuit. Acronym: TTL.

Transitive trust *n.* The standard type of trust relationship between Windows domains in a domain tree or forest. When a domain joins an existing forest or domain tree, a transitive trust is automatically established. Transitive trusts are always two-way relationships. This series of trusts, between parent and child domains in a domain tree and between root domains of domain trees in a forest, allows all domains in a forest to trust each other for the purposes of authentication. For example, if domain A trusts domain B and domain B trusts domain C, then domain A trusts domain C. See also domain, forest, one-way trust, two-way trust.

Translate *vb.* 1. In programming, to convert a programme from one language to another. Translation is performed by special programmes such as compilers, assemblers, and interpreters. 2. In computer graphics, to move an image in the "space" represented on the display, without turning (rotating) the image.

Translated file *n.* A file containing data that has been changed from binary (8-bit) format to ASCII (7-bit) format. BinHex and uuencode both translate binary files into ASCII. Such translation is necessary to transmit data through systems (such as e-mail) that may not preserve the eighth bit of each byte. A translated file must be decoded to its binary form before being used. See also BinHex, uuencode.

Translator *n.* A programme that translates one language or data format into another.

Transmission channel *n.* See channel.

Transmission Control Protocol *n.* See TCP.

Transmission Control Protocol/Internet Protocol *n.* See TCP/IP.

Transmit *vb.* To send information over a communications line or a circuit. Computer transmissions can take place in the following ways: asynchronous (variable timing) or synchronous (exact timing); serial (essentially, bit by bit) or parallel (byte by byte; a group of bits at once); duplex or full-duplex (simultaneous two-way communication), half-duplex (two-way communication in one direction at a time), or simplex (one-way communication only); and burst (intermittent transmission of blocks of information).

Transmit Data *n.* See TXD.

Transmitter *n.* Any circuit or electronic device designed to send electrically encoded data to another location.

Transparency *n.* The quality that defines how much light passes through an object's pixels. If an object is 100 per cent transparent, light passes through it completely and renders the object invisible; in other words, you can see through the object.

Transparency scanner *n.* See scanner.

Transparent *adj.* 1. In computer use, of, pertaining to, or characteristic of a device, function, or part of a programme that works so smoothly and easily that it is invisible to the user. For example, the ability of one application to use files created by another is transparent if the user encounters no difficulty in opening, reading, or using the second program's files or does not even know the use is occurring. 2. In communications, of, pertaining to, or characteristic of a mode of transmission in which data can include any characters, including device-control characters, without the possibility of misinterpretation by the receiving station. For example, the receiving station will not end a transparent transmission until it receives a character in the data that indicates end of transmission. Thus, there is no danger of the receiving station ending communications prematurely.

Transponder *n.* A transceiver in a communications satellite that receives a signal from an earth station and retransmits it on a different frequency to one or more other earth stations.

Transportable computer *n.* See portable computer.

Transport layer *n.* The fourth of the seven layers in the International Organisation for Standardisation's Open Systems Interconnection (OSI) reference model for standardising computer-to-computer communications. The transport layer is one level above the network layer and is responsible for both quality of service and accurate delivery of information. Among the tasks performed on this layer are error detection and correction. See also ISO/OSI reference model.

Transport Layer Security *n.* See TLS.

Transpose1 *n.* The result of rotating a matrix.

Transpose2 *vb.* 1. To reverse, as the order of the letters h and t in hte, in correcting the spelling of the; or reversing two wires in a circuit. 2. In mathematics and spreadsheets, to rotate a matrix (a rectangular array of numbers) about a diagonal axis.

Transputer *n.* Short for transistor computer. A complete computer on a single chip, including RAM and an FPU, designed as a building block for parallel computing systems.

Trap1 *n.* See interrupt.

Trap2 *vb.* 1. To intercept an action or event before it occurs, usually in order to do something else. Trapping is commonly used by debuggers to allow interruption of programme execution at a given spot. See also interrupt, interrupt handler. 2. To slightly overlap adjacent colours in preparing material for printing.

Page layout and prepress programmes trap colour to prevent gaps between colours caused by minor variations in registration during printing.

Trapdoor *n.* See back door.

Trap handler *n.* See interrupt handler.

Trash *n.* An icon on the screen in the Macintosh Finder, resembling a garbage can. To delete a file or eject a diskette, the user drags the icon for the file or diskette to the Trash. However, until the user shuts down the system or chooses the menu option "Empty Trash," a file in the Trash is not actually deleted; the user can retrieve it by double-clicking the Trash icon and dragging the file's icon out of the resulting window.

Traverse *vb.* In programming, to access in a particular order all of the nodes of a tree or similar data structure.

Tree *n.* A data structure containing zero or more nodes that are linked together in a hierarchical fashion. If there are any nodes, one node is the root; each node except the root is the child of one and only one other node; and each node has zero or more nodes as children. See also child (definition 2), graph, leaf, node (definition 3), parent/child (definition 2), root.

Tree network *n.* A topology for a local area network (LAN) in which one machine is connected to one or more other machines, each of which is connected to one or more others, and so on, so that the structure formed by the network resembles that of a tree. See also bus network, distributed network, ring network, star network, token ring network, topology.

Tree search *n.* A search procedure performed on a tree data structure. At each step of the search, a tree search is able to determine, by the value in a particular node, which branches of the tree to eliminate, without searching those branches themselves. See also branch (definition 1), tree structure.

Tree structure *n.* Any structure that has the essential organisational properties of a tree. See also tree.

Tree view *n.* A hierarchical representation of the folders, files, disk drives, and other resources connected to a computer or network. For example, Windows Explorer uses a tree view to display the resources that are attached to a computer or a network. See also resource.

Trellis-coded modulation *n.* An enhanced form of quadrature amplitude modulation that is used by modems that operate at or above 9,600 bps (bits per second). Trellis-coded modulation encodes information as unique sets of bits associated with changes in both the phase and amplitude of the carrier, as well as using extra signal points for error-checking bits. Acronym: TCM. See also quadrature amplitude modulation.

Trendline *n.* A graphic representation of trends in data series, such as a line sloping upward to represent increased sales over a period of months. Trendlines are used for the study of problems of prediction. Also called: regression analysis.

Triage1 *n.* The process of prioritising projects or elements of a project (such as bug fixes) to ensure that available resources are assigned in the most effective, time-efficient, and cost-efficient manner. Traditionally, triage has referred to the prioritisation of treatment to the wounded during wartime or medical disaster situations. More recently, the term also refers to anticipating and preventing computer system crashes brought on by the Year 2000 (Y2K) problem. See also Year 2000 Problem.

Triage2 *vb.* To identify and prioritise the elements of a project or problem to order them in a way that makes best use of labour, funds, and other resources.

Tri-band phone *n.* A wireless phone designed for international travel. Tri-band phones broadcast on the personal communication service (PCS) frequency used in North America as well as PCS frequencies used in other regions of the world.

Trichromatic *adj.* Of, pertaining to, or characteristic of a system that uses three colours (red, green, and blue in computer graphics) to create all other colours. See also colour model.

Trigger1 *n.* 1. In a database, an action that causes a procedure to be carried out automatically when a user attempts to modify data. A trigger can instruct the database system to take a specific action, depending on the particular change attempted. Incorrect, unwanted, or unauthorised changes can thereby be prevented, helping to maintain the integrity of the database. 2. A function built into a virus or worm that controls the release of a malicious payload or similar event. The trigger may be activated at a predetermined time or date or in response to a user-initiated event, such as opening a specific programme or file. In some cases, the trigger may reset itself repeatedly until the virus is neutralised.

Trigger2 *vb.* To activate a function or programme, such as the release of a virus payload, in response to a specific event, date, or time.

Trilinear filtering *n.* A technique used in 3-D computer game rendering and other digital animation applications that produces the illusion of depth of field by making distant objects less distinct and detailed than nearer objects.

Triple-pass scanner *n.* A colour scanner that performs one scanning pass on an image for each of the three primary colours of light (red, green, and blue). See also colour scanner.

Tristimulus values *n.* In colour graphics, the varying amounts of three colours, such as red, blue, and green, that are combined to produce another colour. See also colour, colour model.

Trivial File Transfer Protocol *n.* A simplified version of File Transfer Protocol (FTP) that provides basic file transfer with no user authentication and is often used to download the initial files needed to begin an installation process. Acronym: TFTP. See also communications protocol.

Troff *n.* Short for typesetting run off. A UNIX text formatter often used to format man pages. See also man pages, RUNOFF.

Trojan horse *n.* A destructive programme disguised as a game, utility, or application. When run, a Trojan horse does something harmful to the computer system while appearing to do something useful. See also virus, worm.

Troll *vb.* To post a message in a newsgroup or other online conference in the hopes that somebody else will consider the original message so outrageous that it demands a heated reply. A classic example of trolling is an article in favour of torturing cats posted in a pet lovers' newsgroup. See also YHBT.

Troubleshoot *vb.* To isolate the source of a problem in a programme, computer system, or network and remedy it.

Troubleshooter *n.* A person trained and hired to find and resolve problems or breakdowns in machinery and technical equipment or systems. Troubleshooters often work as short-term consultants or freelancers because many organisations and businesses regard troubleshooting as a short-term effort or possibly an exceptional—unplanned—part of a project or system. See also troubleshoot.

Trouble ticket *n.* A report of a problem with a particular device or system that is tracked through the workflow process. Originally written on paper, electronic trouble tickets are featured by many workflow and help-desk applications. See also help desk (definition 2), workflow application.

True BASIC *n.* A version of Basic created in 1983 by John Kemeny and Thomas Kurtz, the creators of the original Basic, to standardise and modernise the language. True BASIC is a compiled, structured version of Basic that does not require line numbers. True BASIC includes advanced control structures that make structured programming possible. See also Basic, structured programming.

True colour *n.* See 24-bit colour.

True complement *n.* See complement.

TrueType *n.* An outline font technology introduced by Apple Computer, Inc., in 1991 and by Microsoft Corporation in 1992 as a means of including high-grade fonts within the Macintosh and Windows operating systems. TrueType is a WYSIWYG font technology, which means that the printed output of TrueType fonts is identical to what appears on the screen. See also bitmapped font, outline font, PostScript.

TrueType Open version 2 *n.* See OpenType.

Truncate *vb.* To cut off the beginning or end of a series of characters or numbers; specifically, to eliminate one or more of the least significant (typically rightmost) digits. In truncation, numbers are simply eliminated, unlike rounding, in which the rightmost digit might be incremented to preserve accuracy.

Trunk *n.* 1. In communications, a channel connecting two switching stations. A trunk usually carries a large number of calls at the same time. 2. In networking, the cable forming the main communications path on a network. On a bus network, the single cable to which all nodes connect. See also backbone.

Trunking *n.* See link aggregation.

Trusted Computing Base *n.* See TCB.

Trust relationship *n.* A logical relationship established between domains to allow pass-through authentication, in which a trusting domain honors the logon authentications of a trusted domain. User accounts and global groups defined in a trusted domain can be given rights and permissions in a trusting domain, even though the user accounts or groups don't exist in the trusting domain's directory. See also authentication, domain, group, permission, user account.

Truth table *n.* A table showing the value of a Boolean expression for each of the possible combinations of variable values in the expression. See also AND, Boolean operator, exclusive OR, NOT, OR.

Try *n.* A keyword used in the Java programming language to define a block of statements that may throw a Java language exception. If an exception is thrown, an optional "catch" block can handle specific exceptions thrown within the "try" block. Also, an optional "finally" block will be executed regardless of whether an exception is thrown. See also block, catch, exception, finally.

TSAPI *n.* Acronym for Telephony Services Application Programming Interface. The set of standards for the interface between a large telephone system and a computer network server, developed by Novell and AT&T and supported by many telephone equipment manufacturers and software developers.

TSP *n.* See Telephony Service Provider.

TSPI *n.* See Telephony Service Provider Interface.

T-SQL or TSQL *n.* See Transact-SQL.

TSR *n.* Acronym for terminate-and-stay-resident. A programme that remains loaded in memory even when it is not running, so that it can be quickly invoked for a specific task performed while another programme is operating. Typically, these programmes are used with operating systems that are not multitasking, such as MS-DOS. See also hot key.

TSV *n.* Filename extension, short for tab separated values, assigned to text files containing tabular (row and column) data of the type stored in database fields. As the name indicates, individual data entries are separated by tabs.

TTFN *n.* Acronym for Ta ta for now. An expression sometimes used in Internet discussion groups, such as Internet Relay Chat (IRC), to signal a participant's temporary departure from the group. See also IRC.

TTL *n.* See Time to Live, transistor-transistor logic.

TTS *n.* 1. Acronym for Text-to-Speech. The process of converting digital text into speech output. TTS is used extensively in fax, e-mail, and other services for the blind, and for telephone-based informational and financial services. 2. Acronym for Transaction Tracking System. A feature developed to protect databases from corruption caused by incomplete transactions. TTS monitors attempted transactions and in the event of a hardware or software failure, TTS will cancel the update and back out to maintain database integrity.

TTY *n.* Acronym for teletypewriter. A device for low-speed communications over a telephone line, consisting of a keyboard that sends a character code for each keystroke and a printer that prints characters as their codes are received. The simplest video display interface behaves like a TTY. See also KSR terminal, teletype mode.

Tunnel *vb.* To encapsulate or wrap a packet or a message from one protocol in the packet for another. The wrapped packet is then transmitted over a network via the protocol of the wrapper. This method of packet transmission is used to avoid protocol restrictions. See also communications protocol, packet (definition 2).

Tunneling *n.* A method of transmission over internetworks based on differing protocols. In tunneling, a packet based on one protocol is wrapped, or encapsulated, in a second packet based on whatever differing protocol is needed in order for it to travel over an intermediary network. In effect, the second wrapper "insulates" the original packet and creates the illusion of a tunnel through which the wrapped packet travels across the intermediary network. In real-life terms, tunneling is comparable to "encapsulating" a present (the original packet) in a box (the secondary wrapper) for delivery through the postal system.

Tunnel server *n.* A server or router that terminates tunnels and forwards traffic to the hosts on the target network. See also host, router, server, tunnel.

Tuple *n.* In a database table (relation), a set of related values, one for each attribute (column). A tuple is stored as a row in a relational database management system. It is the analog of a record in a nonrelational file. See also relation.

Turing machine *n.* 1. A theoretical model created by British mathematician Alan Turing in 1936 that is considered the prototype for digital computers. Described in a paper ("On Computable Numbers with an Application to the Entscheidungsproblem") published in the Proceedings of the London Mathematical Society, the Turing machine was a logical device that could scan one square at a time (either blank or containing a symbol) on a paper tape. Depending on the symbol read from a particular square, the machine would change its status and/or move the tape backward or forward to erase a symbol or to print a new one. See also status. 2. A computer that can successfully mimic human intelligence in the Turing test.

Turing test *n.* A test of machine intelligence proposed by Alan Turing, British mathematician and developer of the Turing machine. In the Turing test, also known as the Imitation Game, a person uses any series of questions to interrogate two unseen respondents, a human and a computer, to try to determine which is the computer.

Turnaround time *n.* 1. The elapsed time between submission and completion of a job. 2. In communications, the time required to reverse the direction of transmission in half-duplex communication mode. See also half-duplex transmission.

Turnkey system *n.* A finished system, complete with all necessary hardware and documentation and with software installed and ready to be used.

Turnpike effect *n.* The communications equivalent of gridlock; a reference to bottlenecks caused by heavy traffic over a communications system or network.

Turtle *n.* A small onscreen shape, usually a triangle or a turtle shape, that acts as a drawing tool in graphics. A turtle is a friendly, easily manipulated tool designed for children learning to use computers. It takes its name from a mechanical, dome-shaped turtle that was developed for the Logo language and moved about the floor in response to Logo commands, raising and lowering a pen to draw lines.

Turtle graphics *n.* A simple graphics environment, present in Logo and other languages, in which a turtle is manipulated by simple commands. Some versions display the turtle and its track on screen; others use electromechanical turtles that write on paper.

Tutorial *n.* A teaching aid designed to help people learn to use a product or procedure. In computer applications, a tutorial might be presented in either a book or a manual or as an interactive disk-based series of lessons provided with the programme package.

Tux *n.* The mascot of the Linux operating system. Tux is a rotund cartoonish penquin and the Tux image is available for use by any provider of Linux products or services. The name Tux is both short for tuxedo, in reference to a penguin's appearance, and an acronym for Torvalds's UniX, after Linus Torvalds, the creator of the Linux operating system.

TV tuner card *n.* A PCI card that allows a computer to receive television programming and display it on the computer's monitor. See also PCI card.

TWAIN *n.* The de facto standard interface between software applications and image-capturing devices such as scanners. Nearly all scanners contain a TWAIN driver, but only TWAIN-compatible software can use the technology. The TWAIN specification was developed by the TWAIN Working Group, a consortium of industry vendors formed in 1992. The name is thought by some to be an acronym for the phrase "technology without an interesting name," although the TWAIN Working Group maintains the name is not an acronym. Others attribute the name to the quote "Ne'er the twain shall meet," because the TWAIN driver and the application receiving the image are separated. See also scanner.

Tweak *vb.* To make final small changes to improve hardware or software performance; to fine-tune a nearly complete product.

Tween *vb.* In a graphics programme, to calculate intermediary shapes during the metamorphosis of one shape into another.

Twinaxial *adj.* Having two coaxial cables contained in a single insulated jacket. See also coaxial cable.

Twip *n.* A unit of measure used in typesetting and desktop publishing, equal to one-twentieth of a printer's point, or 1/1440th of an inch. See also point1 (definition 1).

Twisted nematic display *n.* A type of passive-matrix liquid crystal display (LCD) in which the glass sheets enclosing nematic liquid crystal material are treated in such a way that the crystal molecules twist 90 degrees between top and bottom—in other words, the orientation at the bottom of the crystal is perpendicular to the orientation at the top. When an electrical charge is applied selectively to these crystals, they become temporarily untwisted and block the passage of polarised light. This blockage is what produces the dark pixels on an LCD display. The nematic part of the description refers to microscopic threadlike bodies that characterise the type of liquid crystals used in these displays. Also called: TN display.

Twisted-pair cable *n.* A cable made of two separately insulated strands of wire twisted together. It is used to reduce signal interference introduced by a strong radio source such as a nearby cable. One of the wires in the pair carries the sensitive signal, and the other wire is grounded.

Twisted-pair wiring *n.* Wiring consisting of two insulated strands of copper twisted around one another to form a cable. Twisted-pair wiring comes in two forms, unshielded twisted pair (UTP) and shielded twisted pair (STP), the latter named for an extra protective sheath wrapped around each insulated pair of wires. Twisted-pair wiring can consist of a single pair of wires or, in thicker cables, two, four, or more pairs of wires. Twisted-pair wiring is typical of telephone cabling.

Two-digit date storage *n.* A limitation in many computer systems and programmes that store the year portion of a date as two digits instead of four. This practice in programming dates from the earliest days of computers when space on punch cards and memory in the computer were very limited, and many programmers used a two-digit year in date fields to economise on space or memory requirements.

Two-digit shortcut *n.* The practice of using two digits to indicate the year in a programme, particularly those written in programming languages or running on systems that have the capability to work with a four-digit year (hence the term shortcut).

Two-dimensional *adj.* Existing in reference to two measures, such as height and width—for example, a two-dimensional model drawn with reference to an x-axis and a y-axis, or a two-dimensional array of numbers placed in rows and columns. See also Cartesian coordinates.

Two-dimensional array *n.* An ordered arrangement of information in which the location of any item is described by two numbers (integers) identifying its position in a particular row and column of a matrix.

Two-dimensional model *n.* A computer simulation of a physical object in which length and width are real attributes but depth is not; a model with x- and y-axes.

Two-nines availability *n.* The availability of a system 99% of the time. Two-nines availability equates to approximately 87.6 hours of downtime in a standard 365-day year. See also high availability.

Two-out-of-five code *n.* An error-sensitive code for data transmission that stores each of the ten decimal digits (0 through 9) as a set of five binary digits: either two of the digits are 1s and the other three digits are 0s or two of the digits are 0s and the other three digits are 1s.

Two's complement *n.* A number in the base-2 system (binary system) that is the true complement of another number. A two's complement is usually derived by reversing the digits in a binary number (changing 1s to 0s and 0s to 1s) and adding 1 to the result. When two's complements are used to represent negative numbers, the most significant (leftmost) digit is always 1. See also complement.

Two-tier client/server *n.* A client/business logic layer and the database layer. Fourth-generation languages (4GL) have helped to popularise the two-tier client/server architecture.

Two-way trust *n.* A type of trust relationship in which both of the domains in the relationship trust each other. In a two-way trust relationship, each domain has established a one-way trust with the other domain. For example, domain A trusts domain B and domain B trusts domain A. Two-way trusts can be transitive or nontransitive. All two-way trusts between Windows domains in the same domain tree or forest are transitive. See also domain, forest, one-way trust, transitive trust.

TXD *n.* Short for Transmit (tx) Data. A line used to carry transmitted data from one device to another, as from computer to modem; in RS-232-C connections, pin 2. See also RS-232-C standard.

Ttxt *n.* A file extension that identifies ASCII text files. In most cases, a document with a .txt extension does not include any formatting commands, so it is readable in any text editor or word processing programme. See also ASCII.

Tymnet *n.* A public data network available in over 100 countries, with links to some online services and Internet service providers.

Type1 *n.* 1. In programming, the nature of a variable—for example, integer, real number, text character, or floating-point number. Data types in programmes are declared by the programmer and determine the range of values a variable can take as well as the operations that can be performed on it. See also data type. 2. In printing, the characters that make up printed text, the design of a set of characters (typeface), or, more loosely, the complete set of characters in a given size and style (font). See also font, typeface.

Type2 *vb.* To enter information by means of the keyboard.

Type-ahead capability *n.* The ability of a computer programme to gather incoming keystrokes in a temporary memory reservoir (buffer) before displaying them on the screen. This capability ensures that keystrokes are not lost if they are typed faster than the programme can display them.

Type ball *n.* A small ball mounted on the print head of a printer or a typewriter (for example, the IBM Selectric) that bears all the characters in the character set on its surface. The ball rotates to align the correct character with the paper and with an inked or carbon ribbon before striking against the paper. See the illustration.

Type checking *n.* The process performed by a compiler or interpreter to make sure that when a variable is used, it is treated as having the same data type as it was declared to have. See also compiler (definition 2), data type, interpreter.

Type declaration *n.* A declaration in a programme that specifies the characteristics of a new data type, usually by combining more primitive existing data types.

Typeface *n.* A specific, named design of a set of printed characters, such as Helvetica Bold Oblique, that has a specified obliqueness (degree of slant) and stroke weight (thickness of line). A typeface is not the same as a font, which is a specific size of a specific typeface, such as 12-point Helvetica Bold

Oblique. Nor is a typeface the same as a typeface family, which is a group of related typefaces, such as the Helvetica family including Helvetica, Helve-tica Bold, Helvetica Oblique, and Helvetica Bold Oblique. See also font.

Type font *n.* See font.

Typematic *adj.* The keyboard feature that repeats a keystroke when a key is held down longer than usual. Also called: auto-key, auto-repeat. See also repeat key, RepeatKeys.

Typeover mode *n.* See overwrite mode.

Type size *n.* The size of printed characters, usually measured in points (a point is approximately 1/72 inch). See also point1 (definition 1).

Type style *n.* 1. The obliqueness, or degree of slant, of a typeface. 2. Loosely, the overall design of a typeface or a typeface family. 3. One of the variant forms of a type character, including roman, bold, italic, and bold italic.

Typography *n.* 1. The art of font design and typesetting. See also computer typesetting, font. 2. The conversion of unformatted text into camera-ready type, suitable for printing. See also camera-ready.

Typosquatter *n.* A form of cybersquatter that takes advantage of typographical errors to snare Web surfers. The typosquatter registers variations of popular trademarked domain names that contain the most likely spelling errors (for example: JCPenny). A user who makes a mistake typing in a Web site address will be taken to the typosquatter's site, which typically is loaded with banner and pop-up ads. The typosquatter is paid by the number of users who see the ads. See also cybersquatter.

U

u-prefix A letter sometimes substituted for the Greek letter m (mu), meaning micro, used as a prefix in measurements denoting one millionth, or 10-6. See also micro- (definition 2).

UA *n.* See user agent.

UART *n.* Acronym for universal asynchronous receiver-transmitter. A module, usually composed of a single integrated circuit, that contains both the receiving and transmitting circuits required for asynchronous serial communication. A UART is the most common type of circuit used in personal computer modems.

Ubiquitous computing *n.* A term coined by Mark Wieser (1988) at the Xerox PARC Computer Science Lab to describe a computing environment so pervasive in daily life that it's invisible to the user. Household appliances such as VCRs and microwave ovens are contemporary low-level examples of ubiquitous computing. In the future, prognosticators say, computers will be so embedded in all facets of life—so ubiquitous—that their presence will fade into the background. Ubiquitous computing is considered to be the third stage in the evolution of computing technology, after the mainframe and the personal computer. Acronym: UC.

UC *n.* See ubiquitous computing.

UCAID *n.* Acronym for University Corporation for Advanced Internet Development. An organisation created to provide guidance in advanced networking development within the university community. UCAID is responsible for the development of the Abilene fiber-optic backbone network that will interconnect over 150 universities into the Internet2 project.

UCE *n.* Acronym for unsolicited commercial e-mail. See spam.

UCITA *n.* Acronym for Uniform Computer Information Transactions Act. Legislation proposed or enacted in several states that will set legal standards and control systems for dealing with computer information. UCITA is a model law intended as an amendment to the Uniform Commercial Code to cover new technology-related issues. One of UCITA's main provisions is a standard for mass market software shrinkwrap and clickwrap agreements. See also clickwrap agreement, shrinkwrap agreement.

UCSD p-system *n.* A portable operating system and development environment that was developed by Kenneth Bowles at the University of California at San Diego. The system was based on a simulated, 16-bit, stack-oriented "pseudomachine." The development environment included a text editor and compilers for several languages, such as FORTRAN and Pascal. Programmes written for a p-system were more portable than programmes compiled to machine language. See also bytecode, pseudomachine, p-system, virtual machine.

UDDI *n.* Acronym for Universal Description, Discovery, and Integration. A platform-independent framework functioning like a directory (similar to a telephone book) that provides a way to locate and register Web services on the Internet. The UDDI specification calls for three elements: white pages, which provide business contact information; yellow pages, which organise Web services into categories (for example, credit card authorisation services); and green pages, which provide detailed technical information about individual services. The UDDI also contains an operational registry, which is available today.

UDP *n.* Acronym for User Datagram Protocol. The connectionless protocol within TCP/IP that corresponds to the transport layer in the ISO/OSI reference model. UDP converts data messages generated by an application into packets to be sent via IP, but it is "unreliable" because it does not establish a path between sender and receiver before transmitting and does not verify that messages have been delivered correctly. UDP is more efficient than TCP, so it is used for various purposes, including SNMP; the reliability depends on the application that generates the message. See also communications protocol, ISO/OSI reference model, packet, SNMP, TCP/IP.

UDT *n.* Acronym for uniform data transfer. The service used in the OLE extensions to Windows that allows two applications to exchange data without either programme knowing the internal structure of the other.

UI *n.* See user interface.

UKnet *n.* 1. The University of Kentucky's campus network. 2. In the United Kingdom, an Internet service provider (ISP) based at the University of Kent. See also ISP.

ULSI *n.* See ultra-large-scale integration.

UltimateTV *n.* A television digital recording technology developed by Microsoft. UltimateTV can record up to 35 hours of DIRECTV broadcasts. Because the television signal is recording on UltimateTV's hard drive, viewers can pause a live show, rewind scenes, and watch previously shown parts of the show in slow or fast motion while UltimateTV records the remainder of the show live.

Ultra DMA/33 *n.* A data transfer protocol, based on direct memory access, for transferring data between a hard drive and a computer's RAM. Ultra DMA/33 improves ATA/IDE performance, doubles burst transfer rates to 33 megabytes per second, and increases data transfer integrity. See also ATA, direct memory access, IDE (definition 1).

Ultrafiche *n.* Microfiche with very high density. The image in ultrafiche is reduced at least 90 times from its original size. See also microfiche.

Ultra-large-scale integration *n.* The highest currently possible density at which components (transistors and other elements) are packed onto an integrated circuit. "Ultra-large-scale" is generally applied to component densities of 1,000,000 or greater. Acronym: ULSI. See also integrated circuit.

Ultralight computer *n.* See portable computer.

UltraSCSI *n.* An extension of the SCSI-2 standard that doubles the transfer speed of Fast-SCSI to allow a transfer rate of 20 megabytes per second (MBps) on an 8-bit connection and 40 MBps on a 16-bit connection. See also SCSI, SCSI-2.

Ultra Wide SCSI *n.* See UltraSCSI.

UMA *n.* 1. Acronym for upper memory area. The portion of DOS memory between the first 640K and 1 MB. 2. Acronym for Uniform Memory Architecture. See SMP.

UMB *n.* Acronym for upper memory block. A block of memory in the UMA (upper memory area) that can be used for device drivers or TSRs. A UMB is allocated and managed by special memory manager programmes such as EMM386.EXE. See also device driver, TSR, UMA (definition 1).

UML *n.* Acronym for Unified Modeling Language. A language developed by Grady Booch, Ivar Jacobson, and Jim Rumbaugh of Rational Software that can be used for specifying, building, and documenting software and non-software systems, such as business models. UML notation provides a common foundation for object-oriented design by providing descriptions of modeling concepts including object class, associations, interface, and responsibility. The UML standard is supported by software developers and vendors and overseen by the Object Management Group (OMG).

UMTS *n.* Acronym for Universal Mobile Telecommunications System. Third-generation wireless communications standard developed to provide a consistent set of packet-based voice, text, video, and multimedia capabilities to users in any communications environment worldwide. When UMTS reaches full implementation, users will be able maintain computer and phone Internet connections from anywhere in the world.

Unary *adj.* Of, pertaining to, or characteristic of a mathematical operation with a single operand (object); monadic.

Unary operator *n.* An operator that takes only one operand —for example, unary minus (as in –2.5). See also operator.

Unbuffered *adj.* Of, pertaining to, or characteristic of something that does not store data characters in memory but instead processes them as they are received. See also buffer.

Unbundle *vb.* To separate the items of a composite sales package; for example, to sell components of a software package separately rather than as a package.

Unbundled *adj.* Not included as part of a complete hardware/software package; the term particularly applies to a product that was previously bundled, as opposed to one that has always been sold separately.

UNC *n.* Acronym for Universal Naming Convention or, sometimes, Uniform Naming Convention. The system of naming files among computers on a network so that a file on a given computer will have the same pathname when accessed from any of the other computers on the network. For example, if the directory c:\path1\path2\...pathn on computer servern is shared under the name pathdirs, a user on another computer would open \\servern\pathdirs\filename.ext to access the file c:\path1\path2\...pathn\ filename.ext on servern. See also URL, virtual path.

Uncompress *vb.* To restore the contents of a compressed file to its original form. Also called: decompress.

Unconditional branch *n.* A transfer of execution to another line of code in a programme without a check for some condition being true or false. The transfer always takes place whenever such an instruction is encountered. See also branch (definition 2).

Undelete1 *n.* The act of restoring deleted information. An undelete is comparable to (and usually included as part of) an undo command; it is more restricted, however, in that "undo" reverses any previous act, but undelete reverses only a deletion. Undelete generally refers only to excised text or deleted files. See also undo.

Undelete2 *vb.* 1. To restore deleted information, usually the last item deleted. 2. In file storage, to restore a file's storage information so that a deleted file becomes available for access again. Also called: unerase. See also file recovery.

Undeliverable *adj.* Not able to be delivered to an intended recipient. If an e-mail message is undeliverable, it is returned to the sender with information added by the mail server explaining the problem; for example, the e-mail address may be incorrect, or the recipient's mailbox may be full.

Undercolour separation *n.* In the CMYK colour model, the process of converting equal quantities of cyan, magenta, and yellow to equivalent gray levels, which are then printed in black ink. This produces grays that are clearer and sharper than those produced by mixing coloured inks. See also CMY, CMYK, colour model.

Underflow *n.* A condition in which a mathematical calculation produces a result too near to zero to be represented by the range of binary digits available to the computer for holding that value in the specified precision. See also precision (definition 2), single-precision.

Underline *vb.* To format a selection of text so that the text is printed with a line slightly below it.

Undernet *n.* An international network of Internet Relay Chat (IRC) servers created in 1992 as an alternative to the larger and more chaotic main IRC network.

Underscore *n.* An underline character often used to emphasize a letter or a word; on nongraphics displays, generally used to indicate italic characters.

Undo *vb.* To reverse the last action—for example, to undo a deletion, thus restoring deleted text to a document. Many application programmes enable the user both to undo and to redo an action. See also undelete (definition 1).

Undock *vb.* 1. To detach a laptop or other portable computer from a docking station. See also docking station, laptop. 2. To move a toolbar from the edge of a window so that the toolbar becomes its own free-floating window. See also toolbar.

Unerase *n.* See undelete1.

Unfold *adj.* See inline (definition 1).

Unhandled exception *n.* An error condition that an application does not internally resolve. When an unhandled exception occurs, the operating system terminates the application that caused the error.

Unibus *n.* A bus architecture introduced by Digital Equipment Corporation in 1970.

Unicast *vb.* To transmit between a single sender and a single receiver over a network. A two-way, point-to-point transmission, unicast is typical of network communications.

Unicode *n.* A 16-bit character encoding standard developed by the Unicode Consortium between 1988 and 1991. By using 2 bytes to represent each character, Unicode enables almost all the written languages of the world to be represented using a single character set. (By contrast, 8-bit ASCII is not capable of representing all the combinations of letters and diacritical marks that are used just with the Roman alphabet.) Approximately 39,000 of the 65,536 possible Unicode character codes have been assigned to date, 21,000 of them being used for Chinese ideographs. The remaining combinations are open for expansion.

Unified messaging *n.* The integration of various communications technologies such as voicemail, fax, and e-mail into a single service. Unified messaging is designed to be a time-saving tool to provide users with a single package with which they can receive, organize, and respond to messages in a variety of media.

Uniform Resource Citation *n.* A description of an object on the World Wide Web, consisting of pairs of attributes and their values, such as the Uniform Resource Identifiers (URIs) of associated resources, author names, publisher names, dates, and prices. Acronym: URC.

Uniform Resource Identifier *n.* A character string used to identify a resource (such as a file) from anywhere on the Internet by type and location. The set of Uniform Resource Identifiers includes Uniform Resource Names (URNs) and Uniform Resource Locators (URLs). Acronym: URI. See also relative URL, Uniform Resource Name, URL.

Uniform Resource Locator *n.* See URL.

Uniform Resource Name *n.* A scheme for uniquely identifying resources that might be available on the Internet by name, without regard to where they are located. The specifications for the format of Uniform Resource Names are still under development by the Internet Engineering Task Force (IETF). They include all Uniform Resource Identifiers (URIs) having the schemes urn:, fpi:, and path:; that is, those that are not Uniform Resource Locators (URLs). Acronym: URN. See also IETF, Uniform Resource Identifier, URL.

UniForum *n.* 1. The International Association of Open System Professionals, an organisation of UNIX users and administrators. 2. A series of UNIX trade shows sponsored by UniForum and managed by Softbank COMDEX, Inc. See also COMDEX.

Unimodem *n.* 1. The universal modem driver, provided with Windows CE, that translates Telephony Service Provider Interface (TSPI) calls into AT commands and sends the commands to a virtual device driver that talks to the modem. 2. A universal modem that supports standard modem AT commands. Windows CE currently supports only PCMCIA modems.

Uninstall *vb.* To remove software completely from a system, including the elimination of files and components residing in system locations such as the registry in Windows 9x, Windows NT, or Windows 2000. Some applications have built-in uninstall utilities, and in other cases a separate uninstall programme can be used. Also called: deinstall.

Uninterruptible power supply *n.* See UPS.

Union *n.* 1. In set theory, the smallest combination of two sets that contains all elements of both sets. 2. In logic, an inclusive OR operation—that is, the result, C, of any union of A and B is true (1) except when A and B are both false (0). See the table. 3. In programming, a structure that can be used to store different types of variables (such as integer, character, or Boolean). 4. In database management, a relational operator. Given two relations (tables), A and B, that are union-compatible (contain the same number of fields, with corresponding fields containing the same types of values), A UNION B builds a new relation containing those tuples (records) that appear either in A or in B or in both.

Table U.1 A Truth Table Showing the Results of Unions.

A	OR	B	=	C
1		1		1
1		0		1
0		1		1
0		0		0

Union-compatible *adj.* In database management, of, pertaining to, or characteristic of two relations (tables) that are of the same order (have the same number of attributes) and whose corresponding attributes are based on the same domain (the set of acceptable values).

Unipolar *adj.* Having one state. In electronics, a unipolar device or signal is one in which the same voltage polarity (positive or negative) is used to represent binary states—on/off or true/false.

Unique user *n.* An individual visitor to a Web site. Tracking unique users is important in ascertaining the success of a given Web site because it indicates how many different visitors access the site, as opposed to the number of hits—visits by the same or different individuals—the site receives. Also called: unique visitor.

Unique visitor *n.* See unique user.

United States of America Standards Institute *n.* The former name of the American National Standards Institute. See also ANSI.

Unit position *n.* The "one's place" in a multiple-digit number—for example, the 3 in the number 473.

UNIVAC I *n.* Short for Universal Automatic Calculator I. The first commercially available electronic computer, designed by J. Presper Eckert and John Mauchly, also the inventors of ENIAC (generally considered the first fully electronic computer). UNIVAC I was the first computer to handle both numeric and textual information.

Universal Server *n.* 1. Software from Oracle Corporation that supplies information from its database in a variety of forms, such as text, sound, and video, in response to HTTP requests. 2. Database software from Informix that works with snap-in software modules to handle user needs for specific data types and ways of processing.

Universal synchronous receiver-transmitter *n.* See USRT.

Universal Time Coordinate *n.* For all practical purposes, the same as Greenwich Mean Time, which is used for the synchronisation of computers on the Internet. Acronym: UTC. Also called: coordinated universal time format.

University Corporation for Advanced Internet Development *n.* See UCAID.

UNIX *n.* A multiuser, multitasking operating system. Originally developed by Ken Thompson and Dennis Ritchie at AT&T Bell Laboratories from 1969 through 1973 for use on mini-computers, UNIX has evolved into a complex, powerful operating system that, because it is written in the C language, is more portable—that is, less machine-specific—than many other operating systems. UNIX has been released in a wide variety of versions, or flavors, including System V (developed by AT&T for commercial release; many current flavors on based on it), BSD UNIX (freeware developed at the University of California Berkeley, which has spun off many related flavors), AIX (a version of System V adapted by IBM to run on RISC-based workstations), A/UX (a graphical version for the Macintosh), Linux (a newer version that runs on the Intel chip), and SunOS (based on BSD UNIX and available on Sun workstations). Many flavors of UNIX are available free.

UNIX shell account *n.* A shell account providing command-line access to a UNIX system. See also shell account.

UNIX shell scripts *n.* Sequences of UNIX commands stored as files that can be run as programmes. In MS-DOS, batch (.bat) files provide similar capabilities. See also batch file, shell, shell script.

UNIX-to-UNIX Copy *n.* See UUCP.

UNIX wizard *n.* A particularly expert and helpful UNIX programmer. Some companies actually use this phrase as a job title. The newsgroup comp.unix.wizards provides answers to many user questions.

Unknown host *n.* A response to a request for a connection to a server that indicates that the network is unable to find the specified address. See also server (definition 1).

Unknown recipients *n.* A response to an e-mail message that indicates that the mail server is unable to identify one or more of the destination addresses.

Unload *vb.* 1. To remove a storage medium, such as a tape or disk, from its drive. 2. To remove software from system memory. See also memory.

Unmanaged code *n.* Code that is executed directly by the operating system, outside of the common language run-time environment. Unmanaged code must provide its own garbage collection, type checking, security support, and so on, unlike managed code, which receives these services from the common language runtime. See also managed code.

Unmoderated *adj.* Of, pertaining to, or characteristic of a newsgroup or mailing list in which all articles or messages received by the server are automatically available or distributed to all subscribers.

Unmount *vb.* To remove a disk or tape from active use.

Unpack *vb.* To restore packed data to its original format.

Unpopulated board *n.* A circuit board whose sockets are empty.

Unread *adj.* 1. Of, pertaining to, or being an article in a newsgroup that a user has not yet received. Newsreader client programmes distinguish between "read" and "unread" articles for each user and download only unread articles from the server. 2. Of, pertaining to, or being an e-mail message that a user has received but has not yet opened in an e-mail programme.

Unrecoverable error *n.* A fatal error—one that a programme is unable to recover from without the use of external recovery techniques.

Unreliable protocol *n.* A communications protocol that makes a "best effort" attempt to deliver a transmission but does not provide for verifying that the transmission arrives without error.

Unroll *adj.* See inline (definition 1).

Unset *vb.* To make the value of a bit position equal to 0.

Unshielded cable *n.* Cable that is not surrounded with a metal shield. If the wires in an unshielded cable are not at least twisted around each other in pairs, the signals they carry have no protection from interference by external electromagnetic fields. Consequently, unshielded cable should be used only over very short distances.

Unshielded twisted pair *n.* See UTP.

Unshielded twisted-pair wiring *n.* See UTP.

Unsolicited commercial e-mail *n.* See spam.

Unsubscribe *vb.* 1. In a newsreader client programme, to remove a newsgroup from the list of newsgroups to which one subscribes. See also newsgroup. 2. To remove oneself as a recipient on a mailing list. See also mailing list.

Untar1 *n.* A utility, available for systems in addition to UNIX, for separating the individual files out of an archive assembled using the UNIX tar programme.

Untar2 *vb.* To separate the individual files out of an archive assembled with the UNIX tar programme.

Unzip *vb.* To uncompress an archive file that has been compressed by a programme such as compress, gzip, or PKZIP.

Up *adj.* Functioning and available for use; used in describing computers, printers, communications lines on networks, and other such hardware.

UPC *n.* Acronym for Universal Product Code. A system of numbering commercial products using bar codes. A UPC consists of 12 digits: a number system character, a five-digit number assigned to the manufacturer, a five-digit product code assigned by the manufacturer, and a modulo 10 check digit. See also bar code.

Update1 *n.* A new release of an existing software product. A software update usually adds relatively minor new features to a product or corrects errors (bugs) found after the programme was released. Updates are generally indicated by small changes in software version numbers, such as 4.0b from 4.0. See also version number.

Update2 *vb.* To change a system or a data file to make it more current.

Update query *n.* A database query that changes a set of records according to search conditions or criteria.

Upflow *n.* In the data warehousing process, the stage during which stored information is checked for completeness, summarised, and readied for distribution. See also data warehouse.

Upgrade1 *n.* The new or enhanced version of a product.

Upgrade2 *vb.* To change to a newer, usually more powerful or sophisticated version.

Uplink *n.* The transmission link from an earth station to a communications satellite.

Upload1 *n.* 1. In communications, the process of transferring a copy of a file from a local computer to a remote computer by means of a modem or network. 2. The copy of the file that is being or has been transferred.

Upload2 *vb.* To transfer a copy of a file from a local computer to a remote computer.

UPnP *n.* Acronym for Universal Plug and Play. A Microsoft initiative which prompted the creation of the UPnP Forum for interconnecting computers, appliances, networks, and services. UPnP extends conventional Plug and Play to include devices connected to networks. It allows peripheral devices to discover and connect to other devices and to enumerate the characteristics of those devices. UPnP is intended to be an element of home networking, in which PCs, appliances, and the services they provide are linked together.

UPnP Device Architecture *n.* A specification developed by the Universal Plug and Play (UPnP) Forum that defines the structure of UPnP networking. The UPnP Device Architecture, formerly known as the DCP Framework, provides information about discovery, description, control, eventing, and presentation in a UPnP network. See also UPnP networking.

UPnP Forum *n.* A consortium of companies and individuals that oversees Universal Plug and Play (UPnP) specifications, protocols, logos, sample implementations, test suites, white papers, and other UPnP-related efforts. See also UPnP, UPnP Device Architecture, UPnP networking.

UPnP networking *n.* The peer-to-peer networking of intelligent machines, appliances, wireless devices, computers, and other devices according to the Universal Plug and Play (UPnP) Device Architecture. UPnP networking uses control points, devices, services, and protocols including GENA, SOAP, SSDP, standard TCP/IP, and other Internet protocols. See also UPnP Device Architecture.

Uppercase *adj.* Of, pertaining to, or characterised by capital letters.

Upper memory area *n.* See UMA (definition 1).

Upper memory block *n.* See UMB.

UPS *n.* Acronym for uninterruptible power supply. A device, connected between a computer (or other electronic equipment) and a power source (usually an outlet receptacle), that ensures that electrical flow to the computer is not interrupted because of a blackout and, in most cases, protects the computer against potentially damaging events, such as power surges and brownouts. All UPS units are equipped with a battery and a loss-of-power sensor; if the sensor detects a loss of power, it switches over to the battery so that the user has time to save his or her work and shut off the computer. See also blackout, brownout.

Upstream1 *n.* The direction in which information is delivered from a client to a (Web) server.

Upstream2 *adj.* 1. The location of a server in relation to another server. 2. The direction in which data moves from an individual computer to the remote network. With certain communications technologies, such as ADSL, cable modems, and high-speed 56-Kbps modems, data flows upstream more slowly than downstream. For example, a 56-Kbps modem can deliver data at a 56-Kbps maximum only downstream; upstream, it delivers data at either 28.8 or 33.6 Kbps.

Uptime *n.* The amount or percentage of time a computer system or associated hardware is functioning and available for use.

Upward-compatible *adj.* Of, pertaining to, or characteristic of a computer product, especially software, designed to perform adequately with other products that are expected to become widely used in the foreseeable future. The use of standards and conventions makes upward compatibility easier to achieve.

Urban legend *n.* A widely distributed story that remains in circulation in spite of the fact that it is not true. Many urban legends have been floating around the Internet and other online services for years, including the request for cards for the sick boy in England (he's long since recovered and grown up), the cookie or cake recipe that cost $250 (it's a myth), and the Good Times or Penpal Greetings virus, which will infect your computer when you read an e-mail message (it does not exist). See also Good Times virus.

URC *n.* See Uniform Resource Citation.

URI *n.* See Uniform Resource Identifier.

URL *n.* Acronym for Uniform Resource Locator. An address for a resource on the Internet. URLs are used by Web browsers to locate Internet resources. A URL specifies the protocol to be used in accessing the resource (such as http: for a World Wide Web page or ftp: for an FTP site), the name of the server on which the resource resides (such as //www.whitehouse.gov), and, optionally, the path to a resource (such as an HTML document or a file on that server). See also FTP(definition 1), HTML, HTTP, path (definition 1), server (definition 2), virtual path (definition 1), Web browser.

URN *n.* See Uniform Resource Name.

Usable *adj.* Of, pertaining to, or characteristic of the ease and adaptability with which a product can be applied to the performance of the work for which it is designed. A high degree of usability implies ease of learning, flexibility, freedom from bugs, and good design that does not involve unnecessarily complicated procedures.

Usage analysis *n.* Data collected to evaluate how a Web site is being used, such as visitor user names, how often each page was visited, and the types of Web browsers used.

USB *n.* Acronym for universal serial bus. A serial bus with a data transfer rate of 12 megabits per second (Mbps) for connecting peripherals to a microcomputer. USB can connect up to 127 peripherals, such as external CD-ROM drives, printers, modems, mice, and keyboards, to the system through a single, general-purpose port. This is accomplished by daisy chaining peripherals together. USB is designed to support the ability to automatically add and configure new devices and the ability to add such devices without having to shut down and restart the system (hot plugging). USB was developed by Intel, Compaq, DEC, IBM, Microsoft, NEC, and Northern Telecom. It competes with DEC's ACCESS.bus for lower-speed applications. See also bus, daisy chain, hot plugging, input/output port, peripheral.

U.S. Department of Defense *n.* The military branch of the United States government. The Department of Defense developed ARPANET, the origin of today's Internet and MILNET, through its Advanced Research Projects Agency (ARPA). See also ARPANET, Internet, MILNET.

Usenet or UseNet or USENET *n.* A worldwide network of UNIX systems that has a decentralised administration and is used as a bulletin board system by special-interest discussion groups. Usenet, which is considered part of the Internet (although Usenet predates it), is comprised of thousands of newsgroups, each devoted to a particular topic. Users can post messages and read messages from others in these newsgroups in a manner similar to users on dial-in BBSs. Usenet was originally implemented using UUCP (UNIX-to-UNIX Copy) software and telephone connections; that method remains important, although more modern methods, such as

NNTP and network connections, are more commonly used. See also BBS (definition 1), newsgroup, newsreader, NNTP, UUCP.

Usenet User List *n.* A list maintained by the Massachusetts Institute of Technology that contains the name and e-mail address of everyone who has posted to the Usenet. See also Usenet.

User account *n.* On a secure or multiuser computer system, an established means for an individual to gain access to the system and its resources. Usually created by the system's administrator, a user account consists of information about the user, such as password, rights, and permissions. See also group1, logon, user profile.

User agent *n.* In the terminology established by the ISO/OSI reference model for LANs (local area networks), a programme that helps a client connect with a server. Acronym: UA. See also agent (definition 3), ISO/OSI reference model, LAN.

User control *n.* In ASP.NET: A server control that is authored declaratively using the same syntax as an ASP.NET page and is saved as a text file with an .ascx extension. User controls allow page functionality to be partitioned and reused. Upon first request, the page framework parses a user control into a class that derives from System.Web.UI.UserControl and compiles that class into an assembly, which it reuses on subsequent requests. User controls are easy to develop due to their page-style authoring and deployment without prior compilation. In Windows Forms: A composite control that provides consistent behaviour and user interface within or across applications. The user control can be local to one application or added to a library and compiled into a DLL for use by multiple applications.

User Datagram Protocol *n.* See UDP.

User-defined data type *n.* A data type defined in a programme. User-defined data types are usually combinations of data types defined by the programming language being used and are often used to create data structures. See also data structure, data type.

User-defined function key *n.* See keyboard enhancer, programmable function key.

User-friendly *adj.* Easy to learn and easy to use.

User group *n.* A group of people drawn together by interest in the same computer system or software. User groups, some of which are large and influential organisations, provide support for newcomers and a forum where members can exchange ideas and information.

User-initiated update *n.* An operating system update mechanism, provided by the dial-up boot loader, which is designed to be used by remote users and field technicians. The operating system image is downloaded using a modem connection. See also automatic update, factory update.

User interface *n.* The portion of a programme with which a user interacts. Types of user interfaces, or UIs, include command-line interfaces, menu-driven interfaces, and graphical user interfaces. Acronym: UI.

User Interface Toolbox *n.* See Toolbox.

Username *n.* The name by which a user is identified to a computer system or network. During the logon process, the user must enter the username and the correct password. If the system or network is connected to the Internet, the username generally corresponds to the leftmost part of the user's e-mail address (the portion preceding the @ sign, as in username@company.com). See also e-mail address, logon.

User name *n.* The name by which a person is known and addressed on a communications network. See also alias (definition 2).

User profile *n.* A computer-based record maintained about an authorised user of a multiuser computer system. A user profile is needed for security and other reasons; it can contain such information as the person's access restrictions, mailbox location, type of terminal, and so on. See also user account.

User state *n.* The least privileged of the modes in which a Motorola 680x0 microprocessor can operate. This is the mode in which application programmes are run. See also 68000.

USnail *n.* 1. Slang for the United States Postal Service. USnail, a term used on the Internet, is a reference to how slow the postal service is in comparison to e-mail. 2. Mail delivered by the United States Postal Service. See also snail mail.

/usr *n.* A directory in a computer system that contains subdirectories owned or maintained by individual users of the computer system. These subdirectories can contain files and additional subdirectories. Typically, /usr directories are used in UNIX systems and can be found on many FTP sites. See also FTP site.

USRT *n.* Acronym for universal synchronous receiver- transmitter. A module, usually composed of a single integrated circuit, that contains both the receiving and transmitting circuits required for synchronous serial communication.

UTC *n.* See Universal Time Coordinate.

UTF-8 *n.* Acronym for UCS Transformation Format 8. A character set for protocols evolving beyond the use of ASCII. The UTF-8 protocol provides for support of extended ASCII characters and translation of UCS-2, an international 16-bit Unicode character set. UTF-8 enables a far greater range of names than can be achieved using ASCII or extended ASCII encoding for character data. See also ASCII, Unicode.

Utility *n.* A programme designed to perform a particular function; the term usually refers to software that solves narrowly focused problems or those related to computer system management. See also application.

Utility programme *n.* A programme designed to perform maintenance work on the system or on system components (for example, a storage backup programme, disk and file recovery programme, or resource editor).

UTP *n.* Acronym for unshielded twisted pair. A cable containing one or more twisted pairs of wires without additional shielding. UTP is more flexible and takes up less space than shielded twisted-pair (STP) cable but has less bandwidth.

.uu *n.* The file extension for a binary file that has been translated into ASCII format using uuencode. Also called: . uud. See also ASCII, binary file, uuencode.

UUCP *n.* Acronym for UNIX-to-UNIX Copy. A set of software programmes that facilitates transmission of information between UNIX systems using serial data connections, primarily the public switched telephone network. See also uupc.

.uud *n.* See .uu.

Uudecode1 *n.* A UNIX programme that converts a uuencoded file back into its original binary format. This programme (along with uuencode) allows binary data, such as images or executable code, to be disseminated through e-mail or newsgroups.

Uudecode2 *vb.* To transform a uuencoded file back into its binary original using the uudecode programme.

.uue *n.* The file extension for a file that has been decoded from ASCII format back into binary format using uudecode. See also ASCII, binary file, uudecode.

Uuencode1 *n.* A UNIX programme that converts a binary file, in which all 8 bits of every byte are significant, into printable 7-bit ASCII characters without loss of information. This programme (along with uudecode) allows binary data, such as images or executable code, to be disseminated through e-mail or newsgroups. A file thus encoded is one-third again as long as the original.

Uuencode2 *vb.* To transform a binary file into printable 7-bit ASCII text using the uuencode programme.

UUID *n.* Acronym for universally unique identifier. A 128-bit value that uniquely identifies objects such as OLE servers, interfaces, manager entry-point vectors, and client objects. Universally unique identifiers are used in cross-process communication, such as remote procedure calling (RPC) and OLE. Also called: GUID.

UUPC *n.* The version of UUCP for IBM PCs and PC-compatibles running DOS, Windows, or OS/2. This version is a collection of programmes for copying files to, logging in to, and running programmes on remote networked computers. See also UUCP.

V

V.120 *n.* The ITU-T (formerly CCITT) standard that governs serial communications over ISDN lines. Data is encapsulated using a protocol similar to the Lightweight Directory Access Protocol (LDAP), and more than one connection may be multiplexed on a communications channel. See also communications channel, communications protocol, International Telecommunications Union, ISDN, Lightweight Directory Access Protocol, multiplexing, standard (definition 1), V series.

V20, V30 *n.* NEC microprocessors that were slight improvements on Intel's 8088 and 8086, using the same command sets but different microcode.

V.2x, V.3x, V.4x, V.5x series *n.* See V series.

V.32terbo *n.* A modem protocol developed by AT&T for 19,200-bps modems, with fallback to the speeds supported by the ITU-T (formerly CCITT) V.32 standard. This protocol is proprietary to AT&T and was not adopted by CCITT or ITU-T. In the V series, V.34 takes the place of V.32terbo. See also International Telecommunications Union, V series.

V.34 *n.* Data transmission standard that provides for up to 28,800 bits per second (bps) communications over telephone lines. It defines a full-duplex (two-way) modulation technique and includes error-correcting and negotiation. See also bits per second, full-duplex, modulation standards, V.90.

V.42 *n.* The ITU-T (formerly CCITT) recommendation specifying procedures for error correction in data communications equipment (DCEs) designed for asynchronous-to-synchronous conversion. See also V series.

V.42bis *n.* The ITU-T (formerly CCITT) recommendation specifying procedures for data compression in data-circuit terminating equipment utilising error-correction operations. See also V series.

V86 mode *n.* See virtual real mode.

V.90 *n.* Data transmission standard that provides for up to 56,000 bits per second (bps) communications over telephone lines. The transmission speed from the client-side modem for uploads is 33,600 bps. The transmission speed for downloads from the host-side modem such as an Internet service provider (ISP) or a corporate network is up to 56,000 bps, with an average speed of 40,000 to 50,000 bps. When the host-side modem does not support this standard, the alternative is V.34. See also bits per second, client, host, ISP, modem, modulation standards, V.34.

VAB *n.* See voice answer back.

VAC *n.* See volts alternating current.

Vacuum tube *n.* A set of metal electrodes and intervening metal grids, contained in a glass or metal tube from which all gas has been removed. Voltages on the grids control electrical currents between the electrodes. Formerly used for amplification and switching in electronic circuits, vacuum tubes are now used in applications such as cathode-ray tubes and those requiring very high power levels. A vacuum tube is known as a valve in Great Britain.

Validation server controls *n.* A set of server controls, included with ASP.NET, that verify user input. The input is checked as it comes from HTML server controls and Web server controls (for example, a Web page form) against programmer-defined requirements. Validation controls perform input checking in server code. If the user is working with a browser that supports DHTML, the validation controls can also perform validation using client script. See also ASP.NET server control, HTML server control, Web server control.

Validation suite *n.* A set of tests that measures compliance with a standard, especially a standard definition of a programming language. See also standard (definition 1).

Valid date interval *n.* A span of time during which a computer will maintain the correct date. For many PCs, the valid date interval is 1980 forward.

Validity check *n.* The process of analysing data to determine whether it conforms to predetermined completeness and consistency parameters.

Value *n.* A quantity assigned to an element such as a variable, symbol, or label. See tone (definition 1).

Value-added network *n.* A communications network that offers additional services, such as message routing, resource management, and conversion facilities, for computers communicating at different speeds or using different protocols. Acronym: VAN.

Value-added reseller *n.* A company that buys hardware and software and resells it to the public with added services, such as user support. Acronym: VAR.

Value list *n.* A list of values used by some application, such as a database, as a search string or as values for a filtered query. See also filter (definition 1), query (definition 1), search string.

Value type *n.* A data type that is represented by the type's actual value. If a value type is assigned to a variable, that variable is given a fresh copy of the value. (This is in contrast to a reference type, where assignment does not create a copy.) Value types are usually created on a method's stack frame, rather than in the garbage-collected heap. A value type can be boxed, which is a process that creates a corresponding reference type. See also reference type.

Valve *n.* See electron tube, vacuum tube.

Vampire tap *n.* A type of transceiver used on Ethernet networks that is equipped with sharp metal prongs that pierce the insulation on thicknet cable to make contact with the copper core over which signals travel.

VAN *n.* See value-added network.

Vanilla *adj.* See plain vanilla.

Vaporware *n.* Software that has been announced but not released to customers. The term implies sarcastically that the product exists only in the minds of the marketing department.

VAR *n.* See value-added reseller.

Variable *n.* In programming, a named storage location capable of containing data that can be modified during programme execution. See also data structure, data type, global variable, local variable.

Variable expression *n.* An expression that depends on the value of at least one variable and, hence, must be evaluated during programme execution. See also run time (definition 1), variable.

Variable-length field *n.* In a record, a field that can vary in length according to how much data it contains. See also field (definition 1).

Variable-length record *n.* A record that can vary in length because it contains variable-length fields, certain fields only under certain conditions, or both of these. See also variable-length field.

VAX *n.* Acronym for virtual address extension. A family of 32-bit minicomputers introduced by Digital Equipment Corporation in 1978. The VAX, like the later 68000 microprocessor, has a flat address space and a large instruction set. The VAX was highly favoured within the hacker community but has been superseded by microprocessors and RISC workstations. See also flat address space, instruction set, microprocessor, minicomputer, RISC.

VBA *n.* See Visual Basic for Applications.

vBNS *n.* Short for very high-speed Backbone Network Service. A network connecting several supercomputer centers and reserved for high-performance, high-bandwidth scientific applications requiring massive computing power. The vBNS was developed by the National Science Foundation and MCI Telecommunications. It began operation in 1995, reaching speeds of 2.4 Gbps, using MCI's network of advanced switching and fiberoptic transmission technologies. Later, vBNS expanded to provide backbone services for Internet2.

VBScript *n.* See Visual Basic, Scripting Edition.

VBS/VBSWG virus *n.* Acronym for Visual Basic Script/Visual Basic Script Worm Generator virus. Any virus created using the VBSWG virus creation toolkit. The tools available in VBSWG worm kit allow individuals to write viruses without having significant computer knowledge. Homepage and the Anna Kournikova virus are examples of VBS/VBSWG viruses.

VBX *n.* Short for Visual Basic custom control. A software module that, when called by a Visual Basic application, produces a control that adds some desired feature to the application. A VBX is a separate executable file, usually written in C, that is dynamically linked to the application at run time and can be used by other applications, including some applications not developed in Visual Basic. Although VBX technology was developed by Microsoft, most VBXs have been written by third-party developers. VBXs are still in use, but the technology has been superseded by OCXs and ActiveX controls. See also control (definition 2), Visual Basic.

VCACHE *n.* The disk caching software used with VFAT driver in Windows 9x. VCACHE uses 32-bit code, runs in protected mode, and automatically allocates space in RAM rather than requiring the user to reserve space for the cache. See also cache, driver, protected mode, RAM, VFAT.

vCalendar *n.* A specification defining the format for applications to exchange scheduling information. The vCalendar specification is based on existing industry standards, including international standards for representing dates and times, and permits the exchange of schedules and "to-do" lists of the sort users commonly enter into personal calendars. Like the companion vCard specification for electronic business cards, it was created by the versit consortium founded by Apple, AT&T, IBM, and Siemens. Handed off to the Internet Mail Consortium (IMC) in 1996, vCalendar is supported by numerous hardware and software vendors. See also vCard.

vCard *n.* A specification for creating an electronic business card (or personal-information card) and for the card itself. Designed to be exchanged through applications such as e-mail and teleconferencing, a vCard includes information such as name, address, telephone and fax number(s), and e-mail address. It can also include time-zone, geographic location, and multimedia data such as photographs, company logos, and sound clips. Based on the ITU's X.500 directory services specification, vCard was developed by versit, a consortium whose principal members include Apple, AT&T, IBM, and Siemens. The specification is under the guidance of the Internet Mail consortium Version 3.0 of the vCard specification has been approved as a proposed standard by the IETF. A companion specification known as vCalendar supports electronic exchange of scheduling information. See also vCalendar, X series.

V-chip *n.* Electronic chip for installation in a television, VCR, cable box, or stand-alone device to provide adults with the ability to block programming they deem inappropriate. Intended to provide parents with a means of controlling the programming viewed by children, the V-chip allows adults to screen programmes based on a rating level transmitted in the portion of the TV signal known as the vertical blanking interval (the same portion that carries closed captioning information). When programmes exceed the chosen level, the V-chip signals the television, which then displays an "unauthorised to receive" message on a blank screen.

VCOMM *n.* The communications device driver in Windows 9x that provides the interface between Windows-based applications and drivers on one side, and port drivers and modems on the other. See also driver.

VCPI *n.* See Virtual Control Programme Interface.

VCR-style mechanism *n.* 1. A user interface for playing movie files that has controls similar to those on a videocassette recorder (VCR). 2. A type of motorised docking mechanism in which a laptop or notebook computer is physically locked into place by the docking station. The advantage to a VCR-style mechanism is that it provides an electrically consistent, secure bus connection. See also docking mechanism, docking station, laptop, portable computer.

VDD *n.* Acronym for virtual display device driver. See virtual device driver.

VDL *n.* Acronym for Vienna Definition Language. A meta-language, containing both a syntactic and a semantic metalanguage, used to define other languages. See also metalanguage.

VDM *n.* See video display metafile.

VDSL *n.* Short for very-high-speed digital subscriber line. The high-speed version of the xDSL (digital subscriber line) communication technologies, all of which operate over existing phone lines. VDSL can deliver up to 52 Mbps downstream, but it is effective only within about 4500 to 5000 feet of the central exchange. The data delivery rate is, in fact, related to the distance the signal must travel. To attain a rate of 52 Mbps, for example, the subscriber must be within 1000 feet of the exchange office. At a distance of 3000 feet, the data rate drops to about 26 Mbps; and at 5000 feet, the data rate drops to about 13 Mbps. See also central office, xDSL.

VDT *n.* Acronym for video display terminal. A terminal that includes a CRT (cathode-ray tube) and keyboard. See also CRT.

VDU *n.* Acronym for video display unit. A computer monitor. See also monitor.

Vector *n.* 1. In mathematics and physics, a variable that has both distance and direction. 2. In computer graphics, a line drawn in a certain direction from a starting point to an endpoint, both of whose locations are identified by the computer using x-y-coordinates on a grid. Vectors are used in the output of some graphics programmes instead of groups of dots (on paper) or pixels (on screen). See also vector graphics. 3. In data structures, a one-dimensional array—a set of items arranged in a single column or row. See also array, matrix.

Vector display *n.* A CRT (cathode-ray tube), commonly used in oscilloscopes and DVST (direct view storage tube) displays, that allows the electron beam to be arbitrarily deflected, based on x-y-coordinate signals. For example, to draw a line on a vector display, the video adapter sends signals to the X and Y yokes to move the electron beam over the path of the line; there is no background composed of scan lines, so the line drawn on the screen is not constructed of pixels. See also CRT, yoke.

Vector font *n.* A font in which the characters are drawn using arrangements of line segments rather than arrangements of bits. See also font.

Vector graphics *n.* Images generated from mathematical descriptions that determine the position, length, and direction in which lines are drawn. Objects are created as collections of lines rather than as patterns of individual dots or pixels.

Vector Markup Language *n.* See VML.

Vector table *n.* See dispatch table.

Velocity Engine *n.* A component of Apple's Macintosh G4 processor that processes data in 128-bit chunks. The Velocity Engine is capable of over one gigaflop of floating-point operations per second.

Venn diagram *n.* A type of diagram, used to express the result of operations on sets, in which a rectangle represents the universe and circles inside the rectangle represent sets of objects. Relationships between sets are indicated by the positions of the circles in relation to one another. The Venn diagram is named after John Venn (1834–1923), an English logician at Cambridge University.

Verbose *adj.* Displaying messages as English text rather than as concise (but cryptic) codes.

Verify *vb.* To confirm either that a result is correct or that a procedure or sequence of operations has been performed.

Veronica *n.* Acronym for very easy rodent-oriented Netwide index to computerised archives. An Internet service developed at the University of Nevada that searches for Gopher archives by keywords. Users can enter Boolean operators, such as AND, OR, and XOR, to help narrow or expand their search. If any matching archives are found, they are listed on a new Gopher menu. See also Boolean operator, Gopher.

Version *n.* A particular issue or release of a hardware product or software title.

Version control *n.* The process of maintaining a database of all the source code and related files in a software development project to keep track of changes made during the project.

Version number *n.* A number assigned by a software developer to identify a particular programme at a particular stage, before and after public release. Successive public releases of a programme are assigned increasingly higher numbers. Version numbers usually include decimal fractions. Major changes are generally marked by a change in the whole number, whereas for minor changes only the number after the decimal point increases.

Verso *adj.* The publishing term for a left-hand page, which is always even-numbered.

Vertex *n.* The highest point of a curve, the point where a curve ends, or the point where two line segments meet in a polygon or freeform.

Vertical application *n.* A specialised application designed to meet the unique needs of a particular business or industry—for example, an application to keep track of billing, tips, and inventory in a restaurant.

Vertical bandwidth *n.* The rate at which a display screen is refreshed entirely, expressed in hertz (Hz). The vertical bandwidth of display systems ranges from 45 Hz to over 100 Hz. Also called: vertical scan rate, vertical sync, V-sync.

Vertical blanking interval *n.* The time required for the electron beam in a raster-scan display to perform a vertical retrace. See also blanking, vertical retrace.

Vertical recording *n.* See perpendicular recording.

Vertical redundancy check *n.* See VRC.

Vertical retrace *n.* On raster-scan displays, the movement of the electron beam from the lower right corner back to the upper left corner of the screen after the beam has completed a full sweep of the screen. See also blanking, vertical blanking interval.

Vertical scan rate *n.* See vertical bandwidth.

Vertical scrolling *n.* Movement up or down in a displayed document. See also scroll bar.

Vertical sync *n.* See vertical bandwidth.

Vertical sync signal *n.* The part of a video signal to a raster display that denotes the end of the last scan line at the bottom of the display.

Very-high-level language *n.* See 4GL.

Very-high-rate digital subscriber line *n.* See VDSL.

Very-high-speed integrated circuit *n.* An integrated circuit that performs operations, usually logic operations, at a very high speed. Acronym: VHSIC.

Very Large Database *n.* A database system containing volumes of data hundreds of gigabytes, or even terabytes, in size. A Very Large Database must often support thousands of users and tables with billions of rows of data, must often be able to operate across several different platforms and operating systems, and must often be able to work with many different software applications. Acronym: VLDB. See also data warehouse.

Very Large Memory *n.* A memory system designed to handle the huge data blocks associated with a Very Large Database. Very Large Memory uses 64-bit RISC technology to allow the use of addressable main memory and file sizes larger than 2 gigabytes (GB) and to cache as much as 14 GB of memory. Acronym: VLM. See also RISC, Very Large Database.

Very-large-scale integration *n.* A reference to the density with which transistors and other elements are packed in an integrated circuit and to the thinness of the connections between them. Very-large-scale integration is generally considered to encompass the range from 5000 to 50,000 components. Acronym: VLSI. See also integrated circuit.

Very Long Instruction Word *n.* See VLIW.

Very-low-frequency electromagnetic radiation *n.* See VLF radiation.

VESA 1 *adj.* Having VL bus expansion slots. Also called: VLB. See also expansion slot, VL bus.

VESA 2 *n.* Acronym for Video Electronics Standards Association. An organisation of hardware manufacturers and vendors dedicated to drafting and improving standards for video and multimedia devices. Standards developed by VESA include the Display Data Channel (DDC), Display Power Management Signaling (DPMS), and VESA local bus (VL bus). See also DDC, DPMS, VL bus.

VESA DDC *n.* See DDC.

VESA Display Data Channel *n.* See DDC.

VESA Display Power Management Signaling *n.* See DPMS.

VESA/EISA *adj.* Having both EISA and VL bus expansion slots. See also EISA, expansion slot, VESA, VL bus.

VESA/ISA *adj.* Having both ISA and VL bus expansion slots. See also expansion slot, ISA, VESA, VL bus.

VESA local bus *n.* See VL bus.

Vesicular film *n.* A coating for optical discs that facilitates erasing and rewriting. The surface is marked by small bumps, which can be flattened and thereby erased, rather than by the pits used in standard CD-ROM discs.

V.everything *n.* A marketing term used by some modem manufacturers to describe modems that comply with both the ITU-T (formerly CCITT) V.34 standard and the various proprietary protocols that were used before the standard was adopted, such as V.Fast Class. A V.everything modem should be compatible with any other modem that operates at the same speed. See also V.Fast Class, V series.

V.Fast Class *n.* A de facto modulation standard for modems implemented by Rockwell International prior to approval of the V.34 protocol, which is the standard. Although both V.Fast Class and V.34 are capable of 28.8-Kbps transmission, V.Fast Class modems cannot communicate with V.34 modems without an upgrade. Acronym: V.FC. See also V series.

VFAT *n.* Acronym for Virtual File Allocation Table. The file system driver software used under the Windows 9x Installable File System Manager (IFS) for accessing disks. VFAT is compatible with MS-DOS disks but runs more efficiently. VFAT uses 32-bit code, runs in protected mode, uses VCACHE for disk caching, and supports long filenames. See also Installable File System Manager, long filenames, protected mode, VCACHE, Windows.

V.FC *n.* See V.Fast Class.

VGA *n.* Acronym for Video Graphics Adapter. A video adapter that duplicates all the video modes of the EGA (Enhanced Graphics Adapter) and adds several more. See also video adapter.

VHLL *n.* Acronym for very-high-level language. See 4GL.

VHSIC *n.* See very-high-speed integrated circuit.

vi1 *n.* Short for visual. The first full-screen text editor under UNIX. The vi editor offers many powerful but not very intuitive keyboard commands. It is still in use on UNIX systems, despite the existence of other editors such as Emacs. See also editor, UNIX.

vi2 *vb.* To edit a file using the vi editor. See also vi1.

VIA *n.* See Virtual Interface Architecture.

VI Architecture *n.* See Virtual Interface Architecture.

Video *adj.* Of or pertaining to the visual component of a television signal. In relation to computers, video refers to the rendering of text and graphics images on displays.

Video accelerator *n.* See graphics engine (definition 1).

Video adapter *n.* The electronic components that generate the video signal sent through a cable to a video display. The video adapter is usually located on the computer's main system board or on an expansion board, but it is sometimes built into the terminal. Also called: video adapter board, video board, video card, video controller, video display adapter.

Video adapter board *n.* See video adapter.

Video board *n.* See video adapter.

Video buffer *n.* The memory on a video adapter that is used to store data to be shown on the display. When the video adapter is in a character mode, this data is in the form of ASCII character and attribute codes; when it is in a graphics mode, the data defines each pixel. See also bit image, bit plane, colour bits, pixel image.

Video capture device *n.* An expansion board that converts analog video signals to digital form and stores them in a computer's hard disk or other mass storage device. Some video capture devices are also capable of converting digital video to analog video for use in a VCR. Also called: video capture board, video capture card. See also expansion board.

Video card *n.* See video adapter.

Video clip *n.* A file that contains a short video item, usually an excerpt from a longer recording.

Video compression *n.* Reduction of the size of files containing video images stored in digital form. If no compression were done, 24-bit colour video at 640 x 480 pixels would occupy almost one megabyte per frame, or over a gigabyte per minute. Video compression can, however, be lossy without affecting the perceived quality of the image. See also lossy compression, Motion JPEG, MPEG.

Video conferencing *n.* Teleconferencing in which video images are transmitted among the various geographically separated participants in a meeting. Originally done using analog video and satellite links, today video conferencing uses compressed digital images transmitted over wide area networks or the Internet. A 56K communications channel supports freeze-frame video; with a 1.544-Mbps (T1) channel, full-motion video can be used. See also 56K, desktop conferencing, freeze-frame video, full-motion video, T1, teleconferencing.

Video controller *n.* See video adapter.

Video digitizer *n.* A device used in computer graphics that uses a video camera, rather than a scan head, to capture a video image and then stores it in memory with the aid of a special-purpose circuit board. See also digitize.

Videodisc *n.* An optical disc used to store video images and associated audio information. See also CD-ROM.

Video display *n.* Any device capable of displaying, but not printing, text or graphics output from a computer.

Video display adapter *n.* See video adapter.

Video display board *n.* A video adapter implementation using an expansion board rather than the computer's main system board. See also video adapter.

Video display card *n.* See video display board.

Video display metafile *n.* A file containing video display information for the transport of images from one system to another. Acronym: VDM.

Video display page *n.* A portion of a computer's video buffer that holds one complete screen image. If the buffer can hold more than one page, or frame, screen updates can be completed more rapidly because an unseen page can be filled while another is being displayed.

Video display terminal *n.* See VDT.

Video display tube *n.* See CRT.

Video display unit *n.* See monitor.

Video DRAM *n.* See video RAM.

Video driver *n.* Software that provides the interface between the video adapter hardware and other programmes, including the operating system. The user can access the video driver to specify the resolution and colour-bit depth of images on the monitor during the setup process. See also driver, monitor, video adapter.

Video editor *n.* A device or programme used to modify the contents of a video file.

Video Electronics Standards Association *n.* See VESA2.

Video game *n.* See computer game.

Video Graphics Adapter or Video Graphics Array *n.* See VGA.

Video graphics board *n.* A video adapter that generates video signals for displaying graphical images on a video screen.

Video look-up table *n.* See colour look-up table.

Video memory *n.* Memory from which a display image is created, located in the video adapter or video subsystem. If both the video processor and the central processing unit (CPU) have access to video memory, images are produced by the CPU's modification of video memory. Video circuitry normally has priority over the processor when both attempt to read or write to a video memory location, so updating video memory is often slower than accessing main memory. See also video RAM.

Video mode *n.* The manner in which a computer's video adapter and monitor display onscreen images. The most common modes are text (character) mode and graphics mode. In text mode, characters include letters, numbers, and some symbols, none of which are "drawn" on screen dot by dot. In contrast, graphics mode produces all screen images, whether text or art, as patterns of pixels (dots) that are drawn one pixel at a time.

Videophone *n.* A device equipped with camera and screen, as well as a microphone and speaker, capable of transmitting and receiving video signals as well as voice over a telephone line. Using conventional telephone lines, a videophone can transmit only freeze-frame video. See also freeze-frame video.

Video port *n.* A cable connector or port on a computer that outputs video signals to a monitor.

Video RAM *n.* A special type of dynamic RAM (DRAM) used in high-speed video applications. Video RAM uses separate pins for the processor and the video circuitry, providing the video circuitry with a back door to the video RAM. The video circuitry can access the video RAM serially (bit by bit), which is more appropriate for transferring pixels to the screen than is the parallel access provided by conventional DRAM. Acronym: VRAM. See also dynamic RAM.

Video server *n.* A server designed to deliver digital video-on-demand and other broadband interactive services to the public over a wide area network.

Video signal *n.* The signal sent from a video adapter or other video source to a raster display. The signal can include horizontal and vertical synchronisation signals, as well as image information. See also composite video display, RGB monitor.

Video terminal *n.* See terminal (definition 1).

Videotex *n.* An interactive information retrieval service designed to be accessed by subscribers over telephone lines. Information can be displayed on a home television screen or a videotex terminal. Subscribers use keypads to choose from menus and to request specific screens, or pages. Also called: videotext.

Videotext *n.* See videotex.

Vienna Definition Language *n.* See VDL.

View 1 *n.* 1. The display of data or an image from a given perspective or location. 2. In relational database management systems, a logical table created through the specification of one or more relational operations on one or more tables. A view is equivalent to a divided relation in the relational model. See also relational database, relational model.

View 2 *vb.* To cause an application to display information on a computer screen.

Viewer *n.* An application that displays or otherwise outputs a file in the same way as the application that created the file. An example of a viewer is a programme to display the images stored in GIF or JPEG files. See also GIF, JPEG.

Viewport *n.* In computer graphics, a view of a document or an image. A viewport is similar to the view in a window, but usually only part of the document or graphical image is visible.

Vine *n.* A means of distributing audiotape copies that is similar to a tape tree. Because vine tapes are digital in format, there is no degradation of sound quality as tapes are copied down the vine from one participant to the next.

Vines *n.* A UNIX-based networking operating system from Banyan Systems.

Viral marketing *n.* A marketing concept that relies on computer users to distribute marketing materials, possibly without even being aware of their participation. Viral marketing is often tied in with free e-mail accounts or other free online services, from which users pass along advertisements with every message they send.

Virgule *n.* The forward slash (/) character.

Virtual *adj.* Of or pertaining to a device, service, or sensory input that is perceived to be what it is not in actuality, usually as more "real" or concrete than it actually is.

Virtual address *n.* In a virtual memory system, the address that the application uses to reference memory. The memory management unit (MMU) translates this address into a physical address before the memory is actually read or written to. See also physical address, virtual memory.

Virtual channel *n.* In Asynchronous Transfer Mode (ATM), the path taken by data sent from one sender to one receiver. See also ATM (definition 1), virtual path (definition 2).

Virtual circuit *n.* A connection between communicating computers that provides the computers with what appears to be a direct link but can actually involve routing data over a defined but longer path.

Virtual community *n.* See online community.

Virtual Control Programme Interface *n.* A specification for MS-DOS programmes to allow access to extended memory under a multitasking environment (for example, Windows) for 386 and higher-level processors. Acronym: VCPI. See also 80386DX, extended memory, multitasking.

Virtual desktop *n.* A desktop enhancement tool that provides access to the desktop when it is covered by open windows or that expands the size of the working desktop. See also desktop.

Virtual device *n.* A device that can be referenced but that does not physically exist. Virtual-memory addressing, for example, uses magnetic disk storage to simulate memory larger than that physically available.

Virtual device driver *n.* Software in Windows 9x that manages a hardware or software system resource. If a resource retains information from one access to the next that affects the way it behaves when accessed (for example, a disk controller with its status information and buffers), a virtual device driver must exist for it. Virtual device drivers are described using three-letter abbreviations beginning with V and ending with D; the middle letter indicates the type of device, such as D for a display, P for a printer, T for a timer, and x when the type of device is not under discussion. Acronym: VD. See also device driver.

Virtual disk *n.* See RAM disk.

Virtual display device driver *n.* See virtual device driver.

Virtual File Allocation Table *n.* See VFAT.

Virtual hosting *n.* A form of hosting that provides a Web server, communication, and other services to customers for their own Web sites. In addition to hardware, software, and communication, virtual hosting can include assistance with domain name registration, e-mail addresses, and other Web-related issues. See also host, hosting.

Virtual image *n.* An image that is stored in computer memory but is too large to be shown in its entirety on the screen. Scrolling and panning are used to bring unseen portions of the image into view. See also virtual screen.

Virtual-image file *n.* A file that specifies the material to be recorded onto a CD-ROM. A virtual-image file generally contains pointers to files that are distributed across a hard disk rather than gathered in one area. Since a complete copy of the material is not assembled, problems may occur in writing the CD-ROM due to delays in assembling the material from a scattered group of files. See also CD-ROM.

Virtual Interface Architecture *n.* An interface specification that defines a standard low-latency, high-bandwidth means of communication between clusters of servers in a System Area Network (SAN). Developed by Compaq, Intel, Microsoft, and more than 100 industry groups, the Virtual Interface Architecture is processor and operating system independent. By reducing the time required for message-passing between applications and the network, it seeks to reduce overhead and thus deliver enterprise-level scalability for mission-critical applications. Acronym: VIA. Also called: VI Architecture. See also cluster, System Area Network.

Virtual LAN *n.* Short for virtual local area network. A local area network consisting of groups of hosts that are on physically different segments but that communicate as though they were on the same wire. See also LAN.

Virtual machine *n.* Software that mimics the performance of a hardware device, such as a programme that allows applications written for an Intel processor to be run on a Motorola chip. Acronym: VM.

Virtual memory *n.* Memory that appears to an application to be larger and more uniform than it is. Virtual memory may be partially simulated by secondary storage such as a hard disk. Applications access memory through virtual addresses, which are translated (mapped) by special hardware and software onto physical addresses. Acronym: VM. Also called: disk memory. See also paging, segmentation.

Virtual monitor *n.* An enhanced monitor viewing system for visually impaired users that uses a virtual-reality headset to move enlarged text across the screen in a direction opposite to head motion. See also virtual reality.

Virtual name space *n.* The set of all hierarchical sequences of names that can be used by an application to locate objects. One such sequence of names defines a path through the virtual name space, regardless of whether the hierarchy of names reflects the actual arrangement of objects around the system. For example, the virtual name space of a Web server consists of all possible URLs on the network on which it runs. See also URL.

Virtual network *n.* A part of a network that appears to a user to be a network of its own. For example, an Internet service provider can set up multiple domains on a single HTTP server so that each one can be addressed with its company's registered domain name. See also domain name, HTTP server (definition 1), ISP.

Virtual path *n.* 1. A sequence of names that is used to locate a file and that has the same form as a pathname in the file system but is not necessarily the actual sequence of directory names under which the file is located. The part of a URL that follows the server name is a virtual path. For example, if the directory c:\bar\sinister\forces\distance on the server miles is shared on the local area network at foo.com under the name \\miles\baz and contains the file elena.html, that file may be returned by a Web request for http://miles.foo.com/baz/elena.html. 2. In Asynchronous Transfer Mode (ATM), a set of virtual channels that are switched together as a unit through the network. See also ATM (definition 1), virtual channel.

Virtual peripheral *n.* A peripheral that can be referenced but does not physically exist. For example, an application might treat a serial port through which data is being transmitted as a printer, but the device receiving the data might be another computer instead.

Virtual printer *n.* A feature in many operating systems that allows printer output to be saved to a file until a printer becomes available.

Virtual printer device driver *n.* See virtual device driver.

Virtual private network *n.* 1. Nodes on a public network such as the Internet that communicate among themselves using encryption technology so that their messages are as safe from being intercepted and understood by unauthorised users as if the nodes were connected by private lines. 2. A WAN (wide area network) formed of permanent virtual circuits (PVCs) on another network, especially a network using technologies such as ATM or frame relay. Acronym: VPN. See also ATM (definition 1), frame relay, PVC.

Virtual reality *n.* A simulated 3-D environment that a user can experience and manipulate as if it were physical. The user sees the environment on display screens, possibly mounted in a special pair of goggles. Special input devices, such as gloves or suits fitted with motion sensors, detect the user's actions. Acronym: VR.

Virtual Reality Modeling Language *n.* See VRML.

Virtual real mode *n.* A feature of the Intel 80386 (SX and DX) and later microprocessors that allows them to emulate several 8086 (real-mode) environments at the same time. The microprocessor provides a set of virtual registers and virtual memory space to each virtual 8086 environment. A programme running in a virtual 8086 environment is completely protected from other virtual 8086 environments in the system and behaves as if it had control of the entire system. Also called: V86 mode, virtual 8086 mode, virtual 86 mode. See also real mode.

Virtual root *n.* The root directory that a user sees when connected to an Internet server, such as an HTTP or FTP server. The virtual root is actually a pointer to the physical root directory, which may be in a different location, such as on another server. The advantages of using a virtual root include being able to create a simple URL for the Internet site and to move the root directory without affecting the URL. Also called: v-root. See also pointer (definition 1), root directory, server (definition 2), URL.

Virtual route *n.* See virtual circuit.

Virtual screen *n.* An image area that extends beyond the dimensions of the physical screen on the monitor, allowing manipulation of large documents or of multiple documents that lie partially outside the normal screen view. See also monitor.

Virtual server *n.* A virtual machine that resides on an HTTP server but has the appearance to the user of being a separate HTTP server. Several virtual servers can reside on one HTTP server, each capable of running its own programmes and each with individualised access to input and peripheral devices. Each virtual server has its own domain name and IP address and appears to the user as an individual Web site. Some Internet service providers use virtual servers for those clients who want to use their own domain names. See also domain name, HTTP server (definition 2), IP address.

Virtual storefront *n.* A company's point of presence on the Web, providing opportunities for online sales. Also called: electronic storefront.

Virtual terminal *n.* See terminal emulation.

Virtual timer device driver *n.* See virtual device driver.

Virtual world *n.* 1. A 3-D modeled environment, often created in VRML, where a user can interact with the viewer to change variables. See also viewer, VRML. 2. An electronic environment that has no basis in the physical world. Multiuser dungeons (MUDs), talkers, and chat rooms are often considered virtual worlds. See also chat(definition 1), MUD, talker.

Virus *n.* An intrusive programme that infects computer files by inserting in those files copies of itself. The copies are usually executed when the file is loaded into memory, allowing the virus to infect still other files, and so on. Viruses often have damaging side effects—sometimes intentionally, sometimes not. For example, some viruses can destroy a computer's hard disk or take up memory space that could otherwise be used by programmes. See also Good Times virus, Trojan horse, worm.

Virus signature *n.* A portion of unique computer code contained in a virus. Antivirus programmes search for known virus signatures to identify infected programmes and files. See also virus.

Visible page *n.* In computer graphics, the image that is being displayed on the screen. Screen images are written into display memory in sections called pages, each of which contains one screen display.

Visio *n.* A software application offered by Microsoft that allows users to create diagrams and visual presentations in electronic form. Visio enables users to share ideas and concepts visually by using diagrams to augment written material in documents or by expanding visual elements in a public presentation. Microsoft acquired the Visio application in 1999, when it purchased Visio Corporation.

Visit *n.* A session during which a person views one or more pages in a particular Web site.

Visitor *n.* A person who views a Web page or Web site.

Visor *n.* A product line of handheld personal digital assistants (PDAs) developed by Handspring Corporation. Features include an address list, an appointments calendar, a to-do list, and memos. Visor also features a 68-pin Springboard socket that allows plug-ins of additional devices offered by Handspring. See also Springboard.

Visual Basic *n.* A trademarked name owned by Microsoft Corporation for a high-level, visual-programming version of Basic. Visual Basic was designed for building Windows-based applications. See also Basic, Visual Basic for Applications, Visual Basic, Scripting Edition, visual programming.

Visual Basic Editor *n.* An environment in which you write new and edit existing Visual Basic for Applications code and procedures. The Visual Basic Editor contains a complete debugging toolset for finding syntax, run-time, and logic problems in your code.

Visual Basic for Applications *n.* A macro-language version of Visual Basic that is used to programme many Windows 9x applications and is included with several Microsoft applications. Acronym: VBA. See also macro language, Visual Basic.

Visual Basic Script *n.* See Visual Basic, Scripting Edition.

Visual Basic, Scripting Edition *n.* A subset of the Visual Basic programming language, optimised for Web-related programming. As with JavaScript, code for Visual Basic, Scripting Edition is embedded in HTML documents. This version is included with the Internet Explorer Web browser. Also called: VBScript, Visual Basic Script. See also Visual Basic for Applications.

Visual C++ *n.* A Microsoft application development system for the programming language C++ that runs under MS-DOS and Windows. Visual C++ is a visual programming environment. See also visual programming.

Visual Café *n.* The Java-based suite of software development tools from Symantec Corporation. Visual Café is available in several product packages. The Standard Edition, intended for beginning Java programmers, includes an integrated editor, debugger, and compiler, as well as a JavaBean library, wizards, and utilities. The Professional Edition provides a larger library of JavaBeans and more sophisticated tools for development and debugging. The Database Edition, as the name indicates, adds support for database functionality. The Enterprise Suite provides a high-end environment for development of enterprise applications. See also Java.

Visual FoxPro Database and Command Language *n.* A Microsoft product for developing database applications that includes a rich object-oriented programming language derived from the Xbase language.

Visual InterDev *n.* Microsoft's integrated development environment for Web applications. Visual InterDev includes tools for end-to-end (design through deployment) development, as well as integrated tools for database programming and design. The first version of Microsoft Visual InterDev was released in 1997.

Visual interface *n.* See graphical user interface.

Visualisation *n.* A feature of an application that displays data in the form of a video image. For example, some databases can interpret and show data in the form of a two- or three-dimensional model.

Visual J++ *n.* Microsoft's Java visual programming environment, which can be used to create applets and applications in the Java language. See also applet, Java, Java applet, visual programming.

Visual programming *n.* A method of programming using a programming environment or language in which basic programme components can be selected through menu choices, buttons, icons, and other predetermined methods.

Visual SourceSafe *n.* A project-oriented version control system designed by Microsoft to manage software and Web site development. Visual SourceSafe stores files in a secure repository that provides easy access to authorised users and tracks all changes made to files. Visual SourceSafe works with any type of file produced by any development language, authoring tool, or application.

Visual Studio *n.* Microsoft's suite of software development tools for rapid development of business applications and components. Visual Studio is provided in two editions. The Professional Edition, for professional programmers, includes the Visual Basic and Visual C++ languages, Visual FoxPro for database development, Visual InterDev for Web development, and Visual J++ for Java development. The Enterprise Edition, for enterprise-level development, also includes Visual SourceSafe (a team-based source code control system) and the Developer Edition of Microsoft BackOffice Server.

Visual Studio .NET *n.* A development environment for creating XML Web services and applications on the Microsoft .NET platform. See also .NET, .NET My Services.

VLAN *n.* See virtual LAN.

VLB1 *adj.* See VESA1.

VLB2 *n.* See VL bus.

VL bus *n.* Short for VESA local bus. A type of local bus architecture introduced by the Video Electronics Standards Association. The VL bus specification allows up to three VL bus slots to be built into a PC motherboard and allows for bus mastering (wherein intelligent adapter cards can do some processing independently of the CPU). A VL bus slot consists of a standard connector plus an additional 16-bit Micro Channel Architecture connector and must be built into the motherboard by the manufacturer. Standard connectors cannot simply be converted to VL bus slots. A non–VL bus adapter card can be used in a VL bus slot, but it cannot use the local bus and so performs as it normally would in a non–VL bus slot. Also called: VL local bus. See also local bus, PCI local bus.

VLF radiation *n.* Short for very-low-frequency radiation. Electromagnetic radiation (radio) at frequencies within the range of approximately 300 Hz to 30,000 Hz (30 kHz). Computer monitors emit this type of radiation. A voluntary standard, MPR II, regulates the amount of VLF radiation that a monitor can emit. See also MPR II.

VLIW *n.* Acronym for Very Long Instruction Word. An architecture that combines many simple instructions into a single long instruction word that uses different registers.

VL local bus *n.* See VL bus.

VLSI *n.* See very-large-scale integration.

VM *n.* Acronym for Virtual Machine. An operating system for IBM mainframes that provides virtual-machine capability. VM was developed by IBM customers and later taken over by IBM itself under the name OS/VM. See virtual memory. See also virtual machine.

VML *n.* Acronym for Vector Markup Language. An XML-based specification for the exchange, editing, and delivery of 2-D vector graphics on the Web. An application of XML (Extensible Markup Language), VML uses XML tags and Cascading Style Sheets to create and place vector graphics, such as circles and squares, in an XML or HTML document, such as a Web page. These graphics, which are rendered in the native operating system, can include colour and are editable in a variety of graphics programmes. See also Cascading Style Sheets, XML.

VoATM *n.* Short for Voice over Asynchronous Transfer Mode. The transmission of voice and other telephony over an ATM network. See also ATM, VoFR, VoIP.

VoFR *n.* Short for Voice over Frame Relay. Voice transmission over a frame relay network. See also frame relay, VoATM, VoIP.

Voice answer back *n.* The use of sound-recorded messages by a computer in responding to commands or queries. Acronym: VAB.

Voice-capable modem *n.* A modem that can support voice messaging applications along with its data-handling functions.

Voice chat *n.* A feature offered by Internet service providers (ISPs) that allows users to converse with each other directly through an Internet connection. See also Internet telephone.

Voice coil *n.* A device that moves a disk drive actuator arm using electromagnetism. It works more quickly than a stepper motor. See also actuator.

Voice-grade channel *n.* A communications channel, such as a telephone line, with an audio bandwidth of 300 to 3000 Hz, suitable for carrying speech. A voice-grade channel can also be used for transmitting facsimile, analog, and digital information at rates up to 33 kilobits per second (Kbps).

Voice input *n.* Spoken instructions that a computer translates into executable commands using speech recognition technology or that are embedded into documents with the aid of a microphone. See also speech recognition.

Voice mail *n.* A system that records and stores telephone messages in a computer's memory. Unlike a simple answering machine, a voice mail system has separate mailboxes for multiple users, each of whom can copy, store, or redistribute messages.

Voice messaging *n.* A system that sends and receives messages in the form of sound recordings.

Voice modem *n.* A modulation/demodulation device that supports a switch to change between telephony and data transmission modes. Such a device might contain a built-in loudspeaker and microphone for voice communication, but more often it uses the computer's sound card. See also modem, sound card, telephony.

Voice navigation *n.* The use of spoken commands to control a Web browser. Voice navigation is a feature of some plug-in applications that embellish Web browsers to allow the user to navigate the Web by means of his or her voice. See also Web browser.

Voice-net *n.* A term used on the Internet to refer to the telephone system, often preceding the user's telephone number in an e-mail signature.

Voice output *n.* See speech synthesis.

Voice over Asynchronous Transfer Mode *n.* See VoATM.

Voice over Frame Relay *n.* See VoFR.

Voice over IP *n.* See VoIP.

Voice recognition *n.* The capability of a computer to understand the spoken word for the purpose of receiving commands and data input from the speaker. Systems that can recognise limited vocabularies as spoken by specific individuals have been developed, but developing a system that deals with a variety of speech patterns and accents, as well as with the various ways in which a request or a statement can be made, is more difficult, although advances are being made in this area. Also called: speech recognition. See also artificial intelligence, dictation software, neural network.

Voice synthesis *n.* See speech synthesis.

VoIP *n.* Acronym for Voice over IP. The use of the Internet Protocol (IP) for transmitting voice communications. VoIP delivers digitised audio in packet form and can be used for transmitting over intranets, extranets, and the Internet. It is essentially an inexpensive alternative to traditional telephone communication over the circuit-switched Public Switched Telephone Network (PSTN). VoIP covers computer-to-computer, computer-to-telephone, and telephone-based communications.

For the sake of compatibility and interoperability, a group called the VoIP Forum promotes product development based on the ITU-T H.323 standard for transmission of multimedia over the Internet. Also called: Internet telephony. See also H.323.

Volatile memory *n.* 1. Memory, such as RAM, that loses its data when the power is shut off. 2. Memory used by a programme that can change independently of the programme, such as memory shared by another programme or by an interrupt service routine.

Volt *n.* The unit used to measure potential difference or electromotive force. One volt is defined as the potential across which 1 coulomb of charge will do 1 joule of work, or the potential generated by 1 ampere of current flowing through 1 ohm of resistance. See also electromotive force.

Voltage *n.* See electromotive force.

Voltage regulator *n.* A circuit or circuit component that maintains a constant output voltage despite variations in input voltage.

Volts alternating current *n.* The measure of the peak-to-peak voltage swing of an electrical signal. Acronym: VAC.

Volume *n.* 1. A disk or tape that stores computer data. Sometimes, large hard disks are divided into several volumes, each of which is treated as a separate disk. 2. The loudness of an audio signal.

Volume label *n.* A name for a disk or tape. MS-DOS systems, which seldom use disk names except in directory listings, use the term volume label. Apple Macintosh systems, which often refer to disks by name, use the term volume name.

Volume name *n.* See volume label.

Volume reference number *n.* See volume serial number.

Volume serial number *n.* The optional identifying volume number of a disk or tape. MS-DOS systems use the term volume serial number. Apple Macintosh systems use the term volume reference number. A volume serial number is not the same as a volume label or volume name.

VON *n.* Acronym for voice on the net. A broad category of hardware and software technology for real-time voice and video transmission over the Internet. The term was coined by Jeff Pulver, who formed a group called the VON Coalition, which opposes regulation of VON technology and promotes VON to the public.

Von Neumann architecture *n.* The most common structure for computer systems, attributed to the mathematician John von Neumann. It uses the concept of a programme that can be permanently stored in a computer and manipulated or made self-modifying through machine-based instructions. Sequential processing is characteristic of von Neumann architecture. Parallel architectures have evolved to improve on the encumbrances of sequential instructions. See also parallel computer.

Von Neumann bottleneck *n.* Competition between data and instructions for CPU time. Mathematician John von Neumann was the first to show that a computer based on architecture linking a single processor with memory will actually spend more time retrieving data from memory than processing it. The bottleneck arises when the processor has to trade off between executing a large number of instructions per second and reading in a large amount of data in the same time. See also CPU.

VPD *n.* Acronym for virtual printer device driver. See virtual device driver.

VPN *n.* See virtual private network.

VR *n.* See virtual reality.

VRAM *n.* See video RAM.

VRC *n.* Acronym for vertical redundancy check. A method for checking the accuracy of transmitted data. VRC generates an extra bit (parity bit) for each character transmitted. The parity bit indicates whether the character contains an odd or an even number of 1 bits. If its value does not match the type of the character, that character is assumed to be incorrectly transmitted. See also parity.

VRML *n.* Acronym for Virtual Reality Modeling Language. A scene description language for creating 3-D interactive Web graphics similar to those found in some video games, allowing the user to "move around" within a graphic image and interact with objects. VRML, a subset of Silicon Graphics' Inventor File Format (ASCII), was created by Mark Pesce and Tony Parisi in 1994. VRML files can be created in a text editor, although CAD packages, modeling and animation packages, and VRML authoring software are the tools preferred by most VRML authors. VRML files reside on an HTTP server; links to these files can be embedded in HTML documents, or users can access the VRML files directly. To view VRML Web pages, users need a VRML-enabled browser or a VRML plug-in for Internet Explorer or Netscape Navigator. See also 3-D graphic, HTML document, HTTP server (definition 1).

V-root *n.* See virtual root.

V series *n.* The series of ITU-T (formerly CCITT) recommendations relating to modems and modem communications over the public phone system, including signaling, coding, and circuit characteristics. See the table.

Table V.1 Recommendations in the V Series for Modem Communications.

Recommendation Number	What It Covers
V.17	14,000-bps two-wire modems used for facsimile applications
V.21	300-bps modems used with dial-up lines; full-duplex transmission; not the same as Bell 103 (in North America)
V.22	1200-bps modems used with dial-up and leased lines; full-duplex transmission; not the same as Bell 212A (in North America)
V.22bis	2400-bps modems used with dial-up and leased lines; full-duplex transmission

V.23	600/1200-bps synchronous or asynchronous modems used with dial-up and leased lines; half-duplex transmission
V.26	2400-bps modems used with four-wire leased lines; full-duplex transmission
V.26bis	1200/2400-bps modems used with dial-up lines; full-duplex transmission
V.26ter	2400-bps modems used with dial-up and two-wire leased lines; DPSK modulation; fallback to 1200 bps; echo canceling to remove phone-line echo; full-duplex transmission
V.27	4800-bps modems used with leased lines; manual equalizer; full-duplex transmission
V.27bis	2400/4800-bps modems used with leased lines; automatic equalizer; full-duplex transmission
V.27ter	2400/4800-bps modems used with dial-up lines; full-duplex transmission
V.29	9600-bps modems used with point-to-point leased circuits; half-duplex transmission or full-duplex transmission
V.32	9600-bps modems used with dial-up lines; echo canceling to remove phone-line echo; full-duplex transmission
V.32bis	4800/7200/9600/12,000/14,400-bps modems used with dial-up lines; echo canceling; full-duplex transmission
V.33	12,000/14,400-bps modems used with four-wire leased lines; synchronous; QAM modulation; time-division multiplexing; full-duplex transmission
V.34	28,800-bps modems; full-duplex transmission
V.35	Group band modems, which combine the bandwidth of more than one telephone circuit

V.54	Operation of loop test devices in modems
V.56	Network transmission model for evaluating modem performance over standard voice-grade telephone connections
V.56bis	Network transmission model for evaluating modem performance over two-wire voice-grade connections
V.56ter	Network transmission model for evaluating modem performance over two-wire, 4-kilohertz duplex modems
V.61	4800-bps modems operating at voice plus data rate or 14,000-bps modems operating at data-only rate over standard switched telephone circuits or on point-to-point, two-wire phone circuits

V-sync *n.* See vertical bandwidth.

VT-52, VT-100, VT-200 *n.* A popular set of control codes used in terminals with those model numbers that were originally manufactured by Digital Equipment Corporation. Appropriate software can enable a microcomputer to use these codes to emulate such terminals.

VTD *n.* Acronym for virtual timer device driver. See virtual device driver.

Vulcan death grip *n.* A warm boot by pressing the Alt+Crl+Delete keys. The name is a reference from Star Trek. See also three-finger salute, warm boot.

V x D *n.* See virtual device driver.

W

W3 *n.* See World Wide Web.

W3C *n.* Abbreviation for the World Wide Web Consortium, a standards body based in the United States, Europe, and Japan. The W3C is dedicated (in part) to encouraging the development of open Web standards, such as the HTML and XML document markup languages, to promote inter-operability and assist the Web in achieving its potential.

Wafer *n.* A thin, flat piece of semiconductor crystal used in the fabrication of integrated circuits. Various etching, doping, and layering techniques are used to create the circuit components on the surface of the wafer. Usually multiple identical circuits are formed on a single wafer, which is then cut into sections. Each integrated circuit then has leads attached and is packaged in a holder. See also integrated circuit, semiconductor.

Wafer-scale integration *n.* The fabrication on a single wafer of different microcircuits that are then connected to form a single circuit the full size of the wafer. See also wafer.

WAI *n.* Acronym for Web Accessibility Initiative. A set of guidelines released by the World Wide Web Consortium (W3C) in May 1999. The WAI is intended to promote Web accessibility for users with disabilities by setting Web design and compatibility guidelines that help assure Web access and usability for all users. See also accessibility.

WAIS *n.* Acronym for Wide Area Information Server. A UNIX-based document search and retrieval system on the Internet that can be used to search over 400 WAIS libraries, such as Project Gutenberg, for indexed files that match keywords entered by the user. WAIS can also be used on an individual Web site such as a search engine. WAIS, developed by Thinking Machines Corporation, Apple Computer, and Dow Jones, uses the Z39.50 standard to process natural language queries. The list of documents returned by WAIS often contains numerous false matches. Users need a WAIS client to use a WAIS server. See also natural language query, Project Gutenberg, search engine, Z39.50 standard.

WAIS client *n.* The programme needed for accessing the WAIS (Wide Area Information Server) system to search its databases. A WAIS client programme must be installed on a user's own machine or accessed from a computer with such a programme already installed. Many freeware and shareware WAIS programmes for various operating systems, including UNIX, MS-DOS, OS/2, and Windows, are available for download on the Internet. To look for documents in a WAIS database, the user selects the database(s) to search and types a query containing keywords to search for. The WAIS client sends this query to the server, communicating with the server via the Z39.50 protocol. The server processes the request using indexes and returns a list of document headlines matching the query to the client. The user can then choose which document to retrieve, send that request to the server, and receive the complete document in return. See also WAIS.

WAIS database *n.* See WAIS.

Waisindex *n.* 1. A UNIX utility for building an index to text files for access using WAIS (Wide Area Information Server) query software. 2. A URL for accessing WAIS. The URL takes the form wais://hostport/database.

WAIS library *n.* A WAIS (Wide Area Information Server) database. A WAIS library is a comprehensive collection of online documents on a specific topic—for example, Project Gutenberg's collection of public-domain literary and historical texts available over the Internet, and the Dow Jones Information Service collection of business and financial information products. Because the hundreds of WAIS free libraries currently accessible are updated and maintained by volunteers, the quality of topic coverage is uneven. See also WAIS, WAIS client, Project Gutenberg.

WAIS server or waisserver *n.* See WAIS.

Wait state *n.* A processing cycle of the microprocessor during which it only waits for data from an input/output device or from memory. While a single wait state is not humanly perceptible, the cumulative effect of wait states is to slow system performance. See also zero wait state.

Wallet *n.* In electronic commerce, a software programme that contains a user's address and credit card information for use in paying for online purchases. When the wallet is opened at the electronic checkout, it identifies the user to the merchant's server and allows the user to authorise the appropriate debit to a credit card.

Wallpaper *n.* In a graphical user interface such as Windows, a pattern or picture in the screen background that can be chosen by the user. See also graphical user interface.

WAN *n.* Acronym for wide area network. A geographically widespread network, one that relies on communications capabilities to link the various network segments. A WAN can be one large network, or it can consist of a number of linked LANs (local area networks).

Wand *n.* Any pen-shaped device used for data entry, such as a graphics tablet's stylus or, most commonly, the scanning instrument used with many bar code readers. See also optical scanner, scan head.

Wanderer *n.* A person who frequently uses the World Wide Web. Many of these people make indexes of what they find.

WAP *n.* See Wireless Application Protocol.

War dialer *n.* A computer programme that calls a range of phone numbers to identify those numbers that make a connection to a computer modem. War dialers are typically used by hackers to search for vulnerable computers and, once a connection is made, the war dialers may automatically probe the computer for potential weaknesses. Early war dialer programmes called demon dialers were used to crack telephone systems in the 1970s and 1980s.

Warez *n.* Illegal copies of computer software distributed through the Internet and other online channels, such as bulletin boards and FTP servers. The spelling is part of the tendency among some online groups to use odd symbols and intentional misspellings.

Warm boot *n.* The restarting of a running computer without first turning off the power. Also called: soft boot, three-finger salute, vulcan death grip, warm start.

Warm start *n.* See warm boot.

Warp *vb.* Sometimes used by computer game developers to describe the need to completely redraw a screen within a game. For example, moving through a door or advancing to a higher level would require a complete screen overhaul. See also computer game.

Watchdog *n.* A hardware device (usually a timer or driver) used to monitor continuing system health and functionality through communications with the system software using a dedicated device driver.

Watermark *n.* A semitransparent image often used for letters and business cards. In currency, a watermark is visible when you hold a bill up to the light.

Watt *n.* The unit of power equal to the expenditure of 1 joule of energy in 1 second. The power of an electrical circuit is a function of the potential across the circuit and the current flowing through the circuit. If E = potential, I = current, and R = resistance, power in watts can be calculated as $I \times E$, $I^2 \times R$, or E^2/R.

.wav *n.* The file extension that identifies sound files stored in waveform (WAV) audio format. See also WAV.

WAV *n.* A file format in which Windows stores sounds as waveforms. Such files have the extension .wav. Depending on the sampling frequency, on whether the sound is monaural or stereo, and on whether 8 or 16 bits are used for each sample, one minute of sound can occupy as little as 644 kilobytes or as much as 27 megabytes of storage. See also sampling, waveform.

Wave *n.* 1. Any disturbance or change that has an oscillatory, periodic nature, for example, a light or sound wave. See also waveform. 2. In electronics, the time-amplitude profile of an electrical signal.

Wave division multiplexing *n.* See dense wavelength division multiplexing.

Waveform *n.* The manner in which a wave's amplitude changes over time. See also period, phase, wavelength.

Wavelength *n.* The distance between successive peaks or troughs in a periodic signal that is propagated through space. Wavelength is symbolised by the Greek letter lambda and can be calculated as speed divided by frequency.

Wavelet *n.* A mathematical function that varies over a limited extent of time. Wavelets are coming into increasing use for analysing signals (such as sound). They have limited duration and sudden changes in frequency and amplitude rather than the infinite duration and constant amplitude and frequency of the sine and cosine functions.

Wave table synthesis or wavetable synthesis *n.* A method of producing sound, especially music, through a PC. Wave table synthesis is based on use of a wave table, which is a collection of digitised sound samples taken from recordings of actual instruments. These samples are typically stored on a sound card and are edited and mixed together to produce music. Wave table synthesis produces higher quality audio output than FM (frequency modulation) techniques.

WBEM *n.* Acronym for Web-Based Enterprise Management. A protocol that links a Web browser directly to a device or an application that monitors a network. See also communications protocol.

WDEF *n.* See window definition function.

WDL *n.* See Windows Driver Library.

WDM *n.* See dense wavelength division multiplexing, Windows Driver Model.

Weak typing *n.* A characteristic of a programming language that allows the programme to change the data type of a variable during programme execution. See also data type, variable.

Wearable computer *n.* A portable personal computer that its user wears like eyeglasses, clothing, or a wristwatch but which, unlike those items, is interactive, responds to commands, and carries out instructions. A wearable computer may be used like a conventional computer for data collection, storage, and retrieval, but without tying the user to a stationary location while operating the computer. The earliest wearable computers were clandestine devices used in the mid-1960s to predict the performance of roulette wheels. Today, wearable computers are used for such applications as inventory and express package tracking.

Web *n.* A set of interlinked documents in a hypertext system. The user enters the web through a home page. See also World Wide Web.

Web *n.* See World Wide Web.

Web Accessibility Initiative *n.* See WAI.

Web address *n.* See URL.

Web application *n.* A set of clients and servers that cooperate to provide the solution to a problem.

Web architect *n.* An individual who analyses the purpose of a Web site and forms a plan for assembling and integrating the hardware, software, and other technical resources necessary to make the site function properly.

Web author *n.* A person who creates content for the World Wide Web. A Web author might be a writer who produces text for a designer to include in a Web page, or a Web designer who writes the text and also adds graphic elements and prepares the HTML code.

Web-Based Enterprise Management *n.* See WBEM.

Web browser *n.* Software that lets a user view HTML documents and access files and software related to those documents. Originally developed to allow users to view or browse documents on the World Wide Web, Web browsers can blur the distinction between local and remote resources for the user by also providing access to documents on a network, an intranet, or the local hard drive. Web browser software is built on the concept of hyperlinks, which allow users to point and click with a mouse in order to jump from document to document in whatever order they desire. Most Web browsers are also capable of downloading and transferring files, providing access to newsgroups, displaying graphics embedded in the document, playing audio and video files associated with the document, and executing small programmes, such as Java applets or ActiveX controls included by programmers in the documents. Helper applications or plug-ins are required by some Web browsers to accomplish one or more of these tasks. Also called: browser. See also ActiveX control, helper application, hyperlink, Internet Explorer, Java applet, Lynx, Mosaic, Netscape Navigator, plug-in.

Web bug *n.* A small, nearly undetectable graphic that links to a Web page and is embedded in a document for use as an eavesdropping device. A Web bug usually takes the form of a 1-by-1-pixel transparent GIF file, so it is nearly invisible. This file is placed in a Web page, Microsoft Word file, or other document that users will access. The application in which the document is opened immediately links to the Web to download and display the embedded graphic. Information about the user, including IP address, browser, referrer, and time viewed, is passed to the author of the file when the application retrieves the invisible graphic information.

Webby Award *n.* Award bestowed annually by the International Academy of Digital Arts and Sciences to Web sites. The academy bestows awards to Web sites in more than 20 categories, which include technical achievement, humour, and best community site.

Web cam or webcam *n.* A video camera whose output appears on a Web page, usually updated on a regular and frequent schedule. Web cams are used to display weather and traffic conditions, to allow customers and other users to observe current activities at the site owner's business or home (for example, at a day care center), for promotional purposes, and as a form of "gee whiz, look at this!" entertainment.

Webcast 1 *n.* Live or delayed audio or video programming delivered to users over the Web. Downloading these broadcasts requires a user to have the appropriate video or audio application, such as RealPlayer. The necessary application is usually available from the webcaster without cost.

Webcast 2 *vb.* To produce and disseminate Web-based audio, video, and text programming.

Webcaster *n.* A company or organisation that produces and disseminates Web-based audio, video, and text programming.

Webcasting *n.* Popular term for broadcasting information via the World Wide Web, using push and pull technologies to move selected information from a server to a client. An emergent technology in 1997, webcasting was developed to provide users with customised content—for example, sports, news, stocks, and weather—that can be updated both regularly and automatically. Webcasting gives users the ability to specify the type of content they want to see, and it gives content providers a means of delivering such information directly to the user's desktop. Also called: netcasting. See also pull, push (definition 2).

Web clipping *n.* A Web service that delivers brief snippets of information to handheld Web-enabled devices, such as wireless phones and personal digital assistants. Rather than opening a Web site and browsing for information, Web clipping allows a customer to request specific types of information from a service. The Web clipping service then downloads the information to the handheld device.

Web CLUT *n.* See browser CLUT.

Web container *n.* A container that implements the Web component contract of Sun Microsystems's Java 2 Platform Enterprise Edition (J2EE) network architecture. This contract specifies a run time environment for Web components that includes security, concurrency, life cycle management, transaction, deployment, and other services. Provided by a Web or J2EE server, a Web container provides the same services as a JavaServer Pages (JSP) container and provides a federated view of the J2EE platform APIs. See also API, container, J2EE, JSP container, servlet container.

Web cramming *n.* A common form of fraud in which Internet Service Providers (ISPs) add charges to the monthly bill for fictitious services or for services the customer had been told were free.

WebCrawler *n.* A World Wide Web search engine operated by America Online. See also search engine.

WebDAV *n.* Short for Web Distributed Authoring and Versioning. A set of extensions to the HTTP protocol that allows users to collaboratively edit, publish, and manage resources on the World Wide Web. WebDAV-enabled additions to HTTP include document writing, editing, and publishing tools and search, storage, and file sharing options.

Web development *n.* The design and coding of World Wide Web pages.

Web directory *n.* A list of Web sites, giving the URL and a description of each. See also URL.

Web Distributed Authoring and Versioning *n.* See WebDAV.

Web Forms *n.* The ASP.NET page framework, which consists of programmable Web pages (called Web Forms pages) that contain reusable server controls. See also ASP.NET server control.

Web hosting *n.* See hosting.

Web index *n.* A Web site intended to enable a user to locate other resources on the Web. The Web index may include a search facility or may merely contain individual hyperlinks to the resources indexed.

Weblication *n.* See Web application. Slang for Web application.

Weblog or weblog or web log *n.* A Web site that has regularly updated content reflecting the interests of the site's host. Often, but not always, the content is in journal form, has highlights of news and information from other Web sites, and is presented from a personal point of view. On some sites, the Weblog is a collaboration between visitors to the site. The high-tech-oriented Slashdot.org is frequently cited as being among the best-known Weblogs.

Webmaster or webmaster *n.* A person responsible for creating and maintaining a World Wide Web site. A Webmaster is often responsible for responding to e-mail, ensuring the site is operating properly, creating and updating Web pages, and maintaining the overall structure and design of the site. Also called: webmistress, webweaver.

Webmistress *n.* See Webmaster.

Webographics *n.* Demographics of Web users specifically focusing on surfing and online shopping habits and on other related information, such as connection method, browser, and platform.

WebPad *n.* A class of wireless Internet appliances offering full Internet and personal digital assistant (PDA) functions. A WebPad features a larger LCD screen than other handheld communications devices and resembles a tablet.

Web page *n.* A document on the World Wide Web. A Web page consists of an HTML file, with associated files for graphics and scripts, in a particular directory on a particular machine (and thus identifiable by a URL). Usually, a Web page contains links to other Web pages. See also URL.

Web page embedding *n.* Embedding a digital streaming media player directly onto a Web page using HTML code. Rather than displaying a hyperlink to the media file, Web page embedding uses browser plug-ins to present the media player as a visual element in the layout of the Web page.

Web phone *n.* See Internet telephone.

Web Presence Provider *n.* A Web hosting and Internet service provider who manages the Web server hardware and software required to make a Web site available on the Internet. Acronym: WPP.

Web rage *n.* 1. Anger or frustration related to the use or operation of the Internet. 2. An intemperate, rude, or angry posting on the Internet; a flame. 3. The latest fad to gain popularity among Web users.

Websafe palette *n.* See browser CLUT.

Web server *n.* See HTTP server.

Web server control *n.* An ASP.NET server control that belongs to the System.Web.UI.WebControls namespace. Web server controls are richer and more abstract than HTML server controls. A Web server control has an <asp:ControlName> prefix on an ASP.NET page. See also ASP.NET server control, HTML server control, namespace.

Web services *n.* A modular collection of Web protocol-based applications that can be mixed and matched to provide business functionality through an Internet connection. Web services can be used over the Internet or an intranet to create products, business processes, and B2B interactions. Web services use standard Internet protocols such as HTTP, XML, and SOAP to provide connectivity and interoperability between companies.

Web Services Description Language *n.* See WSDL.

Web site *n.* A group of related HTML documents and associated files, scripts, and databases that is served up by an HTTP server on the World Wide Web. The HTML documents in a Web site generally cover one or more related topics and are interconnected through hyperlinks. Most Web sites have a home page as their starting point, which frequently functions as a table of contents for the site. Many large organisations, such as corporations, will have one or more HTTP servers dedicated to a single Web site. However, an HTTP server can also serve several small Web sites, such as those owned by individuals. Users need a Web browser and an Internet connection to access a Web site. See also home page, HTML, HTTP server (definition 1), Web browser.

Web Storage System *n.* The storage component of Exchange 2000 Server and SharePoint Portal servers, which integrates Web server, database, file system, and workgroup functionality. The Web Storage System lets you store and share many types of data in a single integrated system. Acronym: WSS.

Web switch *n.* A network device—a switch—designed to optimise Web traffic routing by using the information embedded in HTTP requests to route the requests to the most appropriate servers, no matter where they are located. Web switches are intended to address issues of speed, scalability, and performance for high-volume Web sites. See also switch.

Web terminal *n.* A system containing a central processing unit (CPU), RAM, a high-speed modem or other means of connecting to the Internet, and powerful video graphics, but no hard disk, intended to be used solely as a client to the World Wide Web rather than as a general-purpose computer. Also called: network computer.

Web-to-host *n.* A service that allows remote users to access programmes and data on legacy or mainframe systems through a Web browser. Web-to-host packages typically include a combination of services such as emulation support, legacy access, centralised management, host services, and security options, with some degree of customisation possible. See also legacy system, mainframe computer.

WebTV *n.* A system that provides consumers with the ability to access the Web as well as send and receive -e-mail on a television by means of a set-top box equipped with a modem. Users must have an ISP (Internet service provider) and subscribe to the WebTV Network. Developed by WebTV Networks, WebTV was purchased by Microsoft in 1996.

Webweaver *n.* See Webmaster.

Webzine *n.* An electronic publication distributed primar-ily through the World Wide Web, rather than as an ink-on-paper magazine. See also e-zine.

Weighted code *n.* A data representation code in which each bit position has a specified inherent value, which might or might not be included in the interpretation of the data, depending on whether the bit is on or off.

Weighted fair queuing *n.* A technique used to improve quality of service that prioritises each session flow passing through a network device. With weighted fair queuing, high-bandwidth traffic is given a smaller proportion of network capacity than low-bandwidth traffic. Acronym: WFQ.

Welcome page *n.* See home page.

WELL *n.* Acronym for Whole Earth 'Lectronic Link. A conferencing system based in San Francisco, California, that is accessible through the Internet and through dial-up access points in many major cities. The WELL attracts many computer professionals, along with other people who enjoy participating in one of the Internet's most successful virtual communities. Because of the number of journalists and other prominent people who participate in the WELL, it has substantial influence beyond its own relatively small number of subscribers.

Well-behaved *adj.* 1. Of, pertaining to, or characteristic of a programme that performs properly even when given extreme or erroneous input values. 2. Obeying the rules of a particular programming environment.

Well-formed *n.* An XML or HTML document that follows all the rules of syntax outlined in the protocol's specification. A well-formed XML or HTML document can be read by all Web browsers without difficulty.

Well-mannered *adj.* See well-behaved.

WEP *n.* Acronym for Wired Equivalent Privacy. An encryption algorithm system included as part of the 802.11 standard, developed by the Institute of Electrical and Electronics Engineers as a security measure to protect wireless LANs from casual eavesdropping. WEP uses a shared secret key to encrypt packets before transmission between wireless LAN devices and monitors packets in transit to detect attempts at modification. WEP offers both 40-bit and 128-bit hardware-based encryption options.

Wetware *n.* Slang for human beings—part of the environment that also includes hardware and software. Also called: liveware.

WFC *n.* See Windows Foundation Classes.

WFQ *n.* See weighted fair queuing.

Whatis *n.* 1. A UNIX utility for obtaining a summary of a keyword's documentation. See also man pages. 2. An Archie command for locating software whose description contains desired words.

What You See Before You Get It *adj.* See WYSBYGI.

What You See Is What You Get *adj.* See WYSIWYG.

Wheel printer *n.* See daisy-wheel printer.

Whetstone *n.* A benchmark test that attempts to measure the speed and efficiency with which a computer carries out floating-point operations. The result of the test is given in units called whetstones. The Whetstone benchmark has fallen out of favour because it produces inconsistent results compared with other benchmarks such as the Dhrystone and the sieve of Eratosthenes. See also benchmark[1], Dhrystone, sieve of Eratosthenes.

WHIRLWIND *n.* A digital computer using vacuum tubes, developed at the Massachusetts Institute of Technology in the 1940s and used during the 1950s. The innovations introduced with WHIRLWIND included CRT displays and real-time processing. WHIRLWIND project members included Kenneth H. Olsen, who founded Digital Equipment Corporation in 1957. See also CRT, real-time, vacuum tube.

Whistler *n.* The code name for Microsoft Windows XP that was used during its development cycle. New visual and operational features are designed to make Windows XP easy for the home user to operate. Features include real-time voice, video and application sharing, enhanced mobility, added support for digital photos and video, and download and playback of high-quality audio and video content. Like Microsoft Windows 2000, Windows XP was developed from Windows NT, consolidating consumer and business operating systems into a single code base.

Whiteboard *n.* Software that allows multiple users across a network to work together on a document that is simultaneously displayed on all the users' screens, as though they are all gathered around a physical whiteboard.

Whiteboard *n.* Microsoft NetMeeting feature that opens a separate window in which multiple users can simultaneously review, create, and update graphic information. The Whiteboard is object-oriented, not pixel-oriented, allowing participants to manipulate the contents by clicking and dragging with the mouse. In addition, they can use a remote pointer or highlighting tool to point out specific contents or sections of shared pages. The NetMeeting Whiteboard is T.126 compliant and is interoperable with other T.126-compatible whiteboards.

White box *n.* A nonbranded PC assembled by a reseller, potentially including components from a number of manufacturers. The name refers to the typical colour of the shipping carton, a box unadorned by brand name or logo.

White box testing *n.* A method of testing software that is based on knowledge of how the software is intended to function. Unlike black box testing, which focuses on how the software functions without reference to how it is designed, white box testing relies on detailed knowledge of the programme code itself and is intended to find flaws and/or errors in its design and specification. Also called: glass box testing.

White hat *n.* A hacker who operates without malicious intent. A white hat will not break into a system with the intention of doing damage. White hats may be employed to provide security against other hackers. See also hacker.

White noise *n.* Noise that contains components at all frequencies, at least within the frequency band of interest. It is called "white" by analogy to white light, which contains light at all the visible frequencies. In the audible spectrum, white noise is a hiss or a roar, such as that produced when a television set is tuned to a channel over which no station is broadcasting.

White pages *n.* See DIB (definition 2).

White space *n.* The areas of blank space on a page that can be used in a design for balance, contrast, and visual appeal.

Whois *n.* 1. An Internet service, provided by some domains, that enables a user to find e-mail addresses and other information for users listed in a database at that domain. 2. A UNIX command to access the whois service. 3. A command that displays a list of all users logged onto a Novell network.

Whois client *n.* A programme (such as the UNIX whois command) that enables a user to access databases of usernames, e-mail addresses, and other information. See also whois (definition 1).

Whois server *n.* Software that provides the usernames and e-mail addresses from a database (often listing people who have accounts at an Internet domain) to users who request the information using whois clients. See also whois.

Whole Earth 'Lectronic Link *n.* See WELL.

Whole number *n.* A number without a fractional component—for example, 1 or 173; an integer.

WID *n.* Acronym for Wireless Information Device. Smart phone or other handheld wireless device capable of multiple communications functions, including e-mail and Internet access.

Wide Area Information Server *n.* See WAIS.

Wide area network *n.* See WAN.

Wideband transmission *n.* See broadband network.

Wide SCSI *n.* A form of the SCSI-2 interface that can transfer data 16 bits at a time at up to 20 megabytes per second. The Wide SCSI connector has 68 pins. Also called: Wide SCSI-2. See also SCSI, SCSI-2.

Wide SCSI-2 *n.* See Wide SCSI.

Widow *n.* A last line of a paragraph, shorter than a full line, appearing at the top of a page. A widow is considered visually undesirable on the printed page.

Wildcard character *n.* A keyboard character that can be used to represent one or many characters. The asterisk (*), for example, typically represents one or more characters, and the question mark (?) typically represents a single character. Wildcard characters are often used in operating systems as a means of specifying more than one file by name.

WIMP *n.* Acronym for Windows, Icons, Mouse, and Pointers. A graphical user interface (GUI) such as those provided by the Apple Macintosh and Microsoft Windows operating systems. WIMP is usually said to stand for Windows, Icons, Mouse, and Pointers, but the acronym is sometimes spelled out as either Windows, Icons, Menus, and Pointers or Windows, Icons, Mouse, and Pull-down menus. The WIMP interface was invented at the Xerox Palo Alto Research Center (PARC), where it was first used in the Alto computer in the early 1970s. See also graphical user interface.

Win32 *n.* The application programming interface in Windows 95 and Windows NT that enables applications to use the 32-bit instructions available on 80386 and higher processors. Although Windows 95 and Windows NT support 16-bit 80x86 instructions as well, Win32 offers greatly improved performance. See also 16-bit machine, 32-bit machine, 80386DX, 8086, application programming interface, central processing unit, Win32s.

Win32 Driver Model *n.* See Windows Driver Model.

Win32s *n.* A subset of the Win32 application programming interface that works under Windows 3.x. By including the

Win32s software, which is distributed as freeware, an application can gain in performance from using the 32-bit instructions available on 80386 and higher processors while running on Windows 3.x. See also 32-bit machine, 80386DX, central processing unit, Win32.

Winchester disk *n.* An early IBM name for a hard disk. The term is derived from IBM's internal code name for its first hard disk, which stored 30 megabytes (MB) and had a 30-millisecond access time, reminding its inventors of a Winchester .30-caliber rifle known as a ".30-.30."

Window *n.* In applications and graphical interfaces, a portion of the screen that can contain its own document or message. In window-based programmes, the screen can be divided into several windows, each of which has its own boundaries and can contain a different document (or another view into the same document).

Window definition function *n.* A resource associated with a window in a Macintosh application. The Macintosh Window Manager calls this function to perform such actions as drawing and resizing the window. Also called: WDEF.

Windowing *n.* An approach to remediation (correction of problems) or simply user convenience in which two-digit years are interpreted in relation to a window of time. Logical procedures based on windowing thus enable software to correctly produce accurate four-digit years. In windowing, the century is determined by presuming that the year falls within a 100-year span. So if the window ranges from 1995 to 2094, any year that is 95 or greater is presumed to be in the twentieth century (19xx), while any number less than 95 is presumed to be in the twenty-first century (20xx). Fixed windowing presupposes that a window always starts with the same date, or pivot year. Moving windowing permits a user or another system to specify the pivot year when the programme is installed or started. Sliding windowing is calculated every time a programme runs and can be based on a predetermined span of time, called a slider, that can be added to the current date to produce the pivot year for the window. Potential differences in windows require analysis whenever importing or exporting data between systems. Also called: logic fix. See also pivot year.

Windowing environment *n.* An operating system or shell that presents the user with specially delineated areas of the screen called windows. Windowing environments typically allow windows to be resized and moved around on the display. The Macintosh Finder, Windows, and the OS/2 Presentation Manager are all examples of windowing environments. See also graphical user interface, window.

Window random access memory *n.* See WRAM.

Windows *n.* An operating system introduced by Microsoft Corporation in 1983. Windows is a multitasking graphical user interface environment that runs on MS-DOS–based computers (Windows 3.x. and Windows for Workgroups), and as a self-contained operating system for desktop computers (Windows 9x and Windows Me), workstations (Windows NT Workstation, Windows 2000 Professional), and network servers (Windows NT Server, Windows NT Enterprise Edition, Windows 2000 Server, and Windows 2000 Advanced Server). The most recent versions of Windows are Windows XP Home (home and entertainment use) and Professional (advanced computing, businesses, and large organisations). The next generation of Windows server products will be the Windows .NET Server family. Windows provides a standard graphical interface based on drop-down menus, windowed regions on the screen, and a pointing device such as a mouse.

Windows 95 *n.* An operating system with a graphical user interface for 80386 and higher processors, released by Microsoft Corporation in 1995. Intended to replace Windows 3.11, Windows for Workgroups 3.11, and MS-DOS, Windows 95 is a complete operating system, rather than a shell that requires MS-DOS, as does Windows 3.x. For backward compatibility, Windows 95 can run MS-DOS software. Under Windows 95, filenames can be up to 255 characters long and may include dots and spaces. Windows 95 supports the Plug and Play method for installing and configuring hardware and can access Windows, NetWare, and UNIX networks. The minimum configuration for Windows 95 is an 80386 processor with 4 MB of RAM, but an i486 or higher processor with at least 8 MB of RAM is recommended. Internet functionality is provided in large part in Windows 95 by Microsoft Internet Explorer. See also MS-DOS, NetWare, Plug and Play, Windows.

Windows 98 *n.* An operating system with a graphical user interface for i486 and higher processors, released by Microsoft Corporation in 1998. Building upon Windows 95, Windows 98 features an improved interface and more robust functionality. With the Active Desktop, Windows 98 integrates Internet connectivity even more closely, allowing users to access remote files in the same way they would access files on their hard drives. Hardware support includes USB, IEEE 1394, AGP ports, television tuner cards, DVD drives, multiple modems, and multiple monitors. Windows 98, Second Edition, released in 1999, builds on the features in the initial release and offers home networking and improved maintenance features. See also Windows, Windows 95.

Windows 9x *n.* The architecture upon which Windows 95 and Windows 98 were built. See also Windows 95, Windows 98.

Windows 2000 *n.* A Microsoft operating system, the successor to Windows NT, designed for business rather than consumer use. Like its predecessor, Windows 2000 is a multithreaded, multitasking 32-bit operating system. Implemented in desktop and several server versions, Windows 2000 focuses overall on improved ease of use, networking, management, reliability, scalability, and security.

Windows 2000 Advanced Server *n.* Microsoft's network server for larger organisations. Designed to replace Windows NT 4 Enterprise Edition, it supports up to four-way SMP, large physical memories, and database-intensive work. It integrates clustering and load balancing support. See also SMP, Windows.

Windows 2000 Datacenter Server *n.* Microsoft's network server for larger organisations. Considered the most powerful and functional server operating system ever offered by Microsoft, it supports up to 16-way SMP and up to 64 GB of physical memory (depending on system architecture). Like Windows 2000 Advanced Server, it provides both clustering and load balancing services as standard features. It is optimised for large data warehouses, econometric analysis, large-scale simulations in science and engineering, OLTP, and server consolidation projects. See also OLTP, SMP, Windows.

Windows 2000 Professional *n.* Microsoft's mainstream desktop operating system for businesses of all sizes. Designed to replace Windows NT Workstation 4, which many people are using today as the standard business desktop, Windows 2000 Professional builds upon the interface and kernel in NT 4. It also includes improved security, state-of-the-art features for mobile users, industrial-strength reliability, and better performance.

Windows 2000 Server *n.* Microsoft's network server for small to medium businesses. Designed to replace Windows NT 4 Server, Windows 2000 Server offers improved functionality and supports new systems with up to two-way symmetric multiprocessing (SMP).

Windows application *n.* A software application designed for use with the Microsoft Windows environment.

Windows-based accelerator *n.* A type of super VGA (SVGA) video adapter designed specifically to run Windows and Windows-based applications more quickly. A Windows-based accelerator achieves performance improvements over a standard SVGA video adapter with the help of special routines built into the adapter's read-only memory. These routines relieve the Windows operating system of some of the video-related duties it must perform on a nonaccelerated system. Also called: Windows-based accelerator card. See also SVGA.

Windows CE *n.* A small operating system from Microsoft designed for use with handheld and palm-size PCs and in embedded systems, such as the AutoPC. Windows CE, which has a user interface that is similar to Windows 9x and Windows NT, includes scaled-down versions of several Microsoft applications, including Excel, Word, Internet Explorer, Schedule+, and an e-mail client. See also handheld PC.

Windows CE Services *n.* A set of technologies that makes Windows CE–based devices Web enabled. It provides the functionality to deliver Web content information to Windows CE–based devices from a wireless network or by desktop synchronisation.

Windows Distributed interNet Applications Architecture *n.* See Windows DNA.

Windows DNA *n.* Short for Microsoft **Windows D**istributed inter**N**et **A**pplications Architecture. A framework introduced in 1997 as a means of integrating client/server and Web technologies in the creation of scalable, multitier applications delivered over an enterprise network. Windows DNA is based on a number of technologies, among them COM (Component Object Model), ActiveX, and dynamic HTML.

Windows Driver Library *n.* A collection of hardware device drivers for a Microsoft Windows operating system that were not included in the original Windows package. Acronym: WDL. See also driver.

Windows Driver Model *n.* A 32-bit layered architecture for device and bus drivers that allows for drivers that can be used by both Windows NT and Windows 98. It provides common input/output services understood by both operating systems and supports Plug and Play, USB (Universal Serial Bus), IEEE 1394 bus, and various devices, including input, communication, imaging, and DVD. Acronym: WDM. Also called: Win32 Driver Model.

Windows Explorer *n.* A utility in Windows that enables the user to locate and open files and folders. Windows Explorer resembles the File Manager of Windows 3.1. The user can select folders from a list displayed on the left side of the screen and access files in a selected folder from a list displayed on the right side of the screen.

Windows Forms *n.* A rich Windows client library for building Windows client applications.

Windows Foundation Classes *n.* A Java class library for developing Java applications to run in the Windows environment. Designed by Microsoft to make it easy to write code for the Windows platform using the powerful Java programming language, the Windows Foundation Classes represent an object-oriented framework that encapsulates and unifies the Microsoft Win32 API and Dynamic HTML programming models. This framework enables developers to link Java code directly to Windows APIs. Acronym: WFC. See also Java, Java Foundation Classes.

Windows Image Acquisition *n.* A device-driver interface that supports still digital cameras and low-end and high-end scanners and allows retrieving of still images from IEEE 1394-based DV camcorders and USB-based Web cams. Acronym: WIA.

Windows IP Configuration *n.* See Winipcfg.

Windows Management Instrumentation *n.* A management infrastructure in Windows that supports monitoring and controlling system resources through a common set of interfaces and provides a logically organised, consistent model of Windows operation, configuration, and status. Acronym: WMI. See also resource.

Windows Me *n.* Released in 2000, the Windows Millennium Edition (Windows Me) operating system designed for home users as an upgrade from Windows 95 or Windows 98. Windows Me offers an improved home user experience including making it easier for users to share and manipulate digital photos, music, and videos, enhanced home networking capabilities, a rich Internet experience with support for broadband connections, different Internet communication tools, and online gaming.

Windows Media Audio *n.* A digital audio coding scheme developed by Microsoft that is used in distributing recorded music, usually over the Internet. Windows Media Audio shrinks the size of the audio file by a factor of 20 to 24 without seriously degrading the quality (CD-recording level) of the sound. Windows Media Audio files are given the file extension .wma and can be created with Windows Media Tools and played with the Windows Media Player. Acronym: WMA. See also Windows Media Technologies.

Windows Media Encoder *n.* A Windows Media technology that compresses live or prerecorded audio and video into a Windows Media stream, which can either be distributed immediately or saved as a Windows Media file for later distribution. The technology allows content developers to convert both live and prerecorded audio, video, and computer screen images to Windows Media Format for live and on-demand delivery. Windows Media Encoder also can save a stream as a Windows Media file and convert a file into Windows Media Format. Windows Media Encoder can distribute a stream via HTTP protocol. Also called: (if context is clear) Encoder, the encoder, the encoder engine.

Windows Media Player *n.* A client/control that receives a stream from a Windows Media server or local content for playback. It can run as a stand-alone client executable programme. Windows Media Player can also be embedded in a Web page, a C++ programme, or a Microsoft Visual Basic programme that uses the client ActiveX control.

Windows Media server *n.* A server on which Windows Media Services has been installed.

Windows Media Services *n.* A digital media platform that runs on a server, such as Windows 2000, to support streaming media, such as video and audio.

Windows Media Technologies *n.* Microsoft technologies for the creation, delivery, and playing of streaming audio and video over a network, including both intranets and the Internet. Windows Media Technologies, downloadable from the Microsoft Web site, support both live and on-demand (delivered from storage) content and are based on files delivered in Advanced Streaming Format (ASF). Three major components—Windows Media Tools, Windows Media Services, and Windows Media Player—comprise Windows Media Technologies.

Windows Media Tools *n.* See Windows Media Technologies.

Windows Messenger *n.* See .NET Messenger Service.

Windows Metafile Format *n.* A graphics file format used by Windows to store vector graphics in order to exchange graphics information between applications and to store information between sessions. Acronym: WMF. See also vector graphics.

Windows Movie Maker *n.* Software from Microsoft for capturing, editing, and arranging audio and video source material to create movies. Acronym: WMM.

Windows .NET Server *n.* The next generation of Windows servers. Built on Windows 2000, the Windows .NET Server family includes the functionality, dependability, scalability, and security options to serve as the computing foundation for businesses of all sizes. The flexible computing architecture, built on industry standards, allows businesses to create robust and innovative applications, improve collaboration across the organisation, and connect securely with customers.

Windows NT *n.* An operating system released by Microsoft Corporation in 1993. The Windows NT operating system, sometimes referred to as simply NT, is the high-end member of a family of operating systems from Microsoft. It is a completely self-contained operating system with a built-in graphical user interface. Windows NT is a 32-bit, preemptive multitasking operating system that features networking, symmetric multiprocessing, multithreading, and security. It is a portable operating system that can run on a variety of hardware platforms including those based on the Intel 80386, i486, and Pentium microprocessors and MIPS microprocessors; it can also run on multiprocessor computers. Windows NT supports up to 4 gigabytes of virtual memory and can run MS-DOS, POSIX, and OS/2 (character-mode) applications. See also MS-DOS, operating system, OS/2, POSIX, Windows.

Windows NT Advanced Server *n.* A superset of Windows NT that provides centralised, domain-based network management and security. Windows NT Advanced Server also offers advanced hard disk fault-tolerance features, such as mirroring and additional connectivity. See also Windows NT.

Windows NT Embedded *n.* A version of the Microsoft Windows NT operating system designed for devices and other products that have embedded systems. Windows NT Embedded, released in 1999, targets devices in the midrange to high end of the embedded device industry, including high-speed copiers, patient monitors, private branch exchanges (PBXs), and point-of-sale terminals. Windows NT Embedded features include headless operation (with no keyboard, mouse, or display devices needed), diskless operation, and remote management infrastructure. See also embedded system, Windows NT.

Windows Script Host *n.* The language-independent scripting host for Microsoft Windows platforms. Windows Script Host is a tool that allows users to run VBScript, JScript, or any other scripting language to automate common tasks and to create macros and logon scripts.

Windows Sockets *n.* See Winsock.

Windows terminal *n.* A thin-client solution from Microsoft, designed to enable terminals and minimally configured computers to display Windows applications even if they are not, in themselves, capable of running Windows software. Windows terminals work in conjunction with Windows NT Server, Terminal Server edition. See also thin client.

Windows XP *n.* A member of the Microsoft Windows family of operating systems. Windows XP was released in 2001 in two versions: Windows XP Home Edition for home use and Windows XP Professional for advanced home computing, businesses, and larger organisations. Windows XP features a new visual design that simplifies navigation and search capabilities, improved file management, additional media and Web publishing capabilities, an improved system for device discovery and installation, and advanced features for mobile computing.

WinG *n.* Short for Windows Games. An application programming interface for games in the Windows 9x environment. Under WinG, games can access the video frame buffer directly for increased speed. See also application programming interface, buffer[1], frame buffer.

WinHEC *n.* Short for Microsoft Windows Hardware Engineering Conference. Annual meeting of the computer hardware industry featuring forums, seminars, exhibits, and educational sessions for developers, technical managers, engineers, and product planners who use the Microsoft Windows family of operating systems.

Win.ini *n.* In Windows 3.x and MS-DOS, the initialisation file used to pass the programme configuration information necessary to run the Windows operating environment. The win.ini file has been supplanted by the registry database in Windows 95 and later and Windows NT and later. See also configuration file, ini file, registry.

Winipcfg *n.* Short for Windows IP Configuration. A Windows 9x utility that enables users to access information about their TCP/IP (Transmission Control Protocol/Internet Protocol) and network adapter card settings. Running the Winipcfg programme (winipcfg.exe) opens the IP Configuration window, which reveals the physical address, IP address, subnet mask, and default gateway settings of the primary TCP/IP adapter (or settings of multiple adapters if more than one is installed). This information is also helpful for troubleshooting. See also TCP/IP.

WINS *n.* Acronym for Windows Internet Naming Service. A Windows NT Server method for associating a computer's host name with its address. Also called: INS, Internet Naming Service.

Winsock *n.* Short for Windows Sockets. An application programming interface standard for software that provides a TCP/IP interface under Windows. The Winsock standard developed out of a Birds of a Feather (BOF) discussion that arose among software vendors at a UNIX conference in 1991; it has gained the general support of software developers, including Microsoft. See also application programming interface, BOF, socket (definition 1), sockets API, TCP/IP.

Wintel *adj.* Of, pertaining to, or characteristic of a computer that uses the Microsoft Windows operating system and an Intel central processing unit (CPU). See also Windows.

Wired *adj.* 1. Of, pertaining to, or characteristic of an electronic circuit or hardware grouping in which the configuration is determined by the physical interconnection of the components (as opposed to being programmable in software or alterable by a switch). See also hardwired (definition 1). 2. Knowledgeable about Internet resources, systems, and culture. 3. Having access to the Internet.

Wired Equivalent Privacy *n.* See WEP.

Wired home *n.* See smart home.

Wire-frame model *n.* In computer graphics applications such as CAD programmes, a representation of a three-dimensional object using separate lines that resemble strands of wire joined to create a model.

Wireless *adj.* Of, pertaining to, or characteristic of communications that take place without the use of interconnecting wires or cables, such as by radio, microwave, or infrared light.

Wireless Application Protocol *n.* A specification for a global standard for enabling digital cellular phones and other wireless devices to access Internet and other information services. The Wireless Application Protocol, or WAP, is supported by an organisation known as WAP Forum, which includes such members as Motorola, Nokia, L. M. Ericsson, and Unwired Planet. The goal of the forum is to create an open standard that works with different wireless technologies. Acronym: WAP.

Wireless communication *n.* Communication between a computer and another computer or device without wires. The form of wireless communication provided as part of the Windows operating system uses infrared light to transmit files. Radio frequencies, as used by cellular and cordless telephones, are another form of wireless communication. See also infrared, infrared device, infrared port.

Wireless Information Device *n.* See WID.

Wireless Internet *n.* Version of the Internet designed for use on wireless phones and handheld devices with small display screens, limited memory, and slower data transmission speeds than a personal computer. Most wireless Internet sites offer content as basic text with limited graphics.

Wireless LAN *n.* A LAN (local area network) that sends and receives data via radio, infrared optical signaling, or some other technology that does not require a physical connection between individual nodes and the hub. Wireless LANs are often used in office or factory settings where a user must carry a portable computer from place to place. Also called: WLAN.

Wireless Markup Language *n.* See WML.

Wireless Multimedia Forum *n.* See WMF (definition 2).

Wireless phone *n.* Telephone that operates by means of radio waves without a wire connection. A base station (cell tower) relays the phone's signal to a wireless carrier's network, where it is transmitted to another wireless phone or to a wired telephone network.

Wireless Services server component *n.* A component that allows a content provider or carrier to configure and schedule any number of information acquisition/encoding/transmission components to create a data stream to be transmitted by a carrier to a device. The server component builds on an open architecture to allow new server components to be installed in any part of the stream at any time.

Wireless Transaction Protocol *n.* A lightweight request/reply transaction protocol for devices with limited resources over networks with low to medium bandwidth. It is not called the

Wireless Transport Protocol or the Wireless Transfer Protocol. Acronym: WTP.

Wireless Transport Layer Security *n.* See WTLS.

Wire-pin printer *n.* See dot-matrix printer.

Wire-wrapped circuits *n.* Circuits constructed on perforated boards using wire instead of the metal traces found on printed circuit boards. The stripped ends of insulated wires are wrapped around the long pins of special wire-wrapped integrated circuit sockets. Wire-wrapped circuits are generally handmade, one-of-a-kind devices used for prototyping and research in electrical engineering.

Wiring closet *n.* A room or location in a building where telecommunications and/or networking equipment such as hubs, switches, and routers are installed. Also called: data closet, telecom closet, telecommunications closet.

Wizard *n.* 1. Someone who is adept at making computers perform their "magic." A wizard is an outstanding and creative programmer or a power user. 2. A participant in a multiuser dungeon (MUD) who has permission to control the domain, even to delete other players' characters. See also MUD. 3. An interactive help utility within an application that guides the user through each step of a particular task, such as starting up a word processing document in the correct format for a business letter.

Wizzywig *n.* See WYSIWYG.

WLAN *n.* See wireless LAN.

WMA *n.* Acronym for Windows Media Audio. See Windows Media Audio.

.wmf *n.* A file extension that identifies a vector image encoded as a Microsoft Windows Metafile.

WMF *n.* 1. See Windows Metafile Format. 2. Acronym for Wireless Multimedia Forum. A consortium of technology companies formed to promote open standards for wireless streaming products. WMF members include Cisco Systems, Intel, and the Walt Disney Internet Group. See also ISMA.

WMI *n.* See Windows Management Instrumentation.

WML *n.* Acronym for Wireless Markup Language. A markup language developed for Web sites that are accessed with microbrowsers on Wireless Application Protocol (WAP)-enabled devices. A Web site written with WML would be viewable on handheld devices with small screens, such as cell phones. See also markup language, microbrowser, Wireless Application Protocol.

WMLScript *n.* A scripting language derived from the Java-Script language for use in the development of Wireless Markup Language (WML).

WMM *n.* See Windows Movie Maker.

Word *n.* The native unit of storage on a particular machine. A word is the largest amount of data that can be handled by the microprocessor in one operation and also, as a rule, is the width of the main data bus. Word sizes of 16 bits and 32 bits are the most common.

Word *n.* Microsoft's word processing software, available for the Windows and Macintosh platforms. In addition to extensive editing, formatting, and customisation features, Word provides such tools as automatic text completion and correction. The most recent version, Word 2002 (part of Office XP) adds Web functionality—for example, the ability to save documents in HTML format. The first version, Microsoft Word for MS-DOS 1.00, was introduced in 1983.

Word-addressable processor *n.* A processor that cannot access an individual byte of memory but can access a larger unit. In order to perform operations on an individual byte, the processor must read and write memory in the larger unit. See also central processing unit.

WordPerfect Office *n.* A suite of business application programmes from Corel Corporation. The basic (Standard Edition) WordPerfect Office suite includes the WordPerfect word processor, Quattro Pro spreadsheet, Corel Presentations presentation software, CorelCENTRAL personal information manager, Microsoft Visual Basic for Applications scripting tools, and Trellix Web publisher. A home and small-business package, the Voice-Powered Edition, adds speech recognition and publishing products; a business and corporate package, the Professional Edition, adds database and Internet tools to all of the preceding.

Word processing *n.* The act of entering and editing text with a word processor. Acronym: WP.

Word processor *n.* An application programme for creating and manipulating text-based documents. A word processor is the electronic equivalent of paper, pen, typewriter, eraser, and, most likely, dictionary and thesaurus. Depending on the programme and the equipment in use, word processors can display documents either in text mode (using highlighting, underlining, or colour to represent italics, boldfacing, and other such formatting) or in graphics mode (in which formatting and, sometimes, a variety of fonts appear on the screen as they will on the printed page). All word processors offer at least limited facilities for document formatting, such as font changes, page layout, paragraph indentation, and the like. Some word processors can also check spelling, find synonyms, incorporate graphics created with another programme, align mathematical formulas, create and print form letters, perform calculations, display documents in multiple onscreen windows, and enable users to record macros that simplify difficult or repetitive operations.

Wordwrap or word wrap *n.* The ability of a word processing programme or a text-editing programme to break lines of text automatically to stay within the page margins or window boundaries of a document without the user having to do so with carriage returns, as is typically necessary when using a typewriter. See also hard return, soft return.

Workaround *n.* A tactic for accomplishing a task despite a bug or other inadequacy in software or hardware without actually fixing the underlying problem. See also kludge.

Workbook *n.* In a spreadsheet programme, a file containing a number of related worksheets. See also worksheet.

Workflow application *n.* A set of programmes that aids in the tracking and management of all the activities in a project from start to finish.

Workgroup *n.* A group of users working on a common project and sharing computer files, typically over a LAN (local area network). See also groupware.

Workgroup computing *n.* A method of working electronically in which various individuals on the same project share resources and access to files using a network arrangement, such as a local area network, enabling them to coordinate their separate tasks. This is accomplished through using software designed for workgroup computing. See also groupware.

Workplace Shell *n.* The graphical user interface of OS/2. Like the Mac OS and Windows 95, the Workplace Shell is document-centric. Document files are displayed as icons; clicking an icon starts the corresponding application, and the user can print a document by dragging the document's icon to a printer icon. The Workplace Shell uses the graphical functions of Presentation Manager. Acronym: WPS.

Worksheet *n.* In a spreadsheet programme, a page organised into rows and columns appearing on screen and used for constructing a single table.

Workstation *n.* 1. A combination of input, output, and computing hardware that can be used for work by an individual. 2. A powerful stand-alone computer of the sort used in computer-aided design and other applications requiring a high-end, usually expensive, machine with considerable calculating or graphics capability. 3. A microcomputer or terminal connected to a network.

World Wide Web *n.* The total set of interlinked hypertext documents residing on HTTP servers all around the world. Documents on the World Wide Web, called pages or Web pages, are written in HTML (Hypertext Markup Language), identified by URLs (Uniform Resource Locators) that specify the particular machine and pathname by which a file can be accessed, and transmitted from server to end user under HTTP

(Hypertext Transfer Protocol). Codes, called tags, embedded in an HTML document associate particular words and images in the document with URLs so that a user can access another file, which may be halfway around the world, at the press of a key or the click of a mouse. These files may contain text (in a variety of fonts and styles), graphics images, movie files, and sounds as well as Java applets, ActiveX controls, or other small embedded software programmes that execute when the user activates them by clicking a link. A user visiting a Web page also may be able to download files from an FTP site and send messages to other users via e-mail by using links on the Web page. The World Wide Web was developed by Timothy Berners-Lee in 1989 for the European Laboratory for Particle Physics, or Conseil Européen pour le Recherche Nucléaire, in French (CERN). Acronym: WWW. Also called: w^3, W3, Web. See also ActiveX controls, HTML, HTTP, HTTP server (definition 2), Java applet, URL.

World Wide Web Consortium *n.* See W3C.

Worm *n.* A programme that propagates itself across computers, usually by creating copies of itself in each computer's memory. A worm might duplicate itself in one computer so often that it causes the computer to crash. Sometimes written in separate segments, a worm is introduced surreptitiously into a host system either as a prank or with the intent of damaging or destroying information. See also bacterium, Internet Worm, Trojan horse, virus.

WORM *n.* Acronym for write once, read many. A type of optical disc that can be read and reread but cannot be altered after it has been recorded. WORMs are high-capacity storage devices. Because they cannot be erased and rerecorded, they are suited to storing archives and other large bodies of unchanging information. See also compact disc.

WOSA *n.* Acronym for Windows Open Services Architecture, also known as Windows Open System Architecture. A set of application programming interfaces from Microsoft that is intended to enable Windows-based applications from different vendors to communicate with each other, such as over a network. The interfaces within the WOSA standard include Open Database Connectivity (ODBC), the Messaging Application Programming Interface (MAPI), the Telephony Application Programming Interface (TAPI), Windows Sockets (Winsock), and Microsoft Remote Procedure Calls (RPC). See also MAPI, ODBC, remote procedure call, TAPI, Winsock.

.wp *n.* A file extension used to identify files formatted for the WordPerfect word processor.

WP *n.* See word processing.

WPS *n.* See Workplace Shell.

WRAM *n.* Acronym for window random access memory. A type of RAM used in video adapters. Like video RAM (VRAM), WRAM allows the screen to be repainted while a graphical image is being written, but WRAM is faster.

Wrap around *vb.* To continue movement, as with the cursor or a search operation, to the beginning or to a new starting point rather than stopping when the end of a series is reached. For example, the screen cursor might wrap around to the first column of the next line rather than stopping when it reaches the last column of the current line. Likewise, a programme starting a search or replace operation in the middle of a document might be instructed to wrap around to the beginning rather than stop when it reaches the end of the document.

Wrapper *n.* In the Java programming language, an object that encapsulates and delegates to another object with the aim of altering its behaviour or interface. See also Java, object.

.wri *n.* The file format that identifies document files in the Microsoft Write format.

Wrist support *n.* A device placed in front of a computer keyboard to support the wrists in an ergonomically neutral position, thereby safeguarding against repetitive strain injuries, such as carpal tunnel syndrome. Also called: wrist rest. See also carpal tunnel syndrome, repetitive strain injury.

Write 1 *n.* A transfer of information to a storage device, such as a disk, or to an output device, such as a monitor or a printer.

For example, a disk write means that information is transferred from memory to storage on disk. See also output1.

Write 2 *vb.* To transfer information either to a storage device, such as a disk, or to an output device, such as a monitor or a printer. Writing is the means by which a computer provides the results of processing. A computer can also be said to write to the screen when it displays information on the monitor. See also output1.

Write access *n.* A privilege on a computer system that allows a user to save, change, or delete stored data. Write access is usually set by the system administrator for a networked or server system and by the owner of the computer for a stand-alone machine. See also access privileges.

Write-back cache *n.* A type of cache with the following feature: when changes are made to cached data, they are not simultaneously made to the original data as well. Instead, the changed data is marked, and the original data is updated when the cached data is deallocated. A write-back cache can perform more quickly than a write-through cache. But in some contexts, differences between cached and original data could lead to problems, and write-through caches must be used. See also cache.

Write-behind cache *n.* A form of temporary storage in which data is held, or cached, for a short time in memory before being written on disk for permanent storage. Caching improves system performance in general by reducing the number of times the computer must go through the relatively slow process of reading from and writing to disk. See also CPU cache, disk cache.

Write cache *n.* See write-behind cache.

Write error *n.* An error encountered while a computer is in the process of transferring information from memory to storage or to another output device.

Write mode *n.* In computer operation, the state in which a programme can write (record) information in a file. In write mode, the programme is permitted to make changes to existing information.

Write protect *vb.* To prevent the writing (recording) of information, usually on a disk. Either a floppy disk or an individual file on a floppy disk or a hard disk can be write protected (though not necessarily infallibly). See also write-protect notch.

Write-protect notch *n.* A small opening in the jacket of a floppy disk that can be used to make the disk unwritable. On a 5.25-inch floppy disk, the write-protect notch is a rectangular hole on the edge of the disk jacket. When this notch is covered, a computer can read from the disk but cannot record new information on it. On 3.5-inch micro-floppy disks that are enclosed in plastic shells, the write-protect notch is an opening in a corner. When the sliding tab in this opening is moved to uncover a small hole, the disk is protected and cannot be written to. Also called: write-protect tab. See also write[2].

Write-protect tab *n.* See write-protect notch.

Write-through cache *n.* A type of cache in which changes made to cached data are simultaneously made in the original copy, rather than being marked for later updating. A write-through cache, though not as fast as a write-back cache, is needed in situations where problems would occur if both the original and cached data did not match.

.wrl *n.* File extension required for saving all Virtual Reality Modeling Language (VRML) documents; for example, cube.wrl. See also VRML.

WSDL *n.* Acronym for Web Services Description Language. An XML format developed to allow for better interoperability among Web services and development tools. WSDL describes network services as collections of communication endpoints capable of exchanging messages and is extensible to allow description of endpoints and their messages regardless of what message formats or network protocols are used to communicate.

WSS *n.* See Web Storage System.

WTLS *n.* Acronym for Wireless Transport Layer Security. A security protocol that provides encryption and authentication services for the Wireless Application Protocol (WAP). The WTLS layer uses data integrity, authentication, and encryption mechanisms to provide end-to-end security and privacy for wireless transactions. WTLS is based on Transport Layer Security (TLS), a Secure Socket Layer equivalent used with Internet applications. See also Wireless Application Protocol.

WWW *n.* See World Wide Web.

WYSBYGI *adj.* Acronym for What You See Before You Get It. Providing a preview of the effects of the changes the user has selected before the changes are finally applied. For example, a dialog box in a word processing programme might display a sample of the font a user has chosen before the font is actually changed in the document. The user can cancel any changes after previewing them, and the document will be unaffected. See also WYSIWYG.

WYSIWYG *adj.* Acronym for What You See Is What You Get, pronounced "wizzywig." Allowing a user to view a document as it will appear in the final product, and to directly edit the text, graphics, or other elements within that view. A WYSIWYG language is often easier to use than a markup language, which provides no immediate visual feedback regarding the changes being made.

X

X10 *n.* A popular communications protocol for powerline carrier (PLC) systems that uses existing electrical wiring in a home or building for home networking. X10 uses RF signals to communicate between transmitters and receivers. See also home automation, home network, powerline carrier system.

X.200 *n.* See X series.

X.25 *n.* A recommendation published by the ITU-T (formerly CCITT) international communications standards organisation that defines the connection between a terminal and a packet-switching network. X.25 incorporates three definitions: the electrical connection between the terminal and the network, the transmission or link-access protocol, and the implementation of virtual circuits between network users. Taken together, these definitions specify a synchronous, full-duplex terminal-to-network connection. Packet format, error control, and other features are equivalent to portions of the HDLC (High-level Data Link Control) protocol defined by the International Organisation for Standardisation (ISO). See also CCITT X series, HDLC, packet switching, virtual circuit.

X3D *n.* Acronym for 3D XML. An XML-based 3-D graphics specification incorporating the behaviour capabilities of the Virtual Reality Modeling Language (VRML). X3D is compatible with existing VRML content and tools and supports full integration with other XML-based technologies. The X3D specification was developed and administered by the Web 3D Consortium.

x86 *n.* Any computer based on an 8086, 80286, 80386, 80486, or Pentium microprocessor.

x-axis *n.* The horizontal reference line on a grid, chart, or graph that has horizontal and vertical dimensions. See also Cartesian coordinates.

Xbase *n.* A generic name for a family of database languages based on dBASE, a copyrighted product of the Ashton-Tate Corporation. Xbase languages have since developed characteristics of their own and are now only partly compatible with the dBASE family. Xbase primarily refers to three different file types (.dbf, .dbt, and .ndx). Also called: xBase, xbase, XBase.

Xbox *n.* A video game console developed by Microsoft Corporation and released in 2001. Powered by an Intel 733-MHz processor, the Xbox delivers increased graphics capability over previously released game consoles and provides extensive storage capacity for gaming information. Peripherals plug into four game controller ports. An Ethernet port enables online gaming via a broadband connection. See also computer game, console game, GameCube, PlayStation.

X button *n.* See close button.

XCMD *n.* Short for external command. An external code resource used in HyperCard, a hypermedia programme developed for the Macintosh. See also HyperCard, XFCN.

X Consortium *n.* The body, composed of several hardware firms, that governed the standards for the X Window System. The Open Group's X Project Team now has responsibility for the X Window System. See also X Window System.

xDSL *n.* An umbrella term for all of the digital subscriber line (DSL) technologies, which use a variety of modulation schemes to pack data onto copper wires. The x is a placeholder for the first or first two letters of a member technology, which might be ADSL, HDSL, IDSL, RADSL, or SDSL. See also DSL.

XENIX *n.* A version of UNIX that was originally adapted by Microsoft for Intel-based personal computers. Although it has been sold by many vendors, including Microsoft, Intel, and the Santa Cruz Operation (SCO), it has become principally identified with SCO. See also UNIX.

Xerography *n.* See electrophotography.

Xerox Network System *n.* See XNS.

Xerox PARC *n.* Short for Xerox Palo Alto Research Center. Xerox's research and development facility in Palo Alto, California. Xerox PARC is the birthplace of such innovations as the local area network (LAN), the laser printer, and the graphical user interface (GUI).

XFCN *n.* Short for external function. An external code resource that returns a value after it has completed executing. XFCNs are used in HyperCard, a hypermedia programme developed for the Macintosh. See also HyperCard, XCMD.

XFDL *n.* Short for Extensible Forms Description Language. a document description language introduced and submitted to the World Wide Web Committee in 1998 by the Canadian Internet forms company UWI.Com. XFDL is an XML-based language for describing complex forms, such as legal and government documents. It is designed to allow for interactivity yet remain consistent with Internet standards.

XGA *n.* See Extended Graphics Array.

X-height *n.* In typography, the height of the lowercase letter x in a particular font. The x-height thus represents the height of the body only of a lowercase letter, excluding ascenders (such as the top of the letter b) and descenders (such as the tail on the letter g). See also ascender, descender.

XHTML *n.* Short for Extensible Hypertext Markup Language. A markup language incorporating elements of HTML and XML. Web sites designed using XHTML can be more readily displayed on handheld computers and digital phones equipped with microbrowsers. XHTML was released for comments by the World Wide Web Consortium (W3C) in September 1999. See also HTML, microbrowser, XML.

XIP *n.* See execute in place.

XLANG *n.* A derivative XML language that describes the logical sequencing of business processes, as well as the implementation of the business process by using various application services.

XLink *n.* An XML language that provides a set of attributes that are used to create links between resources. XLink provides complex extended linking, link behaviour, and management capabilities. XLink is able to describe links that connect sets of resources, point to multiple targets, or serve multiple roles within an XML document.

XLL *n.* Acronym for eXtensible Linking Language. Broad term intended to denote the family of XML linking/pointing/ addressing languages, which include XLink, XPointer, and XPath.

XMI *n.* 1. Acronym for XML Metadata Interchange Format. An object-based model for exchanging programme data across the Internet. XMI is sponsored by IBM, Unisys, and others and was submitted as a proposed standard to the Object Management Group (OMG); it is now one of OMG's recommended technologies. XMI is designed to allow for storing and sharing programming information and exchanging data among tools, applications, and storage locations through a network or the Internet so that software developers can collaborate on applications, even if they are not all using the same development tools. 2. As XMI bus, a 64-bit parallel bus supported on certain DEC and Alpha-Server processors. An XMI bus is capable of transferring data, exclusive of addressing overhead, at 100 Mbps.

XML *n.* Acronym for eXtensible Markup Language, a condensed form of SGML (Standard Generalised Markup Language). XML lets Web developers and designers create customised tags that offer greater flexibility in organising and presenting information than is possible with the older HTML document coding system. XML is defined as a language standard published by the W3C and supported by the industry. See also SGML.

XML attribute *n.* Information added to a tag to provide more information about the tag, such as <ingredient quantity="2"units="cups">flour</ingredient>.

XML element *n.* Information delimited by a start tag and an end tag in an extensible Markup Language (XML) document. An example would be <Lastname> Davalio</Last Name>.

XML entities *n.* Combinations of characters and symbols that replace other characters when an XML document is parsed, usually those that have other meanings in XML. For example, < represents the < symbol, which is also the opening bracket for a tag.

XML Metadata Interchange Format *n.* See XMI (definition 1).

XML-RPC *n.* Acronym for eXtensible Markup Language-Remote Procedure Call. A set of XML-based implementations that allows cross-platform and cross-programming language procedure calls over the Internet. XML-RPC permits complex data structures to be transmitted, processed, and returned between different operating systems running in different environments.

XML Schema *n.* A specification providing a common base for data description and validation in XML environments. XML schema replaces Document Type Definition (DTD) by defining a greater set of data types with more explicit data descriptions. XML schema has been developed as an open, vendor-neutral format to enhance information exchange and e-commerce over the Internet. It is also a standard for the description and encoding of data.

XML Schema Description Language *n.* See XSDL.

XML stylesheet *n.* Contains formatting rules that are applied to an XML file referencing the stylesheet. The standard set of rules for XML stylesheets is the Extensible Stylesheet Language (XSL). See also XSL.

XML Web services *n.* Units of application logic providing data and services to other applications. Applications access XML Web services via standard Web protocols and data formats such as HTTP, XML, and SOAP, independent of how each XML Web service is implemented. XML Web services combine the best aspects of component-based development and the Web and are a cornerstone of the Microsoft .NET programming model.

Xmodem *n.* A file transfer protocol used in asynchronous communications that transfers information in blocks of 128 bytes.

Xmodem 1K *n.* A version of the Xmodem file transfer protocol designed for larger, longer-distance file transfers. Xmodem 1K transmits information in 1-kilobyte (1024-byte) blocks and uses a more reliable form of error checking. See also Xmodem.

Xmodem-CRC *n.* An enhanced version of the Xmodem file transfer protocol that incorporates a 2-byte cyclical redundancy check (CRC) to detect transmission errors. See also CRC.

XMS *n.* See extended memory specification.

XMT *n.* Short for transmit. A signal used in serial communications.

XNS *n.* Acronym for Xerox Network System. A set of protocols assigned to five numbered layers (0 through 4) that form a suite designed to handle packaging and delivery of network transmissions.

XON/XOFF *n.* An asynchronous communications protocol in which the receiving device or computer uses special characters to control the flow of data from the transmitting device or computer. When the receiving computer cannot continue to receive data, it transmits an XOFF control character that tells the sender to stop transmitting; when transmission can resume, the computer signals the sender with an XON character. Also called: software handshake. See also handshake.

XOR *n.* See exclusive OR.

XOR encryption *n.* Short for Exclusive-OR encryption. A simple encryption scheme using the "exclusive-or" concept, in which a decision is based on only one of two conditions being met. Using a provided key, XOR encryption performs an exclusive-or process on each byte of data to be encrypted. Because XOR encryption is not a strong security tool used alone, it is typically used as an additional level of security for Internet transmission of sensitive information.

XPath *n.* An XML language for addressing items in an XML document by specifying a path through the document structure. XPath is used by XPointer and XSLT to locate and identify XML document data. XPath is also considered a query language complement to XQuery. XPath is more supported than XQuery even though there is no approved standard yet for either. See also XPointer.

XPointer *n.* An XML language used to locate data within an XML document based on data property descriptions, such as attributes, location, and content. XPointer references the internal structure of a document, allowing links to be made to occurrences of a word, character set, content attribute, or other element, rather than to a specific point within the document. See also XPath.

XQuery *n.* Short for eXtensible Query Language. Designed to be a functional query language that is broadly applicable to a variety of XML data types derived from Quilt, XPath, and XQL. Both Ipedo and Software AG implement their own versions of the W3C's proposed specification for the XQuery language. Also called: XML Query, XQL.

XSD *n.* Acronym for eXtensible Schema Definition. A prefix used by convention to indicate a W3C schema namespace.

XSDL *n.* Acronym for XML Schema Description Language. A World Wide Web Consortium (W3C) recommendation for representing XML structure. XSDL is capable of describing complex XML-based data structures, and provides options not available with Document Type Definitions (DTDs), including namespace support, XML datatypes, and improved extensibility and data type support.

X series *n.* A set of recommendations adopted by the International Telecommunication Union Telecommunication Standardisation Sector (ITU-T), formerly the CCITT, and International Organisation for Standardisation (ISO) for standardising equipment and protocols used in both public access and private computer networks. See the table X.1.

XSL *n.* Acronym for Extensible Stylesheet Language. A World Wide Web Consortium (W3C) standard stylesheet language for XML documents. XSL determines how data in an XML document is displayed on the Web. XSL controls what data will be displayed, in what format, and in what type size and style. XSL contains two major extensions: XSL Transformations (XSLT), a language used to convert XML documents to HTML or other document types, and XSL Formatting Objects (XSL-FO), a language for specifying formatting semantics. See also XSL-FO, XSLT.

Table X.1 Recommendations in X Series for Network Communications.

Recommendation Number	What It Covers
X.25	Interface required to connect a computer to a packet-switched network such as the Internet
X.75	Protocols for connecting two public data networks
X.200	Seven-layer set of protocols known as the ISO/OSI reference model for standardising computer-to-computer connections
X.400	Format at the ISO/OSI application layer for e-mail messages over various network transports, including Ethernet, X.25, and TCP/IP. Gateways must be used to translate e-mail messages between the X.400 and Internet -formats
X.445	Asynchronous Protocol Specification, which governs the transmission of X.400 messages over dial-up telephone lines
X.500	Protocols for client/server systems that maintain and access directories of users and resources in X.400 form
X.509	Digital certificates

XSL-FO *n.* Acronym for Extensible Stylesheet Language Formatting Objects. An XML-based markup language for specifying formatting semantics. XSL-FO allows format and style information to be applied to an XML document and can be used with XSLT to produce source documents. See also XSL.

XSLT *n.* Acronym for Extensible Stylesheet Language Transformations. A language used in transforming an existing XML document into a restructured XML document. Formalised as a W3C Recommendation in 1999, XSLT is primarily intended for use as part of XSL. XSL describes the styling of a document in terms of XSLT transformations into an XML document. See also XML, XSL.

X terminal *n.* An intelligent display device, connected to an Ethernet network, that performs operations on request from client applications in an X Window System. See also Ethernet (definition 1), X Window System.

XT keyboard *n.* See PC/XT keyboard.

XUL *n.* A standards-based interface description language that provides a standard way to exchange data describing a program's user interface. XUL balances simplicity, flexibility, and ease of use with precise layout control. XUL was developed by Netscape and Mozilla and is used with XML, CSS, DOM, and HTML.

X Windows *n.* See X Window System.

X Window System *n.* A nonproprietary standardised set of display-handling routines, developed at MIT. Most often encountered on UNIX workstations, the X Window System is independent of hardware and operating system. An X Window System client calls on the server, which is located on the user's workstation, to provide a window in which the client can generate a display of text or graphics. Also called: X Windows. See also X Consortium.

X-Y display *n.* See vector display.

x-y matrix *n.* An arrangement of rows and columns with a horizontal (x) axis and a vertical (y) axis.

x-y plotter *n.* See plotter.

x-y-z coordinate system *n.* A three-dimensional system of Cartesian coordinates that includes a third (z) axis running perpendicular to the horizontal (x) and vertical (y) axes. The x-y-z coordinate system is used in computer graphics for creating models with length, breadth and depth.

Y

Y2K *n.* See Year 2000 problem.

Y2K BIOS patch card *n.* An ISA board that ensures that system calls to the BIOS return the correct year. The BIOS patch card checks the date the BIOS gets from the real-time clock and sends the correct date to whichever application or process requested it. While a BIOS patch card proved effective for most situations once the year 2000 was reached, some applications and processes that work directly with the real-time clock (not an advisable practice) actually received the wrong date on non-Year-2000-compliant PCs.

Y2K BIOS test *n.* See BIOS test.

Y2K bug *n.* See Year 2000 problem.

Y2K-compliant *adj.* See Year 2000 compliant.

Y2K computer bug *n.* See Year 2000 problem.

Y2K ready *adj.* See Year 2000 compliant.

Yahoo! *n.* The first major online Web-based directory and search engine for Internet resources, which can be found at http://www.yahoo.com. See also search engine (definition 2).

Yahoo! Mail *n.* A popular Web-based e-mail service provided for free by Yahoo! Inc.

Yahoo! Messenger *n.* A popular instant-messaging application provided for free by Yahoo! Inc. on a variety of operating systems. See also instant messaging.

Yanoff list *n.* The informal name of the Internet services list created and maintained by Scott Yanoff. The Yanoff list was one of the earliest directories of Internet services and resources. It is located at http://www.spectracom.com/islist/.

y-axis *n.* The vertical reference line on a grid, chart, or graph that has horizontal and vertical dimensions. See also Cartesian coordinates.

YB *n.* See yottabyte.

Year 2000 compliant *adj.* The criteria for this varied among companies and organisations; however, a general theme was that software or hardware would make the transition from 1999 to 2000 without producing errors. For a PC, the general thinking was that if the real-time clock passed a Year 2000 BIOS test, it was Year 2000 compliant. However, testing the computing environment from end to end, considering the readiness of the operating systems, applications, custom code, data, and system interfaces, was also strongly recommended.

Year 2000 Information and Readiness Disclosure Act *n.* A U.S. statute enacted in October 1998 that required U.S. companies to publicly disclose how they were attempting to make their systems or products ready for the year 2000. Many companies made this information available on the World Wide Web.

Year 2000 problem *n.* Prior to January 1, 2000, a potential software problem stemming from the use of two digits (99) rather than four (1999) as year indicators in computer programmes. Such programmes assumed that 19 preceded every year value, and so could potentially fail or produce incorrect calculations by interpreting the year 2000 (00) as an earlier date than 19xx when the year rolled over into a new century. The use of two-digit year indicators was prevalent in, though not limited to, older programmes that had been written when a saving of two bytes (digits) per year value was significant in terms of computer memory. Because the use of two-digit year indicators was widespread, companies, governments, and other organisations took measures on a large scale to prevent the Year 2000 problem from affecting their computing systems. In the end, however, the problem—luckily—proved largely uneventful.

Year 2000 ready *adj.* See Year 2000 compliant.

Year 2000 rollover *n.* The moment when the year in a computer system changed from 1999 to 2000. Also called: date rollover, millennium transition, rollover, Year 2000 transition.

Year 2000 time problem *n.* See Year 2000 problem.

Year 2000 transition *n.* See Year 2000 rollover.

Yellow Pages *n.* 1. The former name of a UNIX utility, provided by SunSoft (Sun Microsystems system software), that maintains a central database of names and locations of the resources on a network. The Yellow Pages enables processes on any node to locate resources by name. This utility is now known formally as NIS (Network Information Service). 2. InterNIC Registration Services' database of domain names and their IP addresses. See also domain name, IP address. 3. Any of several Internet business directory services. Some are print publications, some are strictly electronic, and some are both.

Yes/No data type *n.* A data type used to define database fields that will contain only one of two values, such as Yes or No and True or False. Null values are not allowed. See also boolean.

Yettie *n.* Short for Young, Entrepreneurial Tech-based Twenty-something or Young, Entrepreneurial Technocrat. A person who works in a technology or Internet-related field and who embraces technological change and opportunity. Yettie is intended to be a successor to the older term "yuppie."

YHBT *n.* Acronym for you have been trolled. An expression used in e-mail and newsgroups to indicate that the receiver has taken a deliberately set bait. See also troll.

YHL *n.* Acronym for you have lost. An expression used in e-mail and newsgroups, often following YHBT. See also YHBT.

Ymodem *n.* A variation of the Xmodem file transfer protocol that includes the following enhancements: the ability to transfer information in 1-kilobyte (1024-byte) blocks, the ability to send multiple files (batch file transmission), cyclical redundancy checking (CRC), and the ability to abort transfer by transmitting two CAN (cancel) characters in a row. See also CRC, Xmodem.

Yocto- prefix A metric prefix meaning 10^{-24} (one septillionth in the U.S. system).

Yoke *n.* The part of a CRT (cathode-ray tube) that deflects the electron beam, causing it to strike a specific area on the screen. Also called: deflection coils. See also CRT.

Yotta- prefix A metric prefix meaning 10^{24} (one septillion in the U.S. system).

Yottabyte *n.* A unit of measure equal to 2^{80} bytes, or approximately 1 septillion (10^{24}) bytes. When calculated as a multiple of 1000 zettabytes (the next highest unit of measure), a yottabyte is 1,000,000,000,000,000,000,000,000 bytes; when calculated as 1024 zettabytes, a yottabyte is 1,208,925,819,614,629,174,706,176 bytes. The prefix yotta- is meant to sound like the Greek letter iota. Abbreviation: YB.

YY *n.* The form in which the year part of a date is stored in some, mostly older, computer systems. Before 2000, the possibility existed that computers that used a 2-digit date would incorrectly interpret the year 2000 (year 00) as the year 1900 and disrupt the computer's operation.

YYYY *n.* Symbolic of providing fully distinguished dates, including 4-digit years. Using 4-digit years was an important step in many Year 2000 remediation programmes—especially those focused on data.

Z

.z *n.* The file extension identifying a UNIX file compressed using the gzip or compact utility. See also gzip.

.Z *n.* The file extension for UNIX files that have been compressed using the compress utility. See also compress.

Z39.50 standard *n.* A specification for a query language based on SQL (structured query language). It is used by WAIS, among other Internet services, to search for files through the use of keywords and is widely used for remote access to library catalogs. See also structured query language, WAIS.

Z80 *n.* An 8-bit microprocessor from Zilog, a company founded by former Intel engineers. The Z80 has a 16-bit address bus, yielding a 64-kilobyte addressable memory space, and an 8-bit data bus. A descendant of the Intel 8080, it was the favoured processor in the days of the CP/M operating system. One of the most popular computers of the early 1980s, the Radio Shack TRS-80, was based on this chip. See also CP/M.

zap *vb.* 1. To erase permanently. For example, to zap a file means to remove it without hope of retrieval. 2. To damage a device, usually by discharging static electricity through it.

Z-axis *n.* The third axis in a three-dimensional coordinate system, used in computer graphics to represent depth. See also Cartesian coordinates, coordinate system.

ZB *n.* See zettabyte.

Zepto- prefix A metric prefix meaning 10^{-21} (one sextillionth in the American system).

Zero1 *n.* The arithmetic symbol (0) representing no magnitude.

Zero2 *vb.* To fill or replace with zeros (for example, to zero a specified portion of memory, a field, or some other limited structure).

Zero divide *n.* A division operation in which the divisor is zero. Division by zero is mathematically undefined, is not allowed in a programme, and is considered a bug.

Zero flag *n.* A flag (bit) in a microprocessor that is set (turned on), typically in a flag register, when the result of an operation is zero. See also flag (definition 1).

Zero-insertion-force socket *n.* See ZIF socket.

Zero-length string *n.* A string that contains no characters. You can use a zero-length string to indicate that you know there's no value for a field. You enter a zero-length string by typing two double quotation marks with no space between them ("").

Zero out *vb.* To set a variable value or a series of bits to zero.

Zero suppression *n.* The elimination of leading (nonsignificant) zeros in a number. For example, zero suppression would truncate 000123.456 to 123.456. See also significant digits.

Zero wait state *n.* The condition of random access memory (RAM) that is fast enough to respond to the processor without requiring wait states. See also wait state.

Zetta- prefix A metric prefix meaning 10^{21} (one sextillion in the American system).

Zettabyte *n.* A unit of measure equal to 2^{70} bytes, or one sextillion (10^{21}) bytes. When calculated as a multiple of 1000 exabytes (the next highest unit of measure), a zettabyte is 1,000,000,000,000,000,000,000 bytes; when calculated as 1024 exabytes, a zettabyte is 1,180,591,620,717,411,303,424 bytes. The prefix (zetta-) is meant to sound like the Greek letter zeta.Abbreviation: ZB.

Z-fold paper *n.* See fanfold paper.

ZIF socket *n.* Short for zero-insertion-force socket. A kind of socket for integrated circuits that can be opened with a lever or screw, allowing the chip to be placed in the socket without the application of pressure. The lever or screw of the socket is then closed, causing the socket contacts to grip the chip's pins. ZIF sockets facilitate frequent insertion and removal of chips, but they take up more space and are more expensive than conventional sockets.

Zinc-air battery *n.* Non rechargeable battery that is relatively inexpensive, offers extended battery life, and contains none of the harsh chemicals or metals found in conventional nickel metal cadmium (NiCad), nickel metal hydride (NiMH), or lithium ion (Li-ion) batteries.

.zip *n.* A file extension that identifies a compressed archive file encoded in ZIP format, as by PKZIP. See also compressed file, PKZIP.

Zip drive *n.* A disk drive developed by Iomega that uses 3.5-inch removable disks (Zip disks) capable of storing 100 megabytes of data. See also disk drive.

Zmodem *n.* An enhancement of the Xmodem file transfer protocol that handles larger data transfers with less error. Zmodem includes a feature called checkpoint restart, which resumes transmission at the point of interruption, rather than at the beginning, if the communications link is broken during data transfer. See also Xmodem.

Zombie *n.* A computer that has become the unwilling host of a DDoS (distributed denial of services) attack programme and that is controlled by remote signals from the attacker. To create a zombie, a hacker utilises security vulnerabilities to crack a Web, mail, news, or application server and plant hidden DDoS tools such as Trinoo and Tribal Flood Network. Later, at a signal from the attacker, the server becomes a zombie that will participate in a coordinated attack on other servers. See also DDoS, hacker.

Zone *n.* 1. On a LAN (local area network), a subgroup of users within a larger group of interconnected networks. 2. In Macintosh programming, a portion of memory that is allocated and reallocated by the memory manager facility as memory is requested and released by applications and by other parts of the operating system. See also heap (definition 1).

Zone header *n.* On the Apple Macintosh, a header at the beginning of a block of memory that contains information needed by the memory management facility in order to use that memory block effectively. See also header (definition 2).

Zone transfer *n.* The process whereby a secondary DNS server obtains information about a zone or domain from the primary server. See also zone (definition 1).

.zoo *n.* The file extension that identifies compressed archive files created with the zoo file compression utility. See also zoo210.

Zoo210 *n.* Version 2.1 of zoo, a programme for creating compressed archive files (whose names have the extension .zoo). The algorithm for zoo210 is based on that of LHARC. Implementations of zoo210 are available for UNIX and Intel systems. See also archive file, LHARC.

Zoom *vb.* To enlarge a selected portion of a graphical image or document to fill a window or the screen. Zooming is a feature of many programmes, including drawing, word processing, and spreadsheet programmes, that allows the user to select a small part of the screen, zoom it, and make changes to the enlarged portion at a finer level of detail. See also window.

Zoom box *n.* A control in the upper right corner of the frame of a window on the Macintosh screen. When the user clicks on the zoom box, the window toggles between the maximum size and the size the user has set for it by dragging. See also window.

Zoomed video port *n.* See ZV port.

Zoo virus *n.* A virus that is kept in an isolated environment for the benefit of anti-virus research and training. Zoo viruses are not found outside the labs of anti-virus companies.

Zope *n.* An open source application server for publishing objects on the Internet. Zope provides tools to integrate data and content from multiple sources into complete Web applications and can be used in conjunction with XML-RPC to form a system for remotely scriptable Web objects. Zope runs on UNIX, Windows NT and later, and most other major operating systems. See also XML-RPC.

Z-order *n.* 1. The order in which objects are drawn on top of one another onscreen to simulate depth (the third dimension) in conjunction with the x and y (height and width) coordinates. 2. The visual layering of windows or controls on a form along the z-axis (depth). The z-order determines which controls are in front of other controls. Each window or control has a unique position in the z-order.

Zulu time *n.* Slang for Greenwich Mean Time.

ZV port *n.* Short for zoomed video port. Port available on many portable computers as an inexpensive multimedia alternative to traditional video input. The ZV port allows data to flow uninterrupted from source to destination without need for buffering. Zoomed video was adopted by the Personal Computer Memory Card International Association (PCMCIA) to enable high transfer rates for portable computers, connected video cameras, and other multimedia devices.

APPENDIX A

Common Character Sets

ANSI Character Set

Character	Unicode Value (Hex)	ANSI code (decimal)	Description
NUL	0000	0	Null
SOH	0001	1	Start of heading
STX	0002	2	Start of text
ETX	0003	3	End of text
EOT	0004	4	End of transmission
ENQ	0005	5	Enquiry
ACK	0006	6	Acknowledge
BEL	0007	7	Bell
BS	0008	8	Backspace
HT	0009	9	Horizontal tabulation
LF	000A	10	Line feed
VT	000B	11	Vertical tabulation
FF	000C	12	Form feed
CR	000D	13	Carriage return
SO	000E	14	Shift out
SI	000F	15	Shift in
DLE	0010	16	Data link escape
DC1	0011	17	Device control 1
DC2	0012	18	Device control 2
DC3	0013	19	Device control 3
DC4	0014	20	Device control 4
NAK	0015	21	Negative acknowledge
SYN	0016	22	Synchronous idle

Character	Unicode Value (Hex)	ANSI code (decimal)	Description
ETB	0017	23	End of transmission block
CAN	0018	24	Cancel
EM	0019	25	End of medium
SUB	001A	26	Substitute
ESC	001B	27	Escape
FS	001C	28	File separator
GS	001D	29	Group separator
RS	001E	30	Record separator
US	001F	31	Unit separator
SP	0020	32	Space
!	0021	33	Exclamation point
"	0022	34	Quotation mark
#	0023	35	Number sign
$	0024	36	Dollar sign
%	0025	37	Per cent
&	0026	38	Ampersand
'	0027	39	Apostrophe
(	0028	40	Left parenthesis
)	0029	41	Right parenthesis
*	002A	42	Asterisk
+	002B	43	Plus sign
,	002C	44	Comma
-	002D	45	Hyphen
.	002E	46	Full stop
/	002F	47	Solidus
0	0030	48	Digit zero
1	0031	49	Digit one
2	0032	50	Digit two
3	0033	51	Digit three
4	0034	52	Digit four

Character	Unicode Value (Hex)	ANSI code (decimal)	Description
5	0035	53	Digit five
6	0036	54	Digit six
7	0037	55	Digit seven
8	0038	56	Digit eight
9	0039	57	Digit nine
:	003A	58	Colon
;	003B	59	Semicolon
<	003C	60	Less-than sign
=	003D	61	Equals sign
>	003E	62	Greater-than sign
?	003F	63	Question mark
@	0040	64	Commercial at
A	0041	65	Latin capital letter A
B	0042	66	Latin capital letter B
C	0043	67	Latin capital letter C
D	0044	68	Latin capital letter D
E	0045	69	Latin capital letter E
F	0046	70	Latin capital letter F
G	0047	71	Latin capital letter G
H	0048	72	Latin capital letter H
I	0049	73	Latin capital letter I
J	004A	74	Latin capital letter J
K	004B	75	Latin capital letter K
L	004C	76	Latin capital letter L
M	004D	77	Latin capital letter M
N	004E	78	Latin capital letter N
O	004F	79	Latin capital letter O
P	0050	80	Latin capital letter P
Q	0051	81	Latin capital letter Q
R	0052	82	Latin capital letter R

Character	Unicode Value (Hex)	ANSI code (decimal)	Description
S	0053	83	Latin capital letter S
T	0054	84	Latin capital letter T
U	0055	85	Latin capital letter U
V	0056	86	Latin capital letter V
W	0057	87	Latin capital letter W
X	0058	88	Latin capital letter X
Y	0059	89	Latin capital letter Y
Z	005A	90	Latin capital letter Z
[	005B	91	Left square bracket
\	005C	92	Reverse solidus
]	005D	93	Right square bracket
^	005E	94	Circumflex accent
_	005F	95	Low line
`	0060	96	Grave accent
a	0061	97	Latin small letter a
b	0062	98	Latin small letter b
c	0063	99	Latin small letter c
d	0064	100	Latin small letter d
e	0065	101	Latin small letter e
f	0066	102	Latin small letter f
g	0067	103	Latin small letter g
h	0068	104	Latin small letter h
i	0069	105	Latin small letter i
j	006A	106	Latin small letter j
k	006B	107	Latin small letter k
l	006C	108	Latin small letter l
m	006D	109	Latin small letter m
n	006E	110	Latin small letter n
o	006F	111	Latin small letter o
p	0070	112	Latin small letter p

Character	Unicode Value (Hex)	ANSI code (decimal)	Description
q	0071	113	Latin small letter q
r	0072	114	Latin small letter r
s	0073	115	Latin small letter s
t	0074	116	Latin small letter t
u	0075	117	Latin small letter u
v	0076	118	Latin small letter v
w	0077	119	Latin small letter w
x	0078	120	Latin small letter x
y	0079	121	Latin small letter y
z	007A	122	Latin small letter z
{	007B	123	Left curly bracket
%	007C	124	Vertical line
}	007D	125	Right curly bracket
~	007E	126	Tilde
DEL	007F	127	Delete
	0080	128	Reserved
	0081	129	Reserved
	0082	130	Reserved
	0083	131	Reserved
IND	0084	132	Index
NEL	0085	133	Next line
SSA	0086	134	Start of selected area
ESA	0087	135	End of selected area
	0088	136	Character tabulation set
	0089	137	Character tabulation with justification
	008A	138	Line tabulation set
PLD	008B	139	Partial line down
PLU	008C	140	Partial line up
	008D	141	Reverse line feed

Character	Unicode Value (Hex)	ANSI code (decimal)	Description
SS2	008E	142	Single shift two
SS3	008F	143	Single shift three
DCS	0090	144	Device control string
PU1	0091	145	Private use one
PU2	0092	146	Private use two
STS	0093	147	Set transmit state
CCH	0094	148	Cancel character
MW	0095	149	Message waiting
	0096	150	Start of guarded area
	0097	151	End of guarded area
	0098	152	Start of string
	0099	153	Reserved
	009A	154	Single character introducer
CSI	009B	155	Control sequence introducer
ST	009C	156	String terminator
OSC	009D	157	Operating system command
PM	009E	158	Privacy message
APC	009F	158	Application programme command
	00A0	160	No-break space
¡	00A1	161	Inverted exclamation mark
¢	00A2	162	Cent sign
£	00A3	163	Pound sign
£	00A4	164	Currency sign
¥	00A5	165	Yen sign
¦	00A6	166	Broken bar
§	00A7	167	Section sign
¨	00A8	168	Diaeresis
©	00A9	169	Copyright sign
ª	00AA	170	Feminine ordinal indicator

Character	Unicode Value (Hex)	ANSI code (decimal)	Description
«	00AB	171	Left-pointing double angle quotation mark
¬	00AC	172	Not sign
-	00AD	173	Soft hyphen
®	00AE	174	Registered sign
¯	00AF	175	Macron
Ú	00B0	176	Degree sign
±	00B1	177	Plus-minus sign
^{2}	00B2	178	Superscript two
^{3}	00B3	179	Superscript three
´	00B4	180	Acute accent
µ	00B5	181	Micro sign
¶	00B6	182	Pilcrow sign
·	00B7	183	Middle dot
¸	00B8	184	Cedilla
^{1}	00B9	185	Superscript one
º	00BA	186	Masculine ordinal indicator
»	00BB	187	Right-pointing double angle quotation mark
¼	00BC	188	Vulgar fraction one quarter
½	00BD	189	Vulgar fraction one half
¾	00BE	190	Vulgar fraction three quarters
¿	00BF	191	Inverted question mark
À	00C0	192	Latin capital letter A with grave
Á	00C1	193	Latin capital letter A with acute
Â	00C2	194	Latin capital letter A with circumflex

Character	Unicode Value (Hex)	ANSI code (decimal)	Description
Ã	00C3	195	Latin capital letter A with tilde
Ä	00C4	196	Latin capital letter A with diaeresis
Å	00C5	197	Latin capital letter A with ring above
Æ	00C6	198	Latin capital ligature AE
Ç	00C7	199	Latin capital letter C with cedilla
È	00C8	200	Latin capital letter E with grave
É	00C9	201	Latin capital letter E with acute
Ê	00CA	202	Latin capital letter E with circumflex
Ë	00CB	203	Latin capital letter E with diaeresis
Ì	00CC	204	Latin capital letter I with grave
Í	00CD	205	Latin capital letter I with acute
Î	00CE	206	Latin capital letter I with circumflex
Ï	00CF	207	Latin capital letter I with diaeresis
Đ	00D0	208	Latin capital letter ETH
Ñ	00D1	209	Latin capital letter N with tilde
Ò	00D2	210	Latin capital letter O with grave
Ó	00D3	211	Latin capital letter O with acute

Character	Unicode Value (Hex)	ANSI code (decimal)	Description
Ô	00D4	212	Latin capital letter O with circumflex
Õ	00D5	213	Latin capital letter O with tilde
Ö	00D6	214	Latin capital letter O with diaeresis
×	00D7	215	Multiplication sign
Ø	00D8	216	Latin capital letter O with stroke
Ù	00D9	217	Latin capital letter U with grave
Ú	00DA	218	Latin capital letter U with acute
Û	00DB	219	Latin capital letter U with circumflex
Ü	00DC	220	Latin capital letter U with diaeresis
Ý	00DD	221	Latin capital letter Y with acute
Þ	00DE	222	Latin capital letter thorn
ß	00DF	223	Latin small letter sharp s
à	00E0	224	Latin small letter a with grave
á	00E1	225	Latin small letter a with acute
â	00E2	226	Latin small letter a with circumflex
ã	00E3	227	Latin small letter a with tilde
ä	00E4	228	Latin small letter a with diaeresis
å	00E5	229	Latin small letter a with ring above

Character	Unicode Value (Hex)	ANSI code (decimal)	Description
æ	00E6	230	Latin small ligature ae
ç	00E7	231	Latin small letter c with cedilla
è	00E8	232	Latin small letter e with grave
é	00E9	233	Latin small letter e with acute
ê	00EA	234	Latin small letter e with circumflex
ë	00EB	235	Latin small letter e with diaeresis
ì	00EC	236	Latin small letter i with grave
í	00ED	237	Latin small letter i with acute
î	00EE	238	Latin small letter i with circumflex
ï	00EF	239	Latin small letter i with diaeresis
ð	00F0	240	Latin small letter eth
ñ	00F1	241	Latin small letter n with tilde
ò	00F2	242	Latin small letter o with grave
ó	00F3	243	Latin small letter o with acute
ô	00F4	244	Latin small letter o with circumflex
õ	00F5	245	Latin small letter o with tilde
ö	00F6	246	Latin small letter o with diaeresis
÷	00F7	247	Division sign

Character	Unicode Value (Hex)	ANSI code (decimal)	Description
ø	00F8	248	Latin small letter o with stroke
ù	00F9	249	Latin small letter u with grave
ú	00FA	250	Latin small letter u with acute
û	00FB	251	Latin small letter u with circumflex
ü	00FC	252	Latin small letter u with diaeresis
ý	00FD	253	Latin small letter y with acute
þ	00FE	254	Latin small letter thorn
ÿ	00FF	255	Latin small letter y with diaeresis

EBCDIC Character Set

Dec	Hex	Name	Character	Meaning
0	00	NUL		Null
1	01	SOH		Start of heading
2	02	STX		Start of text
3	03	ETX		End of text
4	04	SEL		Select
5	05	HT		Horizontal tab
6	06	RNL		Required new line
7	07	DEL		Delete
8	08	GE		Graphic escape
9	09	SPS		Superscript
10	0A	RPT		Repeat
11	0B	VT		Vertical tab

Dec	Hex	Name	Character	Meaning
12	0C	FF		Form feed
13	0D	CR		Carriage return
14	0E	SO		Shift out
15	0F	SI		Shift in
16	10	DLE		Data length escape
17	11	DC1		Device control 1
18	12	DC2		Device control 2
19	13	DC3		Device control 3
20	14	RES/ENP		Restore/enable presentation
21	15	NL		New line
22	16	BS		Backspace
23	17	POC		Programme-operator communication
24	18	CAN		Cancel
25	19	EM		End of medium
26	1A	UBS		Unit backspace
27	1B	CU1		Customer use 1
28	1C	IFS		Interchange file separator
29	1D	IGS		Interchange group separator
30	1E	IRS		Interchange record separator
31	1F	IUS/ITB		Interchange unit separator/ intermediate transmission block
32	20	DS		Digit select
33	21	SOS		Start of significance
34	22	FS		Field separator
35	23	WUS		Word underscore

Dec	Hex	Name	Character	Meaning
36	24	BYP/INP		Bypass/inhibit presentation
37	25	LF		Line feed
38	26	ETB		End of transmission block
39	27	ESC		Escape
40	28	SA		Set attribute
41	29	SFE		Start field extended
42	2A	SM/SW		Set mode/switch
43	2B	CSP		Control sequence prefix
44	2C	MFA		Modify field attribute
45	2D	ENQ		Enquiry
46	2E	ACK		Acknowledge
47	2F	BEL		Bell
48	30			(not assigned)
49	31			(not assigned)
50	32	SYN		Synchronous idle
51	33	IR		Index return
52	34	PP		Presentation position
53	35	TRN		Transparent
54	36	NBS		Numeric backspace
55	37	EOT		End of transmission
56	38	SBS		Subscript
57	39	IT		Indent tab
58	3A	RFF		Required form feed
59	3B	CU3		Customer use 3
60	3C	DC4		Device control 4
61	3D	NAK		Negative acknowledge

Dec	Hex	Name	Character	Meaning
62	3E			(not assigned)
63	3F	SUB		Substitute
64	40	SP		Space
65	41	RSP		Required space
66	42			(not assigned)
67	43			(not assigned)
68	44			(not assigned)
69	45			(not assigned)
70	46			(not assigned)
71	47			(not assigned)
72	48			(not assigned)
73	49			(not assigned)
74	4A		¢	
75	4B		.	
76	4C		<	
77	4D		(	
78	4E		+	
79	4F		%	Logical OR
80	50		&	
81	51			(not assigned)
82	52			(not assigned)
83	53			(not assigned)
84	54			(not assigned)
85	55			(not assigned)
86	56			(not assigned)
87	57			(not assigned)
88	58			(not assigned)
89	59			(not assigned)
90	5A		!	
91	5B		$	
92	5C		*	

Dec	Hex	Name	Character	Meaning
93	5D		)	
94	5E		;	
95	5F		¬	Logical NOT
96	60		-	
97	61		/	
98	62			(not assigned)
99	63			(not assigned)
100	64			(not assigned)
101	65			(not assigned)
102	66			(not assigned)
103	67			(not assigned)
104	68			(not assigned)
105	69			(not assigned)
106	6A	¦		Broken pipe
107	6B		,	
108	6C		%	
109	6D		_	
110	6E		>	
111	6F		?	
112	70			(not assigned)
113	71			(not assigned)
114	72			(not assigned)
115	73			(not assigned)
116	74			(not assigned)
117	75			(not assigned)
118	76			(not assigned)
119	77			(not assigned)
120	78			(not assigned)
121	79		`	Grave accent
122	7A		:	
123	7B		#	

Dec	Hex	Name	Character	Meaning
124	7C		@	
125	7D		"	
126	7E		=	
127	7F		"	
128	80			(not assigned)
129	81		a	
130	82		b	
131	83		c	
132	84		d	
133	85		e	
134	86		f	
135	87		g	
136	88		h	
137	89		i	
138	8A			(not assigned)
139	8B			(not assigned)
140	8C			(not assigned)
141	8D			(not assigned)
142	8E			(not assigned)
143	8F			(not assigned)
144	90			(not assigned)
145	91		j	
146	92		k	
147	93		l	
148	94		m	
149	95		n	
150	96		o	
151	97		p	
152	98		q	
153	99		r	
154	9A			(not assigned)

Dec	Hex	Name	Character	Meaning
155	9B			(not assigned)
156	9C			(not assigned)
157	9D			(not assigned)
158	9E			(not assigned)
159	9F			(not assigned)
160	A0			(not assigned)
161	A1		~	
162	A2		s	
163	A3		t	
164	A4		u	
165	A5		v	
166	A6		w	
167	A7		x	
168	A8		y	
169	A9		z	
170	AA			(not assigned)
171	AB			(not assigned)
172	AC			(not assigned)
173	AD			(not assigned)
174	AE			(not assigned)
175	AF			(not assigned)
176	B0			(not assigned)
177	B1			(not assigned)
178	B2			(not assigned)
179	B3			(not assigned)
180	B4			(not assigned)
181	B5			(not assigned)
182	B6			(not assigned)
183	B7			(not assigned)
184	B8			(not assigned)
185	B9			(not assigned)

Dec	Hex	Name	Character	Meaning
186	BA			(not assigned)
187	BB			(not assigned)
188	BC			(not assigned)
189	BD			(not assigned)
190	BE			(not assigned)
191	BF			(not assigned)
192	C0		{	Opening brace
193	C1		A	
194	C2		B	
195	C3		C	
196	C4		D	
197	C5		E	
198	C6		F	
199	C7		G	
200	C8		H	
201	C9		I	
202	CA	SHY		Syllable hyphen
203	CB			(not assigned)
204	CC			(not assigned)
205	CD			(not assigned)
206	CE			(not assigned)
207	CF			(not assigned)
208	D0		}	Closing brace
209	D1		J	
210	D2		K	
211	D3		L	
212	D4		M	
213	D5		N	
14	D6		O	
15	D7		P	
16	D8		Q	

Dec	Hex	Name	Character	Meaning
217	D9		R	
218	DA			(not assigned)
219	DB			(not assigned)
220	DC			(not assigned)
221	DD			(not assigned)
222	DE			(not assigned)
223	DF			(not assigned)
224	E0		\	Reverse slash
225	E1	NSP		Numeric space
226	E2		S	
227	E3		T	
228	E4		U	
229	E5		V	
230	E6		W	
231	E7		X	
232	E8		Y	
233	E9		Z	
234	EA			(not assigned)
235	EB			(not assigned)
236	EC			(not assigned)
237	ED			(not assigned)
238	EE			(not assigned)
239	EF			(not assigned)
240	F0		0	
241	F1		1	
242	F2		2	
243	F3		3	
244	F4		4	
245	F5		5	
246	F6		6	
247	F7		7	

Dec	Hex	Name	Character	Meaning
248	F8		8	
249	F9		9	
250	FA			(not assigned)
251	FB			(not assigned)
252	FC			(not assigned)
253	FD			(not assigned)
254	FE			(not assigned)
255	FF	EO		Eight ones

APPENDIX B

Common File Extensions

File Extension	Type of File
.0	File containing information on hard disk compressed with DoubleSpace.
.123	Spreadsheet file in Lotus 123.
.4th	Source file in Forth.
.a	Source file in Macintosh Assembly.
.ad	Screensaver file in After Dark.
.ada	Source file in Ada.
.ai	Vector graphic file in Adobe Illustrator.
.aif	See .aiff.
.aifc	See .aiff.
.aiff	Audio file in the Apple Audio Interchange Format originally used on Apple and Silicon Graphics (SGI) computers.
.ani	• Animated cursor file in Microsoft Windows 9x and Windows NT. • Animation file.
.aol	File related to America Online.
.aps	Source file in Microsoft Visual C++.
.arc	Archive file compressed with ARC.
.arj	Archive file compressed with ARJ.
.asc	1. ASCII text file. 2. File encrypted with PGP (Pretty Good Privacy).
.asf	File in Microsoft Advanced Streaming Format.
.asm	Source file in Assembler.

File Extension	Type of File
.asp	File in Active Server Page format, generally found on the World Wide Web.
.atm	File in Adobe Type Manager.
.au	Sound file, generally on UNIX systems or the World Wide Web.
.avi	Audio visual interleaved data file in the Microsoft RIFF format.
.bac	See .bak.
.bak	Backup file.
.bas	Source file in Basic.
.bat	Batch programme file.
.bfc	Briefcase file in Microsoft Windows 9x.
.bin	1. Archive file compressed with MacBinary.
	2. Binary file.
.bk	See .bak.
.bmk	Bookmarked file.
.bmp	Raster graphics file stored in bitmap format.
.box	Mailbox file in Lotus Notes.
.c	Source file in C.
.c++	Source file in C++.
.cab	Microsoft cabinet file—multiple files compressed into one and extractable with the extract.exe utility.
.cas	Comma-delimited ASCII text file.
.cb	Clean boot file in Microsoft Windows.
.cbl	Source file in Cobol.
.cca	E-mail message in Lotus cc:mail.
.cda	CD audio track.
.cdf	1. File in Microsoft Channel Definition Format.
	2. File in Common Data Format.
.cdi	File in Phillips Compact Disk Interactive format.
.cdr	Vector graphics file in CorelDraw.

File Extension	Type of File
.cgi	File containing Common Gateway Interface scripts, generally for use on the World Wide Web.
.cgm	Vector graphics file in Computer Graphics Metafile format.
.chk	Portions of unidentifiable files saved in Windows by the Disk Defragmentor or ScanDisk utilities.
.chm	File containing compiled HTML.
.cil	Microsoft Clip Gallery download package.
.class	Class file in Java.
.clp	Temporary file created by Microsoft Windows Clipboard utility.
.cmd	Command file in Windows NT, OS/2, MS-DOS, and CP/M.
.cmf	File in Corel Metafile.
.cob	Source file in Cobol.
.com	Command file or programme.
.cpl	Control Panel file in Microsoft Windows 9x.
.cpp	Source file in C++.
.crt	Certificate file.
.css	Cascading Style Sheet file, generally used in conjunction with Web sites.
.csv	Comma-delimited text file.
.ct	Graphics file in Paint Shop Pro.
.cur	Cursor file in Windows.
.cxx	Source file in C++.
.dat	Data file.
.dbf	Database in dBASE and FoxPro.
.dcr	Multimedia file in Macromedia Shockwave.
.dib	Graphics file in Device Independent Bitmap format.
.dif	File in Data Interchange Format.
.dll	Dynamic-link library file.

File Extension	Type of File
.doc	1. Document file in Microsoft Word. 2. In the past, document file in Adobe FrameMaker or WordStar. 3. Document file formatted for a word processor.
.dos	MS-DOS–related files in Microsoft Windows 9x.
.dot	Document template in Microsoft Word.
.drv	Device driver.
.dtd	Document Type Definition file in SGML or XML.
.dtp	Document file in Microsoft Publisher or PublishIt!
.dv	Video file.
.dvi	Document file in TEX Device Independent File format.
.emf	File in Enhanced Windows Metafile format.
.eml	Mail message in Microsoft Outlook Express.
.eps	Encapsulated PostScript file.
.exe	Executable programme or file.
.F	Source file in Fortran.
.F77	Source file in Fortran 77.
.F90	Source file in Fortran 90.
.fax	Fax file in many Fax programmes.
.fdf	File in Adobe Acrobat Forms.
.fla	Movie file in Macromedia Flash.
.fli	Animation file in AutoDesk FLIC file.
.flf	Device driver in OS/2.
.fm	Document file in Adobe FrameMaker.
.fon	System font file in Windows.
.for	Source file in Fortran.
.fp	File in FileMaker Pro.
.fpt	See .fp.
.frm	Document file in Adobe FrameMaker.
.gid	Index file in Windows 9x.

File Extension	Type of File
.gif	Raster image file in GIF format.
.giff	See .gif.
.gtar	UNIX archive file compressed in GNU tar utility.
.gz	UNIX archive file compressed by gzip.
.gzip	See .gz.
.h	Header file.
.hdf	File in Hierarchical Data Format.
.hex	File encoded with Macintosh BinHex utility.
.hlp	Help file in Microsoft Windows.
.hqx	File encoded with BinHex utility.
.htm	See .html.
.html	HTML file, most commonly used as a Web page.
.ico	Icon file in Microsoft Windows 9x.
.iff	1. Image or sound file in IFF format. 2. Data file on Amiga systems.
.image	Image file in Macintosh Disk Image format.
.inf	Device information file, which contains scripts used to control hardware operations.
.ini	In MS-DOS and Windows 3.x, an initialisation file, which contains user preferences and startup information about an application programme.
.ins	File containing InstallShield install script.
.isu	File containing InstallShield uninstall script.
.jas	Image file in JAS format.
.jav	See .java.
.java	Source file in Java.
.jff	See .jpg.
.jfif	See .jpg.
.jpe	See .jpg.
.jpeg	See .jpg.

File Extension	Type of File
.jpg	Graphic image file encoded in the JPEG File Interchange Format.
.js	Source file in JavaScript.
.l	Source file in LISP.
.latex	Text file in LaTeX.
.lha	Archive file compressed with LZH.
.lib	Library file in many programming languages.
.lnk	Shortcut file in Windows 9x and Windows NT 4.
.log	Log file.
.lsp	Source file in LISP.
.lzh	See .lha.
.mac	Image file in MacPaint.
.mak	Project file in Microsoft Visual Basic or Microsoft Visual C++.
.man	Manual page in UNIX.
.mbox	Mailbox file in BSD UNIX.
.mbx	1. Address file in Microsoft Outlook. 2. Mailbox file in Eudora.
.mcw	Document file in Microsoft Word for the Macintosh.
.mdb	Database in Microsoft Access.
.mic	Image file in Microsoft Image Composer.
.mid	Music file in MIDI format.
.midi	See .mid.
.mime	File encoded in MIME format.
.moov	Video file in Apple QuickTime.
.mov	See .moov.
.movie	See .moov.
.mp2	Audio file compressed and encoded according to the MPEG Audio Layer-2 standard.

File Extension	Type of File
.mp3	Audio file compressed and encoded according to the MPEG Audio Layer-3 standard.
.mpe	See .mpg.
.mpeg	See .mpg.
.mpg	Compressed video and audio file in MPEG format.
.mpp	1. Graphics file in CAD format.
	2. File in Microsoft Project.
.msg	E-mail message in Microsoft Outlook.
.ncb	File in Microsoft Developer Studio.
.ncf	Command file in Novell NetWare.
.ncf	Temporary file created by Microsoft Windows Clipboard utility.
.net	Network configuration file.
.newsrc	Setup file for UNIX-based newsreaders.
.nlb	Data file in Oracle 7.
.nlm	Module file in Novell NetWare.
.nsf	Database in Lotus Notes.
.nws	News message file in Microsoft Outlook Express.
.obd	File in Microsoft Office Binder.
.ocx	Microsoft OLE control.
.ole	Microsoft OLE object.
.opt	See .ncb.
.p	Source file in Pascal.
.p65	Document file in PageMaker 6.5.
.pab	Address book file in Microsoft Outlook.
.pcd	Image file in Kodak Photo-CD.
.pcl	File in Hewlett-Packard Printer Control Language.
.pcx	Bitmapped image file in PC Paintbrush.

File Extension	Type of File
.pdf	Document file encoded in Adobe Portable Document Format.
.pgp	File encrypted in PGP (Pretty Good Privacy).
.pic	1. Image file in PC Paint format.
	2. See .pict.
.pict	Image file in the Macintosh PICT.
.pl	1. Source file in Perl.
	2. Source file in Prolog.
.png	Bitmap image file in PNG format.
.pps	1. Image file in Paint Shop Pro.
	2. Slide show file in Microsoft PowerPoint.
.ppt	Presentation file in Microsoft PowerPoint.
.prc	Text or programme file for 3Com PalmPilot.
.prg	File in Microsoft FoxPro, Ashton-Tate dBase, or CA Clipper.
.ps	PostScript printer file.
.psd	Image file in Adobe PhotoShop.
.pst	Personal File Folder file in Microsoft Outlook.
.pub	Document file in Ventura Publisher, Adobe PageMaker, or Microsoft Publisher.
.pwd	Document file in Microsoft Pocket Word for handheld and palm-size computers.
.pwl	Password file in Microsoft Windows 9x.
.pxl	Spreadsheet file in Microsoft Pocket Excel for handheld and palm-size computers.
.qic	Backup file in Microsoft Backup.
.qif	See .qti.
.qt	See .qtm.
.qti	Image file in Apple QuickTime.

File Extension	Type of File
.qtif	See .qti.
.qtm	Movie file in Apple QuickTime.
.qts	See .qti.
.qtx	See .qti.
.qxd	Document file in QuarkXPress.
.ra	Sound file in RealAudio.
.ram	Metafile in RealAudio.
.ras	Raster image bitmap on Sun systems.
.rast	See .ras.
.raw	Bitmap file in RAW format.
.rdf	Resource Description Framework file in XML.
.rgb	See .raw.
.rif	Bitmap file in RIFF format.
.riff	See .rif.
.rle	Bitmap file in RLE compression scheme.
.rm	Video file in RealAudio.
.rtf	Document file in Rich Text Format.
.s	1. Source file in Assembler. 2. Source file in Scheme.
.sam	Document file in Lotus Ami Professional.
.sav	1. Saved file in many games. 2. Saved backup file.
.scc	File in Microsoft SourceSafe.
.scd	File in Microsoft Schedule+.
.scr	Screensaver file in Microsoft Windows.
.sea	Self-extracting Macintosh archive file compressed with StuffIt.
.set	File set in Microsoft Backup.
.sgm	File in SGML.

File Extension	Type of File
.sgml	See .sgm.
.shtml	1. File in HTML format that has SSI (server side includes). 2. Secure file in HTML.
.sig	Signature file for e-mail or Internet newsgroup use.
.sit	Macintosh archive file compressed with StuffIt.
.sm	Source file in Smalltalk.
.snd	1. Interchangeable sound file format used on Sun, NeXT, and Silicon Graphics computers, consisting of raw audio data preceded by a text identifier. 2. Sound resource file on the Macintosh.
.spl	File in Macromedia Shockwave Flash.
.sql	Query or report file in SQL.
.stm	See .shtml.
.sun	Raster graphics file in Sun systems.
.swa	Audio file in Macromedia Shockwave.
.swf	File in Macromedia Shockwave Flash.
.swp	Swap file in Microsoft Windows.
.sys	System configuration file.
.tar	Uncompressed UNIX archive in tar format.
.taz	UNIX archive file in Gzip or tar format.
.tcl	Source file in TCL.
.tga	Bitmap file in Targa format.
.tif	Bitmap images in TIFF format.
.tiff	See .tif.
.tmp	Temporary file in Windows.
.tsv	Tab separated values file.
.ttf	TrueType font file.
.txt	ASCII text file.

.udf	Database file in Microsoft Windows NT.
.uri	File containing list of URIs.
.url	Shortcut file on the Internet for a URL.
.uu	See .uud.
.uud	Binary file that has been translated into ASCII format using uuencode.
.uue	File that has been decoded from ASCII format back into binary format using uudecode.
.vbx	Custom control in Microsoft Visual Basic.
.vda	See .tga.
.vp	Document file in Ventura Publisher.
.vrm	1. See .vrml. 2. Source file in Visual ReXX.
.vrml	A 3-D graphics file in VRML.
.vst	Bitmap image file in Targa.
.vxd	Virtual device driver in Microsoft Windows.
.wab	E-mail file in Microsoft Outlook Express.
.wav	Sound file stored in waveform (WAV) audio format.
.wmf	Vector image file encoded as a Microsoft Windows Metafile.
.wp	Document file in Corel WordPerfect.
.wp6	Document file in Corel WordPerfect 6.x.
.wpd	See .wp.
.wpg	Graphic file in Corel WordPerfect.
.wps	Document file in Microsoft Works.
.wri	Document file in Microsoft Write.
.xls	Spreadsheet file in Microsoft Excel.
.z	UNIX file archive compressed with gzip.
.Z	UNIX file archive compressed with compress utility.
.zip	Archive file compressed in ZIP format with PKZIP or WinZip.
.zoo	Archive file compressed with zoo.

APPENDIX C

Instant Messaging Emoticons and Acronyms

Instant messaging, chat, and other Internet communications formats have led to a variety of shorthand indicators and clarifiers meant to enhance the user experience.

Emotags: Emotags were first used in e-mail and newsgroups to clarify a message for the reader. Typically, emotags consist of a word or words in brackets or parentheses, such as <joke>, and appear right after or both before and after the text they refer to.

Smileys: The most common emoticons are faces and expressions composed of standard keyboard punctuation marks and symbols, and which are viewed sideways. These are known as "smileys" in reference to the first emoticons, which represented a smile, such as: :-). Smileys are indicators of the emotional "tone of voice" intended by the writer.

Smileys

Text	Meaning
:-)	smile
(-:	left-handed smile
:o)	smile with a large nose (or clown smiley)
:)	smile with no nose
:->	smirk (or wry smile)
:-}	wry smile (or leer)
:-t	unsmiley
:*)	just clowning around (or inebriated)
:-))))	extreme happiness (or sarcastic happiness)
:-D	very happy (or laughing)
(-D	laughing hard

Text	Meaning
:-) :-) :-)	loud guffaw
:"-)	laughing and crying
%-)	amused (and possibly confused)
:-/	chagrined (or skeptical)
:-I	indifferent
:~)	touched (or ill with a cold)
(:-(	sad (or bald and sad)
:-(	frown (or unhappy)
:-c	very unhappy
:-((((	extremely unhappy (or sarcastic unhappiness)
:-<	forlorn
>:-(	annoyed
:-[	pouting
(:-& or %-(	angry
>:-<	very angry
~ :-(	very angry (or fuming mad)
%-(or :/)	not amused
:-%	expressionless
:-% or :-(	have an ordinary day
:-e	disappointed
:-X	lips are sealed (or not saying a word)
:-v	talking
:-I	hmmm
:-8(	condescending stare
:-O	shouting (or shocked)
:-@	screaming
:,-(or :"-(	crying
~:-o	baby
]:-)>	devilish

Text	Meaning
):-)	impish
;->	lewd
:-x	kiss
:-*	ready for a kiss (or just ate something sour)
8-]	wow
:-J	tongue-in-cheek
:-&	tongue-tied (or biting tongue)
:-p	no way! (or nyah nyah)
;-)	wink
″-)	one-eyed wink
:-7	wry statement (or tongue-in-cheek)
:-% :-%	déjà vu
?-(	sorry, I don't know what went wrong (or black eye)
:-C	that's unbelievable! (or incredible!)
B-D	serves you right
:-B	drooling
:-*)	drunk
:-9	licking lips
%-p	yuck!
:-b	sticking out tongue
-]:-)[-	impressed
3-I or 8-%	in suspense
%:-%	excessively rigid
:-]	obnoxious
%-)	bored (or asleep)
%-I	asleep
I^o	snoring
%-O	yawning

Text	Meaning
:-"	whistling (or pursing lips)
:-s	incoherent statement
:-#	just said the wrong thing (or braces)
:-!	foot in mouth
:-() or :-D	big mouth
(:-$ or :-(*)	ill
(:~) or :-")	ill with a cold
:-R	ill with the flu
%+% or %+{	lost a fight
X-(	unconscious (or dead)
<:-)	dunce
*:o)	bozo
@;-)	flirt
X:-)	child
:>)	big nose
&:-)	curly hair (or girl smiley)
#:-)	matted hair
8-)	wearing glasses
8:-)	glasses on forehead (or little girl, or hair in curlers)
B-)	wearing horn-rimmed glasses (or sunglasses)
B-]	wearing cool sunglasses
O:-)	angel
&8-%	nerd
c:-) or (:-)	bald
:-{	has a moustache
:-)} or :-)#	has a beard
:-Q or :-I	smoker
:-d~	heavy smoker

Text	Meaning
:-?	pipe smoker
:-/I	no smoking
:-) X	wearing a bow tie
{(:-)	wearing a toupee
:-{}	lipstick
[:-)	stereo headphones
d :-o	hats off
~:-(	has been flamed (or is on fire)
~~:-(	has been flamed repeatedly
)	Cheshire cat
(:-I	egghead
3:-o	cow
[: %]	robot
M-)	see no evil
:X)	hear no evil
:-M	speak no evil
*8((:	strange
O+	female
O->	male
%%*(	handshake offered
%%*)	handshake accepted
<{:-)}	message in a bottle
(-: :-)	putting heads together
[] or ()	hug given (name or initials can be included between the brackets)
((( )))	lots of hugs
((( ))):**	hugs and kisses
(::()::)	Band-Aid (or comfort)
@->–	a rose

Text	Meaning
@—>—	a long-stemmed rose
@==	atomic bomb
<“)))))-<	a fish
^	giggles

Alternate (Japanese) Smileys

Alternate smileys, which do not require users to tilt their heads sideways, were developed by Internet users in Japan and are becoming more common worldwide. Some versions of these emoticons leave out the ( ) brackets around the faces.

Alternate Smileys

Text	Meaning
(^_^)	male smiley
(^.^)	female smiley
(^L^) or (^(^)	happy
(-_-)	secret smile
(^o^)	laughing out loud
(^_^;)	laughing to cover nervousness
(^_^)/	waving hello
(;_;)/	waving good-bye
(^_~) or (^_-)	winking
(*^o^*) or (*^.^*)	exciting
\(^_^)/	joyful
(;_;) or (~~>.<~~)	crying
(>.<) or (>_<)	angry
(v_v)	expressionless
(^o^;>	excuse me?
(*^_^*)	blushing (or shy)
(^_^;;;)	embarrassed (or in a cold sweat)

Text	Meaning
(?_?)	confused (or wondering)
(!_!) or (o_o)	shocked
(*_*)	frightened (or in love)
(=_=)~	sleepy
(u_u)	sleeping
(@_@)	stunned
"\=o-o=/"	wearing glasses
m(_)m	humble bow of thanks or apology

Acronyms and Shorthand

The first emotional indicators in newsgroups and e-mail were acronyms designed to give readers clues to the attitude and intent of the sender. Acronyms also quickly developed as keyboarding shortcuts. Use of acronyms is particularly prevalent in instant messaging, primarily to maintain the pace of real-time conversation.

Acronyms

Text	Meaning
AAMOF	as a matter of fact
AAR	at any rate
ADN	any day now
AFAIK	as far as I know
AFK	away from keyboard
AFKBRB	away from keyboard, be right back
ASAP	as soon as possible
A/S/L	age/sex/location
B2W	back to work
B4N (or BFN)	bye for now
BAK	back at keyboard
BBL	be back later
BBS	be back soon

Text	Meaning
BCNU	be seeing you
BF (or B/F)	boyfriend
BMN	but maybe not
BRB	be right back
BTDT	been there, done that
BTDTBTT	been there, done that, bought the tape
BTDTGTTS	been there, done that, got the t-shirt
BTDTGTTSAWIO	been there, done that, got the t-shirt, and wore it out
BTW	by the way
BYKT	but you knew that
CIO	cut it out
CMIIW	correct me if I'm wrong
CU (or CYA)	see you
CUL (or CUL8R)	see you later
DIY	do it yourself
DYJHIW	don't you just hate it when
EAK	eating at keyboard
EOL	end of lecture
EOM	end of message
F2F (or FTF)	face to face
FAPP	for all practical purposes
FOFL (or FOTFL)	falling on the floor laughing
FTR	for the record
FWIW	for what it's worth
FYA	for your amusement
FYEO	for your eyes only
FYI	for your information
g (or <g>)	grin
G (or <G>)	big grin
G2G (or GTG)	got to go

Text	Meaning
GAL	get a life
GD&H	grinning, ducking, and hiding
GD&R	grinning, ducking, and running
GD&RVVF	grinning, ducking, and running, very, very fast
GF (or G/F)	girlfriend
GG	gotta go (or good game)
GIWIST	gee, I wish I said that
GMTA	great minds think alike
GoAT	go away, troll
HAK	hugs and kisses
HAGD	have a great day
HAND	have a nice day
HEH	a courtesy laugh
HHOS	ha-ha, only serious
HTH	hope this helps (or hope that helps)
IAE	in any event
HW	homework (or hardware)
IANAL	I am not a lawyer
IC	I see
ICBW	I could be wrong (or it could be worse)
IDTS	I don't think so
IINM	if I'm not mistaken
IIRC	if I recall correctly
IIUC	if I understand correctly
IMCO	in my considered opinion
IME	in my experience
IMHO	in my humble opinion
IMNSHO	in my not-so-humble opinion
IMO	in my opinion
IOW	in other words

Text	Meaning
IRL	in real life
ISTM	it seems to me
ISWYM	I see what you mean
ITRW	in the real world
J (or <J>)	joking
JC	just chillin'
JIC	just in case
JK (or J/K)	just kidding (or that was a joke)
JTYWTK	just thought you wanted to know
JW	just wondering
K	okay
KWIM	know what I mean?
L (or <L>)	laughing
L8R	later
LJBF	let's just be friends
LOL	laughing out loud
LTNS	long time no see
MHBFY	my heart bleeds for you
MHOTY	my hat's off to you
MOTAS	member of the appropriate sex
MOTD	message of the day
MYOB	mind your own business
NBD	no big deal
NBIF	no basis in fact
NOYB	none of your business
NP	no problem
NRN	no response necessary (or no reply necessary)
OIC	oh, I see
OM	oh my (or old man, as in husband)
OOI	out of interest

Text	Meaning
OOTB	out of the box
OTL	out to lunch
OTOH	on the other hand
OTTH	on the third hand
PAW	parents are watching
PC	politically correct
PDA	public display of affection
PEST	please excuse slow typing
PI (or PIC)	politically incorrect
PKB (or P/K/B)	pot, kettle, black (or pot calling the kettle black)
PMBI	pardon my butting in
PMFJI	pardon me for jumping in
POS	parent over shoulder (or parents over shoulder)
POV	point of view
PPL	people
PTB	powers that be
R (or r)	are
REHI	re-hello (following a short time away) (or hi again)
RFC	request for comment
RL	real life
ROTFL	rolling on the floor laughing
ROTFLOL	rolling on the floor laughing out loud
RSN	real soon now
S (or <S>)	smile
SCNR	sorry, could not resist
SITD	still in the dark
SOP	standard operating procedure
SPMD	some people may differ
SUP	what's up?

Text	Meaning
TBE	to be expected
THX (or TX)	thanks
TIA	thanks in advance
TANJ	there ain't no justice
TIC	tongue-in-cheek
TPHB	the pointy-haired boss
TPTB	the powers that be
TTBOMK	to the best of my knowledge
TTFN	ta-ta for now
TTYL	talk to you later
TVM	thanks very much
TVMIA	thanks very much in advance
TYVMIA	thank you very much in advance
U	you
UW	you're welcome
VBG (or <VBG>)	very big grin
WB	welcome back
WCD	what's cookin' doc?
WHBT	we have been trolled
WOA	work of art
WRT	with regard to (or with respect to)
WTG	way to go
WTH	what the heck?
Y (or <Y>)	yawning
YHBT	you have been told (or you have been trolled)
YHBW	you have been warned
YHGMTPOTG	you have greatly misinterpreted the purpose of this group
YHM	you have mail
YMMV	your mileage may vary
YOYO	you're on your own
YWSYLS	you win some, you lose some

APPENDIX D

Internet Domains

Top-Level Domains: Organisational

Domain	Type of Organisation
.aero	Air-transport industry
.biz	Businesses
.com	Commercial
.coop	Cooperatives
.edu	Educational
.gov	Nonmilitary agency, United States federal government
.info	Unrestricted use
.int	International organisation
.mil	United States military
.museum	Museums
.name	Individuals
.net	Network provider
.org	Nonprofit organisation
.pro	Professional workers

Top-Level Domains: Geographic

Domain	Country/Region
.ac	Ascension Island
.ad	Andorra
.ae	United Arab Emirates
.af	Afghanistan
.ag	Antigua and Barbuda

Domain	Country/Region
.ai	Anguilla
.al	Albania
.am	Armenia
.an	Netherlands Antilles
.ao	Angola
.aq	Antarctica
.ar	Argentina
.as	American Samoa
.at	Austria
.au	Australia
.aw	Aruba
.az	Azerbaijan
.ba	Bosnia and Herzegovina
.bb	Barbados
.bd	Bangladesh
.be	Belgium
.bf	Burkina Faso
.bg	Bulgaria
.bh	Bahrain
.bi	Burundi
.bj	Benin
.bm	Bermuda
.bn	Brunei
.bo	Bolivia
.br	Brazil
.bs	Bahamas, The
.bt	Bhutan
.bv	Bouvet Island
.bw	Botswana
.by	Belarus
.bz	Belize

Domain	Country/Region
.ca	Canada
.cc	Cocos (Keeling) Islands
.cd	Congo (DRC)
.cf	Central African Republic
.cg	Congo
.ch	Switzerland
.ci	Côte d'Ivoire
.ck	Cook Islands
.cl	Chile
.cm	Cameroon
.cn	China
.co	Colombia
.cr	Costa Rica
.cu	Cuba
.cv	Cape Verde
.cx	Christmas Island
.cy	Cyprus
.cz	Czech Republic
.de	Germany
.dj	Djibouti
.dk	Denmark
.dm	Dominica
.do	Dominican Republic
.dz	Algeria
.ec	Ecuador
.ee	Estonia
.eg	Egypt
.er	Eritrea
.es	Spain
.et	Ethiopia
.fi	Finland

Domain	Country/Region
.fj	Fiji Islands
.fk	Falkland Islands (Islas Malvinas)
.fm	Micronesia
.fo	Faroe Islands
.fr	France
.ga	Gabon
.gd	Grenada
.ge	Georgia
.gf	French Guiana
.gg	Guernsey
.gh	Ghana
.gi	Gibraltar
.gl	Greenland
.gm	Gambia, The
.gn	Guinea
.gp	Guadeloupe
.gq	Equatorial Guinea
.gr	Greece
.gs	South Georgia and the South Sandwich Islands
.gt	Guatemala
.gu	Guam
.gw	Guinea-Bissau
.gy	Guyana
.hk	Hong Kong SAR
.hm	Heard Island and McDonald Islands
.hn	Honduras
.hr	Croatia
.ht	Haiti
.hu	Hungary
.id	Indonesia
.ie	Ireland

Domain	Country/Region
.il	Israel
.im	Man, Isle of
.in	India
.io	British Indian Ocean Territory
.iq	Iraq
.ir	Iran
.is	Iceland
.it	Italy
.je	Jersey
.jm	Jamaica
.jo	Jordan
.jp	Japan
.ke	Kenya
.kg	Kyrgzstan
.kh	Cambodia
.ki	Kiribati
.km	Comoros
.kn	St. Kitts and Nevis
.kp	North Korea
.kr	Korea
.kw	Kuwait
.ky	Cayman Islands
.kz	Kazakhstan
.la	Laos
.lb	Lebanon
.lc	St. Lucia
.li	Liechtenstein
.lk	Sri Lanka
.lr	Liberia
.ls	Lesotho
.lt	Lithuania

Domain	Country/Region
.lu	Luxembourg
.lv	Latvia
.ly	Libya
.ma	Morocco
.mc	Monaco
.md	Moldova
.mg	Madagascar
.mh	Marshall Islands
.mk	Macedonia, Former Yugoslav Republic of
.ml	Mali
.mm	Myanmar
.mn	Mongolia
.mo	Macau SAR
.mp	Northern Mariana Islands
.mq	Martinique
.mr	Mauritania
.ms	Montserrat
.mt	Malta
.mu	Mauritius
.mv	Maldives
.mw	Malawi
.mx	Mexico
.my	Malaysia
.mz	Mozambique
.na	Namibia
.nc	New Caledonia
.ne	Niger
.nf	Norfolk Island
.ng	Nigeria
.ni	Nicaragua
.nl	Netherlands, The

Domain	Country/Region
.no	Norway
.np	Nepal
.nr	Nauru
.nu	Niue
.nz	New Zealand
.om	Oman
.pa	Panama
.pe	Peru
.pf	French Polynesia
.pg	Papua New Guinea
.ph	Philippines
.pk	Pakistan
.pl	Poland
.pm	St. Pierre and Miquelon
.pn	Pitcairn Islands
.pr	Puerto Rico
.ps	Palestinian Authority
.pt	Portugal
.pw	Palau
.py	Paraguay
.qa	Qatar
.re	Reunion
.ro	Romania
.ru	Russia
rw	Rwanda
.sa	Saudi Arabia
sb	Solomon Islands
.sc	Seychelles
sd	Sudan
se	Sweden
sg	Singapore

Domain	Country/Region
.sh	St. Helena
.si	Slovenia
.sj	Svalbard and Jan Mayen
.sk	Slovakia
.sl	Sierra Leone
.sm	San Marino
.sn	Senegal
.so	Somalia
.sr	Suriname
.st	São Tomé and Príncipe
.sv	El Salvador
.sy	Syria
.sz	Swaziland
.tc	Turks and Caicos Islands
.td	Chad
.tf	French Southern and Antarctic Lands
.tg	Togo
.th	Thailand
.tj	Tajikistan
.tk	Tokelau
.tm	Turkmenistan
.tn	Tunisia
.to	Tonga
.tp	East Timor
.tr	Turkey
.tt	Trinidad and Tobago
.tv	Tuvalu
.tw	Taiwan
.tz	Tanzania
.ua	Ukraine
.ug	Uganda

Domain	Country/Region
.uk	United Kingdom
.um	U.S. Minor Outlying Islands
.us	United States
.uy	Uruguay
.uz	Uzbekistan
.va	Vatican City
.vc	St. Vincent and the Grenadines
.ve	Venezuela
.vg	Virgin Islands, British
.vi	Virgin Islands
.vn	Vietnam
.vu	Vanuatu
.wf	Wallis and Futuna
.ws	Samoa
.ye	Yemen
.yt	Mayotte
.yu	Yugoslavia
.za	South Africa
.zm	Zambia
.zw	Zimbabwe

APPENDIX E

Numeric Equivalents

Decimal (Base 10)	Hexadecimal (Base 16)	Octal (Base 8)	Binary (Base 2)
1	01	01	00000001
2	02	02	00000010
3	03	03	00000011
4	04	04	00000100
5	05	05	00000101
6	06	06	00000110
7	07	07	00000111
8	08	10	00001000
9	06	11	00001001
10	0A	12	00001010
11	0B	13	00001011
12	0C	14	00001100
13	0D	15	00001101
14	0E	16	00001110
15	0F	17	00001111
16	10	20	00010000
17	11	21	00010001
18	12	22	00010010
19	13	23	00010011
20	14	24	00010100
21	15	25	00010101
22	16	26	00010110
23	17	27	00010111
24	18	30	00011000

Decimal (Base 10)	Hexadecimal (Base 16)	Octal (Base 8)	Binary (Base 2)
25	19	31	00011001
26	1A	32	00011010
27	1B	33	00011011
28	1C	34	00011100
29	1D	35	00011101
30	1E	36	00011110
31	1F	37	00011111
32	20	40	00100000
33	21	41	00100001
34	22	42	00100010
35	23	43	00100011
36	24	44	00100100
37	25	45	00100101
38	26	46	00100110
39	27	47	00100111
40	28	50	00101000
41	29	51	00101001
42	2A	52	00101010
43	2B	53	00101011
44	2C	54	00101100
45	2D	55	00101101
46	2E	56	00101110
47	2F	57	00101111
48	30	60	00110000
49	31	61	00110001
50	32	62	00110010
51	33	63	00110011
52	34	64	00110100
53	35	65	00110101

Decimal (Base 10)	Hexadecimal (Base 16)	Octal (Base 8)	Binary (Base 2)
54	36	66	00110110
55	37	67	00110111
56	38	70	00111001
57	39	71	00111000
58	3A	72	00111010
59	3B	73	00111011
60	3C	74	00111100
61	3D	75	00111101
62	3E	76	00111110
63	3F	77	00111111
64	40	100	01000000
65	41	101	01000001
66	42	102	01000010
67	43	103	01000011
68	44	104	01000100
69	45	105	01000101
70	46	106	01000110
71	47	107	01000111
72	48	110	01001000
73	49	111	01001001
74	4A	112	01001010
75	4B	113	01001011
76	4C	114	01001100
77	4D	115	01001101
78	4E	116	01001110
79	4F	117	01001111
80	50	120	01010000
81	51	121	01010001

Decimal (Base 10)	Hexadecimal (Base 16)	Octal (Base 8)	Binary (Base 2)
82	52	122	01010010
83	53	123	01010011
84	54	124	01010100
85	55	125	01010101
86	56	126	01010110
87	57	127	01010111
88	58	130	01011000
89	59	131	01011001
90	5A	132	01011010
91	5B	133	01011011
92	5C	134	01011100
93	5D	135	01011101
94	5E	136	01011110
95	5F	137	01011111
96	60	140	01100000
97	61	141	01100001
98	62	142	01100010
99	63	143	01100011
100	64	144	01100100
101	65	145	01100101
102	66	146	01100110
103	67	147	01100111
104	68	150	01101000
105	69	151	01101001
106	6A	152	01101010
107	6B	153	01101011
108	6C	154	01101100
109	6D	155	01101101

Decimal (Base 10)	Hexadecimal (Base 16)	Octal (Base 8)	Binary (Base 2)
110	6E	156	01101110
111	6F	157	01101111
112	70	160	01110000
113	71	161	01110001
114	72	162	01110010
115	73	163	01110011
116	74	164	01110100
117	75	165	01110101
118	76	166	01110110
119	77	167	01110111
120	78	170	01111000
121	79	171	01111001
122	7A	172	01111010
123	7B	173	01111011
124	7C	174	01111100
125	7D	175	01111101
126	7E	176	01111110
127	7F	177	01111111
128	80	200	10000000
129	81	201	10000001
130	82	202	10000010
131	83	203	10000011
132	84	204	10000100
133	85	205	10000101
134	86	206	10000110
135	87	207	10000111
136	88	210	10001000
137	89	211	10001001
138	8A	212	10001010
139	8B	213	10001011

Decimal (Base 10)	Hexadecimal (Base 16)	Octal (Base 8)	Binary (Base 2)
140	8C	214	10001100
141	8D	215	10001101
142	8E	216	10001110
143	8F	217	10001111
144	90	220	10010000
145	91	221	10010001
146	92	222	10010010
147	93	223	10010011
148	94	224	10010100
149	95	225	10010101
150	96	226	10010110
151	97	227	10010111
152	98	230	10011000
153	99	231	10011001
154	9A	232	10011010
155	9B	233	10011011
156	9C	234	10011100
157	9D	235	10011101
158	9E	236	10011110
159	9F	237	10011111
160	A0	240	10100000
161	A1	241	10100001
162	A2	242	10100010
163	A3	243	10100011
164	A4	244	10100100
165	A5	245	10100101
166	A6	246	10100110
167	A7	247	10100111
168	A8	250	10101000
169	A9	251	10101001

Decimal (Base 10)	Hexadecimal (Base 16)	Octal (Base 8)	Binary (Base 2)
170	AA	252	10101010
171	AB	253	10101011
172	AC	254	10101100
173	AD	255	10101101
174	AE	256	10101110
175	AF	257	10101111
176	B0	260	10110000
177	B1	261	10110001
178	B2	262	10110010
179	B3	263	10110011
180	B4	264	10110100
181	B5	265	10110101
182	B6	266	10110110
183	B7	267	10110111
184	B8	270	10111000
185	B9	271	10111001
186	BA	272	10111010
187	BB	273	10111011
188	BC	274	10111100
189	BD	275	10111101
190	BE	276	10111110
191	BF	277	10111111
192	C0	300	11000000
193	C1	301	11000001
194	C2	302	11000010
195	C3	303	11000011
196	C4	304	11000100
197	C5	305	11000101
198	C6	306	11000110
199	C7	307	11000111

Decimal (Base 10)	Hexadecimal (Base 16)	Octal (Base 8)	Binary (Base 2)
200	C8	310	11001000
201	C9	311	11001001
202	CA	312	11001010
203	CB	313	11001011
204	CC	314	11001100
205	CD	315	11001101
206	CE	316	11001110
207	CF	317	11001111
208	D0	320	11010000
209	D1	321	11010001
210	D2	322	11010010
211	D3	323	11010011
212	D4	324	11010100
213	D5	325	11010101
214	D6	326	11010110
215	D7	327	11010111
216	D8	330	11011000
217	D9	331	11011001
218	DA	332	11011010
219	DB	333	11011011
220	DC	334	11011100
221	DD	335	11011101
222	DE	336	11011110
223	DF	337	11011111
224	E0	340	11100000
225	E1	341	11100001
226	E2	342	11100010
227	E3	343	11100011
228	E4	344	11100100
229	E5	345	11100101

Decimal (Base 10)	Hexadecimal (Base 16)	Octal (Base 8)	Binary (Base 2)
230	E6	346	11100110
231	E7	347	11100111
232	E8	350	11101000
233	E9	351	11101001
234	EA	352	11101010
235	EB	353	11101011
236	EC	354	11101100
237	ED	355	11101101
238	EE	356	11101110
239	EF	357	11101111
240	F0	360	11110000
241	F1	361	11110001
242	F2	362	11110010
243	F3	363	11110011
244	F4	364	11110100
245	F5	365	11110101
246	F6	366	11110110
247	F7	367	11110111
248	F8	370	11111000
249	F9	371	11111001
250	FA	372	11111010
251	FB	373	11111011
252	FC	374	11111100
253	FD	375	11111101
254	FE	376	11111110
255	FF	377	11111111